Florida A&M University, Tallahassee
Florida Atlantic University, Boca Raton
Florida Gulf Coast University, Ft. Myers
Florida International University, Miami
Florida State University, Tallahassee
University of Central Florida, Orlando
University of Florida, Gainesville
University of North Florida, Jacksonville
University of South Florida, Tampa
University of West Florida, Pensacola

Women and Gender in Early Jewish and Palestinian Nationalism

Sheila H. Katz

University Press of Florida

Gainesville · Tallahassee · Tampa · Boca Raton
Pensacola · Orlando · Miami · Jacksonville · Ft. Myers

08 07 06 05 04 03   6 5 4 3 2 1

Library of Congress Cataloging-in-Publication Data
Katz, Sheila H.
Women and gender in early Jewish and Palestinian nationalism / Sheila H. Katz.
p. cm.
Includes bibliographical references (p.) and index.
ISBN 0-8130-2618-0 (cloth : alk. paper)
1. Women in politics–Israel–History–20th century. 2. Women in politics–Palestine–History–
20th century. 3. Nationalism and feminism–Israel–History–20th century. 4. Nationalism and
feminism–Palestine–History–20th century. 5. Jewish women–Israel–Political activity–His-
tory–20th century. 6. Jewish women–Palestine–Political activity–History–20th century. 7.
Women, Palestinian Arab–Political activity–History–20th century. 8. Jews–Israel–Identity. 9.
Palestinian Arabs–Israel–Ethnic identity. I. Title.
HQ1236.5.I75K38   2003
305.42'095694–dc21   2003040245

The University Press of Florida is the scholarly publishing agency for the State University
System of Florida, comprising Florida A&M University, Florida Atlantic University, Florida
Gulf Coast University, Florida International University, Florida State University, University
of Central Florida, University of Florida, University of North Florida, University of South
Florida, and University of West Florida.

University Press of Florida
15 Northwest 15th Street
Gainesville, FL 32611–2079
http://www.upf.com

In memory of
my father,
Murray Katz
(1910–1991),
and my mother,
Dorothy Wekstein Katz
(1919–2000),
who loved knowledge, justice, and peace.

It ought to be possible for historians to "make visible the assignment of subject positions," not in the sense of capturing the reality of objects seen, but of trying to understand the operations of the complex and changing discursive process by which identities are ascribed, resisted, or embraced, and which processes themselves are unremarked and indeed achieve their effect because they are unnoticed.

Joan Wallach Scott, "Evidence of Experience"

Contents

Preface

The way we tell the stories of our past has life and death consequences. Both peoples in Israel and Palestine have interpreted their histories in (at least) two antagonistic ways that obliterate the truth of the other. The stories become sources of and justifications for war. This book goes against the grain of a century of historical writing about Jews and Arabs in Palestine and Israel. It grows out of scholarship of the past decade or so by and about Israelis and Palestinians that demythologizes national histories and breaks down the dichotomy between two opposing tellings. Yet most of the scholars who attempt these exposés do not challenge the male-centeredness of the stories. While the history contained in this book acknowledges the legitimacy and interdependency of both peoples' political identities, it honors the importance of women in formulating them.

There are very few books that attempt to address the histories of both Arab and Jewish women in the region. There are still fewer that seek to understand the roles that these women played in the formative years of their national movements. This book traces some of the ways that issues of women and gender contributed to the creation of new political identities for Jews and Arabs of Palestine before the creation of the state of Israel. It seeks to unmask the hidden discourse of gender in international conflict. Historian Joan Scott observed that "those absent from official accounts partook nonetheless in the making of history; those who are silent speak eloquently about the meanings of power and the uses of political authority."[1] This study helps put to rest the illusion that political history and international conflict are gender neutral. During one hundred years of conflict over the one land, Palestinian Arabs' and Israeli Jews' ideas about male and female roles played a central yet often invisible part in shaping nationalism and fueling conflict.

Telling the history of Jews' and Arabs' struggle for existence and independence in one land is a difficult task. For each people viewed the other and served the other as a primary obstacle to achieving dignity and security in their land. Part of the historian's task is to explore painful realities about the past to make possible a newly imagined future. A study of women and politics enables us to deconstruct exclusive notions of national "self" and "other" and expose unacknowledged battles for survival by subgroups obscured within a nationalist rubric. For identity, whether sexual or political, is to a large extent a social construct even as it claims hearts, minds, and lives.

Women, real and imagined, were central to the notions of who each people wished to be and wished not to be, of how they envisioned their enemies and allies. Women were entangled in discussions of male traits lauded by nationalists, in relationships between people and land, in clashes between self-appointed modernizers and so-called guardians of tradition, and in perceptions of difference and power between the peoples of Palestine. Women were present in Zionist conceptions of Arab Palestinians, in images of the Jewish pioneer, in Arab defense of honor and land, in Arab rage at Jewish colonists, in dismissal and demonization of the "other."

Scholars still lament that "explorations of the gendering of the national imagination have been conspicuously paltry."[2] Yet there is a growing understanding of the ways in which women influenced and were influenced by political struggles. Although this study explores the unique situation of Arab and Jewish women in a particular place and time, it nevertheless underscores the commonality of women's struggles everywhere.

One does not have to haunt distant archives to discover how central women were to the two conflicting narratives of nationalism in Palestine. This work asks new questions of old published sources written by men and women, read by men and women who took part in formulating new national identities before and during the British Mandate years, from around the 1860s through the 1940s. In *Palestinians*, Kimmerling and Migdal describe these published works as "furnishing the shared aesthetic and intellectual material for a concrete expression of the new Palestinism—a cultural glue helping to keep the society together. The principal medium was the printing press, producing textbooks, fiction, history, political tracts, translations, and . . . poetry."[3] It is the very accessibility of these materials that underscores the way power operated to obscure the obvious role women and gender played in these narratives.

Thirty years ago, I began to wrestle with issues of women and gender in Palestinian and Jewish history. In the 1970s, I lived in Jerusalem for six years. During that time I helped organize some of the early feminist (1971–72) and Arab-Jewish (1975–80) grassroots movements. I witnessed how Israeli women labored under a myth of liberation that actually veiled limits on their lives then invisible in Israeli society. I saw that the so-called powerlessness of Arab women, a notion that I had imbibed from Western media and early second-wave feminism, obscured different kinds of power I had never encountered among women. The Palestinian and Israeli men and women that I met during my early years there helped to formulate my questions here.

I learned that no matter how angered I was by injustices incurred by Israel's creation or its contradictions as a democratic and Jewish state, that it and its peoples' survival were a victory. I learned that no matter how angered I was by tragedies wrought by Palestinian violence or their rejection of Israel, Palestinians' dignity and independence were paramount.

The apparent impossibility of celebrating both peoples' nationalist achievements set me on a course of investigation. Inspiration gained from those six years of work and friendship with Israeli and Palestinian women and men eventually propelled me to return to the university for formal study of Middle East history. Unfortunately, but not surprisingly, I found that the polarization and tensions so characteristic of the conflict permeated academia. Yet by then I was determined to reject the dismissal or vilification of one people's national aspirations to legitimize or romanticize the other.

When gender emerged as a mode of analysis in the late 1980s, I began research for a dissertation that forms the basis of this book. In this work, "gender" is a vehicle for exposing contradictions within each people's historical narratives and for underscoring the legitimacy of each people's desire for political empowerment. Since the 1993 signing of the Declaration of Principles for a negotiated settlement, this position has become less subversive and more imperative as setbacks to peace return us to an outmoded and tragically untenable future.

The book explores issues of women and gender from the late nineteenth through mid-twentieth centuries. It contends that the two national movements in Palestine turned women and gender into linchpins of conflict and possibilities of interconnection. These processes do not end in 1948 but evolve within new political contexts created with the state of Israel and the Palestinian exile. The consequences for gender and politics in Israel and Palestine after 1948 are beyond the scope of this book and indeed enjoy significantly more scholarly attention than the pre-1948 period.

I have divided the study into four parts. Part I provides a context for the work both in terms of scholarship and history. Chapter 1 introduces objectives, sources, methodological approaches, and problems of an exploration of "(en)gendering nations," of two peoples claiming one land. Chapter 2 of this first part peruses the scholarship that grounds this study and shows how it is unique. Chapters 3 and 4 construct a narrative history of the conflict from the nineteenth to mid-twentieth centuries highlighting the evolution of two new national identities.

Part II contains three chapters that probe the ways nationalists imagined their communities through particular gender tropes. It examines representations of manhood and masculinity (chapter 5), the feminization of the land as the central symbol of both national movements (chapter 6), and nationalist fantasies about "their" women (chapter 7).

Part III investigates how women and gender operated in the construction of hierarchies of difference and power between the two peoples. At the intersection of nationalism and modernization, treatment of women became a gauge of progress and civilization (chapter 8). Debates about the importance and content of girls' education nuanced discourse on national progress (chapter 9). Narratives in film, plays, and literature turned women and issues of gender into validation of the national "self" and invalidation of the enemy "other." Each group formed attitudes towards the other in part through judgments about the others' women and by characterizing the enemy with gendered metaphors (chapter 10).

Part IV returns to a historical chronology of conflict, this time with focus on the actions, writings, desires, and protests of the women for whom nationalism opened unprecedented opportunities (chapter 11). So the chronological context of historical narrative (chapters 3, 4, and 11) brackets the six chapters of discourse analysis (chapters 5 through 10). Chapter 12, the final chapter, probes Jewish and Arab women's interactions with each other that transgressed conventional boundaries between the two peoples. It examines how women contested standard narratives of conflict and created alternative modes of understanding and action.

Issues of women and gender were an intricate part of creating, defining, and perpetuating conflict in Palestine. This is true for all national movements. What was unique to Arab and Jewish nationalisms was that each side constructed its identities in part on the belief that the other's movement was so utterly different and irreconcilable from its own. Yet a deconstruction of sexual and political identities also reveals hidden possibilities of interconnectedness.

I want to thank the *Arab Studies Journal* for granting me permission to use material from my article on "*Shahada* and *Haganah*." I also thank I. B. Tauris for allowing me to use material previously published in a chapter of *Gendering the Middle East* and the volume's editor, Deniz Kandiyoti, for encouraging me to summarize my research in her cutting-edge collection. Chapter 9 was originally presented as a paper at the World Union of Jewish Studies Conference in Jerusalem in 1997.

Zachary Lockman guided this project in the initial research phase for a dissertation as my advisor at Harvard. Susan Miller, then associate director of the Center for Middle East Studies at Harvard, labored over the details and theoretical implications with intelligent precision. Judith Tucker read the manuscript in its entirety as a dissertation and contributed sage insight. Most recently, Roger Owen found time while director of the Center for Middle East Studies at Harvard to read this work and pose tough questions that helped to morph it from dissertation to book.

The spirit of my teachers infuses these pages: Lisa Anderson, Ali Asani, Leila Fawaz, William Graham, Stanley Hoffman, Herbert Kelman, Roy Mottahedeh, Nadav Safran, and Paula Sanders. My students at Harvard and Berklee demanded clarification of my ideas in ways that enlivened the text.

Awards granted by Harvard University, the Center for Middle East Studies at Harvard, Foreign Language and Area Studies, and the U.S. Department of Education made it possible to begin this work. Financial support from the Berklee College of Music for travel and research made it possible to continue the work. A year as Scholar-in-Residence at Brandeis University's International Research Institute on Jewish Women freed me from teaching responsibilities and provided the intellectual and practical support that enabled me to complete the work.

Collegial conversations and collaborations in this country and in the Middle East helped me through the difficulties of the work. My appreciation goes to Leila Ahmed, Janet Aviad, Bishara Bisharat, Ghada Bisharat, Lisa Blum, Palmyra Brummett, Esther Eillam, Sara Graham-Brown, Huda Lufti, Elias Jabbour, Afsaneh Najmabadi, Julie Peteet, Najwa al-Qattan, and Gershon Shafir.

Michael, Ari, Lily, and Noah Appel are constant sources of love and humor vital for productivity. In addition, many women and men around the world sustain me with their clear thinking, brazen courage, and persistence in pursuing progressive change. Among them, individual Israeli and Palestinian women and men—who made six years in Jerusalem as well as countless meetings and wild adventures in Israel, the Sinai, the West Bank, Cyprus, Egypt and Europe, a learning and loving experience—remain the inspiration for this book.

I

Texts and Contexts

1

(En)Gendering Nations

Introduction

All nationalisms are gendered; all are invented; and all are dangerous . . . in the sense that they represent relations to political power
and to the technologies of violence.

Anne McClintock, *Dangerous Liaisons*

Political identity . . . never exists in the forces of an absolute, inte-
rior self or community, but always as an already-divided relation
of self/other. Political identity, this means to say, is no more sin-
gular or absolute than the identity of words in a system of writing. . . . There are no political 'units,' no atomistic, undivided
selves; only relations or forces of difference, out of which identities are formed as something always self-divided and contingent.

Tim Mitchell, *Colonizing Egypt*

In the latter half of the nineteenth century and first half of the twentieth
century, Jews and Arabs began to articulate hopes for a new future in
which their children might live independent lives in newly imagined
communities, or nations. From the beginning, old dreams of a new future
offered fertile ground for conflict not only over the hills and valleys of
Palestine and Israel but over the hearts, minds, and bodies of women.
Arab and Jewish women became central to new national identities and to
the conflict between them.

Yet nowhere does gender seem more remote than in the narratives of
political history where women are absent and men ubiquitous. Volumes
of Palestinian and Israeli historical and political analyses yield hardly a
word about the roles or concerns of women, generating an overwhelming
impression that gender is irrelevant to politics. But it is on this seeming
irrelevance that particular political arrangements depend. The maintenance of power relations that bolster complex hierarchies of difference
depend on the exclusion of women from political discourse.

The obliteration of women from politics perpetuates violence just as narratives of nationalism justify war. My aim is to expose the myths of nationalism and the marginalization of women in politics, both of which exacerbate conflict in Palestine. I want to show how conflicting political discourses that were overtly or covertly gendered contributed to the creation of two national communities and the conflict between them. McClintock, Mufti, and Shohat have argued that "nation, community, race, class, religion, gender, sexuality—each names a site for the re-enactment of the great drama of origins, loyalty, belonging, betrayal, in short, of identity and identification."[1] Cynthia Enloe's work demonstrates that these great dramas within and between nations are dependent not only on economic and military factors, but on the construction of gender.[2]

The growth of nationalism and international conflict thus depends at least in part on control of actual women and of women as symbols. This is also true for men. Interpretations of international conflict based on conventional notions of nations often mask multiple layers of hostility within and between nations based on gender, class, race, or ethnicity. Cynthia Cockburn commented that "a feminist is likely to see 'community' and 'people' as seductive words that hide gender and class inequalities within. Because she has seen how the innocent notion of 'home' conceals confinement, divisions, oppression, and violence, she is the more likely to be skeptical of 'homeland.'"[3]

The idea that gender undergirds the evolution of nationalism and political violence is not new. For the past thirty years there has been a growing understanding of ways in which women and gender were part of bloody battles in the world and in texts over colonization, independence, westernization, and preservation of traditions. The present study explores some of the particular ways this happened in Palestine. This chapter opens the investigation by introducing (1) gender as a unit of analysis, (2) nationalism as discourse, (3) sources and methodologies, (4) problems of studying both peoples in one book, and (5) terms of discourse.

Gender as a Unit of Analysis

Joan Scott defines gender as the changing social roles assigned to men and women in different historical periods and in different places; it is neither the sole nor most important element to analyze, but a remarkably significant one.[4] In a study of gender in Islamic law in Ottoman Syria and Palestine, Judith Tucker approached gender in two ways. On one hand, "gender is the symbolic construction produced . . . by Muslim thinkers who developed a consciously Islamic legal discourse."[5] On the other hand, Tucker continued, "gender as a social relationship is the product of the historical development of human experience."[6] The same can be said for Jewish and Palestinian Arab nationalists who consciously describe elements of a new modern political identity that include what it means to be a man or a woman.

By using gender as a unit of analysis, one can venture beyond old categories, insular historical visions, and the "international relations" paradigms that dominate writings on Palestine and Israel. Gender encompasses political, cultural, economic, and social constructs. Some change over time and place and others do not. Studying gender in politics can expose unequal power relations, power/knowledge matrices, dominant and subaltern discourses that contribute to ideas about womanhood, manhood, and nationhood.

For Simona Sharoni, gender relations both within and between Palestinian and Israeli communities constitute a central role in shaping international conflict.[7] I agree with Sharoni that prospects for a peaceful solution to the conflict "depend upon our ability and courage to call into question the gendered language and assumptions that inform dominant interpretations and practices of the Israeli-Palestinian conflict."[8] Yet one must go beyond her investigation of the past decade or two to a far-reaching look at the formative years of the conflict. This was a time when Arabs and Jews in Palestine were cantankerously figuring out what it meant to be a national community.

Several aspects of gender-nation relations were evident in the formative stages of Arab and Jewish political identities before 1948. They were present in the ways that nationalist discourse (1) constructed manhood and womanhood in the process of defining peoplehood, (2) feminized and masculinized certain central symbols of "nation-ness," and (3) developed ideologies of modernization which seized upon "woman" as signifier of "progress" or "backwardness." Changing roles of women and men in Jewish and Arab society played an important, though often hidden, role in the formation of national identity, just as the formation of new national identities made an impact on the evolving roles of women and men.

Rashid Khalidi in *Palestinian Identity* stated that "if one takes identity to be the answer to the question, 'who are you?' it is clear that the response of the inhabitants of Palestine has changed considerably over time."[9] The transformation of pre-nationalist loyalties into national identity entailed a new articulation of "who are we?" and "who are they?" The three aspects of nation-gender relations mentioned above contributed to an ongoing creation and contestation of answers to those questions. Imagining and describing differences, whether between Jews and Arabs, and later Israelis and Palestinians, or between men and women, were part of the new relationships of power in Palestine and Israel.

Discourse on nation and gender was neither unchanging nor univocal, and evolved in the context of relations between and among the two peoples. Political and social processes fostered hegemonies of men over women, Arabs over Jews as a Middle Eastern minority, and finally, Israelis over Palestinians when Israel became a state backed by world powers. Yet although the historical context continually shifted from the 1860s to 1940s, gender continued to operate in the construction of two opposing political movements.

Study of the discourses of nation and gender does not eclipse the reality of women's agency; women actively colluded with, resisted, and created fluctuating constructs of identity. This research, however, is not so much a retrieval of women's history as an uncovering of the operations of gender that include women's changing roles. The uncovering of new information about the histories of women is a project of critical importance that exceeds the parameters of this work.[10] Yet national histories of Jews and Palestinians before 1950 were, in Joan Scott's words, "enacted on a field of gender," so that the politics of nationalism constructed gender and the politics of gender constructed nationalism.[11]

When Benedict Anderson elaborated his seminal theory of the nation as an "imagined community," he overlooked gender as a significant cultural artifact.[12] Several years later, however, Patricia Yaeger opened a conference at Harvard devoted to the study of "Nationalisms and Sexualities" with the assertion that the social construction of differences between men and women, and the power relationships between them, were at both the "heart and margins" of nationalism.[13] During the years between Anderson's publication and Yaeger's remarks, researchers exposed gender's imbrication in politics. In 1989, the same year as the conference, Elaine

Showalter introduced *Speaking of Gender* with an assertion that the study of gender in politics and social science was the most significant intellectual breakthrough, or paradigm shift, of the decade.[14]

The assumption that politics was a gender-neutral domain was under attack not only in the academy but in the media as well. By 1990, media coverage of the U.S.–Iraqi confrontation, for example, attended to issues of women and gender in unprecedented ways. There were articles about roles of women in the U.S. military and images of Iraqi women on television. Women appeared on television as hostages or in amiable conversation with Saddam Husayn. Articles foregrounded Arab masculinity and conflated sexuality and violence in descriptions of Saddam himself.[15] These were a few instances of ways that gender entered discourse on nationalism and international conflict, marking boundaries between "us" and "them" and justifying war.

Thus in addition to historical, political, and social configurations of gender, there were sexual constructs, too. Evelyn Accad located sexuality as central to "motivations of war."[16] Accad defined sexuality as "not only the physical and psychological relations between men and women . . . but the customs . . . involved in relations between men and women . . . as well as the notion of territory attached to possession and jealousy."[17] Defending and delineating sexuality was a raison d'etre of nationalism and intrinsic to its formation of identities and conflict.

Nationalism as Discourse

Untold numbers of intricately detailed and well-researched narrative histories of Palestine and Israel exclude, distort, or attack each "other." In fact, these writings of the histories of Palestine and Israel are inextricably linked to the creation of the political movements themselves. Ted Swedenburg's work suggests that the remembering of national history can not include the "other" as equal.[18] Each history portrays the "other" as a threat to national existence. Yet revisionist histories over the past two decades have expanded the discourse on the history of Palestine and Israel to include more nuanced and less mythological narratives of "national self" and "enemy other."[19]

Nationalism is not biologically determined but rather a social construct composed of competing interpretations of real and imagined phenomena. Lynn Hunt's work on the French Revolution showed "how political language could be used rhetorically to build a sense of community and at the same time to establish new fields of social, political, and cultural struggle—that is, make possible unity and difference at the same time."[20] When Benedict Anderson wrote about nation as "imagined community," he took an early step in applying some of the insights of postmodernists such as Michel Foucault to deconstruct the formation of modern political identity.[21] This book emerges from these and many other analyses of nationalism.[22] It treats nationalism as "collective identities contingent in nature," stating that it "emerges and declines under specific historical circumstances."[23] Ran Greenstein evoked Hobsbawm's work when he argued that "much national mythology is a conscious creation by intellectuals who take it upon themselves to construct a viable identity for their own group."[24]

Helena Lindholm Schulz referred to nationalism as an ideology of "boundedness" in both political and social terms, dependent on the creation and maintenance of an "us" and a "them." By its nature, nationalism contains two opposing forces. On one hand, it is inclusive: a means for collective security, belonging, identity, emancipatory, liberating, anticolonial, and capable of embracing different ethnic groups under one citizenship. On the other hand, it is also exclusive: aggressive, expansionist, incorporating racist stereotyping of an "other."[25] In considering the specific case of Palestinian women, Nahla Abdo concurred that nationalism is both a force of domination/oppression that subordinates different groups (including women) and a force of liberation.[26]

Palestinian and revisionist Zionist historians have been exposing old nationalist narratives for the implicit power/knowledge matrices they contain. This study is part of the attempt by historians to adopt what Zachary Lockman referred to as a "critical stance toward categories of historical analysis." These categories are developed, in the case of Palestine and Israel, by two opposing nationalist narratives written "from within (and implicitly accepting the premises of) either Zionist or Arab Palestinian nationalist historical narratives."[27] The study of gender can expose nationalism to be what Lockman described as "a more subtle and flexible conception . . . a complex of ideas, symbols, sentiments, and practices which people . . . deploy selectively and contingently."[28]

Jonathan Boyarin argued that we are at a critical juncture in our choice of political identity, which can be either "ahistorical, rigid, exclusive" or a "transcultural reintegration of our own history and the history of the "Other." Boyarin remarked that

> formulations of both Zionism and Palestinian nationalism are marked by a curious combination on the one hand, of claims of priority, of being the nation that 'really' belongs to the land, and on the other hand, of claims to representing the side of progress in this national struggle. The Israeli–Palestinian conflict is thus a struggle for both land and history, space and time. . . . [In fact history is] one of the major stakes over which Israelis and Palestinians still contend.[29]

Beshara Doumani critiqued the conventional nationalist narratives by Palestinians and Israelis, stating that "throughout this century, the interplay between power and knowledge has produced a series of tunnel visions, each of which questions the legitimacy of the other."[30]

Yet for women their location in the national narrative is even more problematic than for their people as a whole. Cynthia Enloe stated that nationalisms have "typically sprung from masculinized memory, masculinized humiliation and masculinized hope."[31] Davida Wood critiqued Benedict Anderson's work on nationalism from a gendered perspective by pointing out that he

> fails to address the putative decline of concepts of hierarchical political authority in the societies to which their national model is transplanted. Do all other concepts of political authority simply lose their grip once nationalism appears?[32]

Wood has shown in her own research that "the elaboration of national identity is intertwined with Palestinian critiques of kinship and gender orderings."[33]

Reading the Sources

This work brings new questions to old materials. Most of the sources are available to the general reader in English translated from Arabic, Hebrew, and other languages in nationalist anthologies. But in these familiar writings, there is a discovery of issues previously unnoticed and overlooked. It is the very accessibility of these sources that accentuates previous failures to see the ubiquity of women and gender in the development of political identity and conflict. These are not obscure archival documents but rather published writings, which make it all the more remarkable that operations of gender in formative political processes have been ignored.

Discourse on women and gender in nationalism appeared in the published nonfiction and fiction writings about Palestine by Jews and Arabs who lived in and out of Palestine. It is in these published texts written by men and women, read by men and women who took part in formulating national identity, that one can glimpse rich evidence of the intersection between nation and gender. The sources include excerpts from old polemical tracts on the ancient and future nation, detailed revisionist histories, memoirs of nationalists, biographies, recorded interviews, newspaper and magazine editorials and letters, poetry, plays, short stories, film, and novels.

Men and women who authored these sources wrote mostly before and during the British Mandate years, from around the 1860s to the 1940s. But the arguments and attitudes of nationalists about issues of women and gender don't magically start in 1860 or end in 1948. Some memoirs, biographies, and studies were written later. Memoirs written in the 1970s, such as Golda Meir's or Atallah Mansour's, are in some ways more about the 1970s than about the period of their focus but nevertheless contain valuable information about the period they attempt to evoke. Works by authors who lived through the pre-1948 period but published in the 1950s can still be informative, such as Tibawi's study on education in the Mandate period or films such as "Hill Twenty-Four Does Not Answer" or "Tomorrow Is a Wonderful Day."

The use of published sources poses a problem for understanding class. Writers and readers of these materials were primarily from the literate middle and upper classes; they often wore blinders in regards to their peoples' class distinctions. In the case of Palestinian Arabs, the nationalist writers were primarily from urban areas. Important distinctions of class tended to disappear. Yet the differences in experience and perception around issues of women and gender between urban middle classes and rural peasants were significant. It was the urban literate Palestinian classes, however, whose vision of "the woman question" prevailed in these literatures.

The sources do reveal differences of content and intent, male and female authorship, ideological positions on politics and sexuality, and literary format. English-language translations, nonarchival and secondary sources by no means create an exhaustive survey but rather an array of voices. Arabs and Jews in Palestine wrote some of these sources; Arabs and Jews outside Palestine authored other texts. One characteristic that distinguished Palestinian and Jewish nationalism from other nationalisms was that Arabs and Jews who did not live in Palestine contributed to the discourse. Egyptians, Lebanese, and others Arabs, as well as Jews who had never been to Palestine or who visited it on occasion, also took part in imagining the new national community there and the nature of gender relations within it.

In his book *Palestine and Modern Arab Poetry*, Khalid Sulaiman argued that Palestinian issues had profound impact on the content and essence of all Arab poetry. One may also argue that poets and writers throughout the Arab world had impact on culture and politics within Palestine. Jews, too, from outside Palestine who visited or fantasized about it took part in the construction of manhood, womanhood, and peoplehood. The idea of "rebuilding" a nation in Zion fired the imagination of certain Jews around the world who wrote about it in a myriad of forms. Elements of these literatures had bearing on the thought and action of Jews in Palestine.

The texts must be read as much for omission as commission. Ella Shohat, in her work on Israeli film, described cinematic images that "provoke a rupture with the text, by unveiling, where necessary, its mythical tendencies . . . to expose the text's other face, to make its silence speak."[34] Joan Scott dealt with silence and evasion within texts when she wrote that "'non-actors. . .' are acting according to rules established in the public realm; the private sphere is a public creation.[35] Miriam Cooke wrote that war was conceived as man's affair not because women were absent from battlefields but because they were absent from its histories.

In *War's Other Voices*, Cooke exposed the battles of high diplomacy, waged in a familiar succession of seemingly endless hostilities expressed in texts as well as embassies and battlefields. Nationalism, like war, persisted through writing as well as through weaponry. "Men called themselves generals, leaders, warriors, ideologues, and then they assigned supporting roles to women, naming their experiences."[36] Close reading of primary and secondary sources from within and outside Palestine by men and women offer glimpses of these processes for Arabs and Jews.

One can mine nationalist texts for issues of gender even if women are ostensibly absent. Gender exists in ideological presuppositions, in who is doing the speaking, seeing, or acting, in who has no right to speak, in whose views are not expressed, in whose actions are considered irrelevant, in what the speaker finds important to include in narratives or to omit. It is fascinating to reread old nationalist texts within these interpretive guidelines. It becomes possible to read for implicit and explicit assumptions about identity and conflict, for values of nationalism and modernity, for omissions and misinformation. This kind of reading reveals how writers co-opted women and gender for central national symbols, for portraits of ideal men and women, for constructions of heroism, and for enforcement of inequalities between sexes and inequalities between peoples.

Some sources self-consciously, often vociferously, address "the woman question," while others offer muted inferences and unspoken assumptions regarding gender in the new nation. Almost all share the conscious sense that women and issues of gender are irrelevant, or at best marginal, to the national project. Yet when taken together, the writings illuminate the centrality of women and gender in the construction of new political identities.

Problems of Asymmetry

The study of women and gender in two national movements provides a historiographical opportunity to further an integrative or relational approach to the history of Palestine. The use of gender as a category of analysis is one way to hold both histories up to a fresh light, and to ask similar questions of each people's history. But an attempt to hold both sides accountable to similar questions about gender implies a symmetry to both sides that simply did not exist.

There is no symmetry in Israeli–Palestinian relations, politics, or histories. Yet there are many reasons why this truth is often lost. Similarities between the two movements can seduce one into a sense of mutuality: both are nationalist, focus on the same land, construct the other as the major obstacle to peace and independence, and think the other is to blame for past injustice and responsible for future resolution. There is a sense that each has irrevocably wounded the other and that each must change policies and actions towards the other for protracted war to end. Nissim Rejwan captured some of the appearance of symmetry in his observations about similarities and differences between Zionism and pan-Arabism:

> In truth, the Zionists and the pan-Arabs have too much in common—too great an ideological affinity with each other, the lines of their respective political development are too parallel, and their national aspirations too obviously fixed on the same object—for them to be able to come together or even accept each other's presence. In pure ideological terms, at least, they have been in agreement on almost every issue, with the crucial exception of one: the right of the other side to lead a sovereign political existence in that strip of territory that both consider their homeland. . . . The two positions are also entirely a-historical. Jews and Muslim Arabs lived side by side through at least fifteen centuries of their history—and they did so in a way that no adherents of any other two faiths have ever managed to do.[37]

Thus a sense of symmetry tends to obscure the power imbalances that always existed and continue to exist in relations between the two peoples. For the centuries that Jews lived in Muslim Arab lands they were a subordinated minority living on the good will of their hosts, whose guidelines were legal policies protecting non-Muslims or *dhimmis*.[38] In the current situation Palestinians live within the limits of what Israel is willing or not willing to give, but Jews of Israel remain a minority within the Arab majority of the region.

Asymmetries of history and of power relations between two peoples constitute a challenge for any study that seeks to address aspects of both peoples' realities. This study operates under the constraints and premises articulated in the most recent works by Rogan, Shlaim, Boyarin, and Bernstein. In Eugene Rogan's and Avi Shlaim's volume on revisionist history of Palestine, there is an awareness of the asymmetry of sources. By its political victory, Israel had official political and military archives. Israeli revisionist historians could work with new materials released from archives. But due in large part to political defeat of statehood for

Palestinians, they had no formal archives bolstered by government funds. Instead there were personal narratives and eyewitness accounts. Furthermore, Arab archives in several countries are still closed.[39]

When Jonathan Boyarin told a fellow anthropologist that he was planning to study the "rhetorical construction of Palestinian and Israeli national identity," the colleague adamantly advised: "Don't try to do both of them. There is no way you'll have comparable information from both sides." Boyarin concurred that this was "sensible advice" but nevertheless served to reinforce old boundaries. So instead he strove not to have "illusions or demands on myself to 'obtain equal access' to Israelis and Palestinians."[40] Deborah Bernstein's study of Jewish and Arab workers in Mandatory Palestine also attempted to break down false historical dichotomies of internal Jewish settlement development separate from an external Arab world. Yet in her attempt to work with materials on both sides she clarified her limits: "I do not claim to be able to present both groups with as much detail, or with anything like as much sensitivity. I do not know if anyone can."[41] Thus, this study, too, loses depth of detail of each side's history but gains a breadth of perspective on the conflict between them.

Asymmetries apply to realities about gender in the conflict as well. There are voluminously more materials on each side about Arab and Jewish men than about women. Men and women had unequal access to writing and publishing during this period. But focusing on women's experience alone produces its own imbalances. There are more writings by Jewish women than by Arab women, and they had more access to public action, debate, writing, and reading than their Palestinian sisters. Most significantly, each side had different notions about gender that grew out of differences in the two communities' political leadership, social structure, cultural norms, and historical development.

Another issue regarding the sources concerns the writings of Jews and Arabs living in Palestine versus those beyond its borders. Neither Arabs nor Jews of Palestine wrote or formulated their ideas on nation and gender in a vacuum. This study takes into account ideas beyond the borders of Palestine that had bearing on the political development there. Drawing on Egyptian, Lebanese, or Syrian sources, on one hand, or European Jewish writings, on the other, evokes the breadth and complexity of cross-cultural fertilization of competing strands of nationalism. This does not mean that Palestinian Arabs were merely pan-Arabs, or that Palestinian

Jews were merely European. Yet it is as useful to read ideas about gender and nation written by Egyptians and Lebanese as to examine *Altneuland,* a fictional fantasy of the future of Palestine by Theodor Herzl, a liberal Viennese Jew living at the turn of the century.

Another difficulty of this work concerns the multivalent nature of nationalism itself. There has never been one Jewish or Palestinian nationalist movement but instead multiple factions and ideologies that compete with, defeat, or complete each other. Jewish and Palestinian nationalisms changed over time, were contested from within and without. In *Comrades and Enemies,* Zachary Lockman stated that it is counter-productive to "essentialize discourses . . . as if they were unitary, internally unconflicted and unchanging over time" and that "in Palestine neither Jewish nor Arab nationalisms were unitary or static objects."[42]

In proceeding with this study despite these pitfalls, it is necessary to clarify the terms of discourse which in themselves are politically charged. In this book, Palestine refers to the land on which both peoples lived; Israel and Israelis did not yet exist. In this work Jewish settlers in Palestine are referred to as Jews or as Zionists or as Palestinian Jews. Arab inhabitants of Palestine are referred to as Arabs or Palestinians or Palestinian Arabs. "Zionism" is a term synonymous with modern political "Jewish nationalism"; I use both terms interchangeably to refer to the modern political movement for Jewish national liberation. I assume that both peoples' development of modern collective identity and international conflict had its roots in political, economic, and social changes of the nineteenth and twentieth centuries, and not in ancient religious or civilizational orientations.

This study assumes the underlying legitimacy of both movements in Palestine. This simple notion has been attacked or dismissed from both sides. On one hand, some argue that Palestinians were never a people before 1948: that they did not think of themselves as separate from the Ottoman Empire or later from a pan-Arab entity. This argument assumes they did not come to their Palestinian-ness until after 1948 (or even after 1967). The argument continues that the claim that there was an earlier Palestinian identity is the result of propaganda aimed in classic anti-Semitic fashion at the undermining of Jewish national existence.

Others argue that Jews are not a nation but a religion. Jewish culture, they argue, encompasses so many nationalities, races, ethnicities, and linguistic categories that Jewish nationalism is an artifice brought about by foreign colonial agitation and propaganda to right the wrongs of European anti-Semitism by robbing the Palestinians of their rightful sovereignty over Palestine.

This work rejects these assumptions and instead presumes the development of a distinct modern political Palestinian Arab identity with roots as far back as the eighteenth century. It also presumes that a modern political identity began to take shape for Jews in Europe after the French Revolution, with Jewish *Haskala* or Enlightenment. One of the many responses Jews made to the challenges of modernity was nationalist. But acknowledging the early growth of national consciousness also means recognizing the fluidity and flux of national identities. Collective identity everywhere was a construct that changed over time. Nadim Rouhana's work on collective identity of Palestinians in Israel argued that not only does national identity change but it must change to end the conflict.[43]

In his work on the "genealogies" of the conflict, Ran Greenstein stated that "we should treat national and racial groups as unstable in nature, not as immutable entities."[44] He reminds us that "Arab" was a term used in the late–nineteenth-century Ottoman Empire to describe only desert nomads. By the 1920s, "Arab" described Arabic speakers throughout the Middle East excluding only those Arabic speakers who were Jews. By then Arab was a term universally accepted by the group itself. Those called Jews were seen in a variety of changing ways over the past two centuries: for example, as a non-Muslim religious minority (Middle East), as foreign nationals (pre-Enlightenment Eastern Europe), or as a white ethnic or religious group (United States).

Because of the challenges of this kind of study, the attempt to examine gender in two antagonistic national movements faces the danger of becoming "orientalist" (oversimplifying or invalidating Arab life in Palestine) or "anti-Zionist" (distorting or invalidating Jewish life in Palestine). This is not my intention. I hope the reader will recognize any invalidation of legitimacy or dignity as my own shortcomings as a student of these histories and not the limits of the peoples themselves. It is useful to acknowledge any such shortcomings explicitly in all scholarship that attempts a re-vision of these intersecting, politically charged histories.

Reframing Questions

Scaffolds of Scholarship

> In Palestine many powerful and contradictory views of self and of
> history are conjoined.
>
> Rashid Khalidi, *Palestinian Identity*

Although women were absent from most historical accounts of Palestine
before 1948, they were present in its historical realities. For the past
twenty-five years, scholars have been involved in a process of discovery
of their roles. For the past fifteen years, in addition to uncovering information about women, there has been an investigation into operations of
gender in political processes. New questions and methodologies now
make it possible to examine the roles of women and men in early nationalism in new ways.

This chapter examines some of the literature on women and gender in
political processes and specifically in nationalism around the world. It
also explores writings about gender and nationalism in Middle Eastern,
Palestinian, and Israeli contexts. An analysis of this growing body of literature reveals both the scaffold of scholarship that makes this study possible and the omissions of scholarship that make this study unique.

Textual Contexts I: Women and Gender in Nationalism

It is not an accident that, at the same time Israeli and Palestinian women
began to challenge patriarchal strictures in their respective societies in
the 1970s, scholars began to explore connections between women and
their political movements. Their actions opened up a new terrain of writing about women and gender. This section focuses on literature that

raised new questions about women and gender in the construction of political identities.

One of the early examples of this kind of analysis can be found in the writings of Frantz Fanon concerning the Algerian revolution (1954–62). Fanon described a battle for control of the country waged literally and figuratively over the bodies of Algerian women by French colonial administrators and Algerian resistance leaders, both of whom equated the flesh of woman with the flesh of the nation. *A Dying Colonialism* detailed the French administration's attempt to usurp Algerian "manhood" by seeking control over one profound aspect of Algerian culture, women's dress, encouraging Algerian women to unveil in order to modernize the country. Algerian men, on the other hand, fought to retain control of "their" women's dress to preserve cultural authenticity symbolized in their traditional garb. French "experts" on "native affairs" believed that if they won over Algerian women to their conception of "modernization," the rest of Algeria would follow:

> After each success the authorities were strengthened in their conviction that the Algerian woman would support Western penetration into native society. Every rejected veil disclosed to the eyes of the colonists horizons until then forbidden, and revealed to them, piece by piece, the flesh of Algeria laid bare.[1]

The explosion of second-wave feminism in the West in the early 1970s made an indelible impact on academia. Some of the new writings turned to the previously hidden connections between men and women, colonizer and colonized, and developed and developing nations. In 1972, for example, Sheila Rowbotham identified the "noble savage" and the "earth mother" as "impotent self-binding symbols of the qualities the white man in capitalism has destroyed for himself." She exposed some of the contradictions for women in male-dominated national liberation movements:

> Only in the abnormal circumstances of political revolt . . . is it possible to take uncustomary actions. It has been national independence movements which have created the impetus for the active involvement of women outside the small social elite. . . . [Yet] bourgeois nationalism has proved consistently incapable of answering the needs of . . . poor Third World women.[2]

Throughout the 1970s, scholars uncovered hitherto unacknowledged roles of women in nationalism. Temma Kaplan studied political movements in Spain, noting that leaders made their appeals to women and men in different ways and organized men and women differently to contribute to the revolution.[3] Other scholars studied women under the most virulent and militant form of nationalism, fascism in Nazi Germany.[4] By the end of the decade the focus began to include men in ways that challenged the unspoken assumption that there existed gender-neutral universalist political processes. Klaus Theweleit was working in Germany at this time on a provocative study titled *Male Fantasies*, which would not be published in English until the 1980s.

Theweleit read the diaries of German World War I soldiers in the *Freikorps* for references to women or gender to describe the political culture out of which fascism arose. *Male Fantasies* illustrates the binding of self-identity to manhood and nationality, as boys came to see themselves first and foremost as German men. Their desire was to rid themselves of tormenting feelings of failure acquired in a German society infused with bourgeois values. They experienced the anti-eroticism of marital relations, the formal quality of neighborly relations "united as wearers of granite expressions," limitations based on "impenetrable circles of refusals and prohibitions," bullying as schoolboys, terror as cadets, and the severe wounds of war. Women were perceived as part of men's lives and the nation. They were either indistinct, nameless, disembodied women (absent wives and fiancées, women left behind, and the chaste German upper-middle-class "white nurses" on the battle front) or class enemies (lower-class or "red women" perceived as whores, as figures in angry mobs, or as individuals who must be killed).[5]

Theweleit's work dealt with the "political symbolism and the sexual component of the idea of nationhood, masses, and power" in a kind of psychological history of nationalism.[6] Fascism was portrayed not merely as a form of government, economy, or system but rather as a social psychology of male sovereignty in which "love of women and love of country are at opposite poles."[7] Men were permitted to love and admire guns, horses, other powerful men, the nation, homeland, native soil, and other members of the community: church, nation, or troops. But they had to leave their women behind to become real men—capable of defending the nation and able to eventually return home as "real" men to real women for whom they nurtured unreal fantasies. Theweleit wrote:

only a German war victory . . . will enable soldiers to become lovers
and husbands, Germany must first attain the status of a 'nation. . . .'
Personal sexual life is so closely bound up with concepts like . . .
'nation,' these concepts must be intimately related to the man's
body and to its ability to make love to women. . . . Male self-esteem
is dependent on the status of Germany, *not* on his actual relationship with a woman. [The New Man of the new bourgeois nationalist
society of Germany saw] women as mere appendages of developments in question . . . . Marriage was clearly tantamount to an oath
to uphold the state's notion of order, as well as an agreement to work
and to forego the vice of idleness.[8]

The study of gender thus assumed that understanding men's experience could deepen an understanding of women's experience in history by
exposing distortions in both their lives. Studies of nationalist narratives
in Europe, America, India, Africa, South America, and Asia theorized
gender (men's and women's roles) in diverse political contexts. George
Mosse, for example, discussed men and male homosexuality in European
nationalisms. He portrayed the ideals of manliness as limited concepts of
virility basic to bourgeois European society and its nation-states. Nationalism, according to Mosse, "co-opted the male search for friendship and
community" as manliness "symbolized the nation's spiritual and material vitality."[9] Woman was idealized and put firmly in her place while
symbolizing the sedate and immutable aspects of the nation; men came to
symbolize that which was dynamic and progressive.

The core ideals of what Mosse labeled "respectability" in European
bourgeois society, out of which modern nationalism developed, were constructed with contrasting stereotypes of the normal, the beautiful, and
the healthy versus the outsider, the diseased, and the dangerous whether
they be homosexual, Jew, foreigner, insane, or criminal. R. K. Martin
drew on both Mosse and Anderson when he discussed nationalism as an
"imagined brotherhood" which excluded homosexual men by appeal to a
specific kind of virility and by the stress on heterosexual love for spawn-
ing a larger and stronger nation, symbolized by royal families and first
ladies.[10]

Other studies addressed how essential notions of masculinity and
femininity contributed to new political symbolism of the nation. Lynn
Hunt treated "the diverse utterances of revolutionary politicians...as

constituting one text," finding that the Jacobins used concepts of masculinity to represent key notions of the revolution.[11] Marina Warner focused upon representations of idealized women as symbolic elements in the political culture of Europe. Idealized unnamed women portrayed ideals of "Justice" and "Liberty" in eighteenth- and nineteenth-century European art, at a time when women were denied these rights.[12]

Much of the work on gender in history in the 1980s focused on colonial and postcolonial struggles. Gayatri Spivak underlined the tensions between the oppression of colonized women and the male-led and male-conceived nationalist struggles that left intact gender limitations for both men and women.[13] Yet resistance and nationalist movements also provided women with new possibilities. Kumari Jayawardena argued that early indigenous feminist movements of the late–nineteenth and early–twentieth centuries flourished in different parts of Asia and the Middle East because of expanding nationalist consciousness.[14] Jayawardena linked expanding rights for women with nationalist, reformist, anticolonial impulses of this period. Several years later, Kumkum Sangari problematized this relationship between women's rights and nationalism. She argued that an understanding of a relationship between women's liberation and national liberation did not often take into account "the complexities of relations between class and patriarchy and the increasing politicization of 'religious' identities."[15]

At the 1989 Nationalisms and Sexualities Conference held at Harvard University, scholars investigated issues of gender in political processes that included the sexual body as an arena for nationalism; ties between the bourgeoisie, sex, soul, and nation; the construction of eros and polis upon each other; the eroticization of nationalism in literature; and the intertwining of longing and belonging in India, Ireland, Latin America, Africa, Asia, and the Middle East. English literature, for example, portrayed Irish men as barbaric, demasculinized, and impotent; it accused the men of living like women, and likened them to prostitutes. Irish women were seen as symbols of disorder and sedition.[16] Irish writers themselves feminized Ireland by treating their country as the mother or the ruined maid whose virginity was either saved by male Irish nationalists or trespassed.[17] English literature linked "feminine virtues" to a Celtic race represented as emotional, ineffectual, appreciative of beauty, and infantile.[18]

Using gender as a framework for analysis deconstructed not only colonizers but resistance leaders as well. Purnima Bose posed Gandhi's female imagery, constructed along traditional lines for anticolonial purposes, against Gandhi's actions that opened up nontraditional choices for Indian women and created for them more egalitarian, more public opportunities.[19] Ketu Katrak detailed the gendering of national symbols such as the policy of buying homespun goods made by Indian women, or the practice of choosing national heroines. Rather than picking an actual woman in Indian history who was renowned for dressing like a man to fight the British, male nationalists chose the mythical Draupadi, a woman in Hindu tradition who looked to Krishna for leadership. Katrak critiqued male patronage of women's liberation movements as serving their own purposes of furthering nationalists' goals.[20]

Some scholars compared the situation of women with the situation of colonized peoples who experienced economic and cultural exploitation. Paul Brophy, for example, likened women's bodies to territories under colonization, forced to produce offspring just as colonized peoples are forced to produce certain crops or to labor in certain sectors for the benefit of the colonizers. He compared the situation of colonization to rape, as colonizers exploited women and land, ravishing and deflowering both.[21]

Still others delineated differences between women as colonizers and women as colonized. Nancy Paxton showed how the British colonizers in India considered the rape of their women by Indian men the epitome of sacrifice for the national struggle. The figure of the English woman raped by the Indian man harboring feelings of revenge was thought to constitute English women's passive self-sacrifice to the British Empire.[22] In a book published the same year as the Harvard conference, Yuval-Davis underscored the problematic relationship between colonizer women and colonized women, asserting that "women themselves participate in the oppression and exploitation of women from other ethnic groups as well as from other economic classes."[23]

This research on the ways men and women, manhood, and womanhood shaped and were shaped by nationalism, colonialism, and political processes provides a groundwork for examining the intersections of gender and nationalism that were unique to Palestine and Israel. We now turn to the studies of gender that focused on societies of the Middle East, specifically on Palestine and Israel.

Textual Contexts II: Women and Gender in the Middle East

One aspect of the way nationalism affected women in the Middle East had to do with alternately mobilizing or marginalizing them depending on the stage of nationalist struggle. During nationalist crisis, women were mobilized to fight for the emerging nation. At these times, unprecedented opportunities emerged for public action and personal courage. Yet once the crisis passed, limitations on women's lives tightened. Elizabeth Fernea observed that

> prolonged violent conflict encourages men and women to cast off old roles and to develop new and more egalitarian male-female relationships. . . . After the immediate situation of common danger ends, women and men revert to older patterns.[24]

Nationalist crises, resistance movements, and especially the situation of outright war often expanded women's opportunities. Minecke Schipper found a reflection of this reality in Arab women's writings:

> Women have always played a vital role in the struggles to liberate their country. . . . Women in resistance movements have often had to work twice as hard to overcome the prejudices of their male comrades and prove they were the equal to men. Once independence is achieved, however, men often prefer to return to 'normal.'[25]

When national crises turned into protracted war, however, women also paid a steep price. "Where warfare has not consumed [women's] . . . relatives and their friends, destroyed their homes and their sources of livelihood, it has blunted aspirations and ideals, shifted personal goals and disrupted traditional family patterns."[26]

For women, nationalist pressures extended beyond the demands of war. Peacetime exerted heavy demands as well. Algerian women, for example, were in the crossfire of the battle for modernization: some nationalists argued for dramatic social change while others argued that survival was dependent on preservation of traditional values and women's traditional roles. Nowhere were women consulted about priorities for change or cultural preservation in national liberation. This was true for Palestinian women. National victories and defeats were predicated on their subordination to an emerging male leadership. In times of national crises in

Palestine in 1929, from 1936 to 1939, and in 1948, gender boundaries became more fluid. Palestinian women were admired for their courage and held up as symbols of national continuity, yet were refused basic social, economic, or political equality.

National wars depleted resources so that it devolved on women to re-plenish demographic strength through reproduction. Women were caught up in the issues of competing demographics and were supposed to provide the social conditioning that would ready their sons to die for the nation. Daughters, too, had to be taught to accept giving up lovers and husbands for the nation. After the state of Israel was created, Jewish women who gave birth to more than four children were rewarded mon-etarily by the state. Palestinian women attained one of the highest birth-rates in the world. Both sets of women were prized for their ability to strengthen sheer numbers of their people in the land.

Most works on Palestinian women focus on their current plight.[27] Historical studies before 1948 are the exceptions. Sarah Graham-Brown's photo-essay on the history of Palestinians was a breakthrough of sorts for making Arab women visible.[28] Yet the text and photos told two differ-ent stories. The written narrative, like almost every other narrative on Palestinian history, excluded women almost entirely. But the photos re-vealed a history and society replete with women, showing Palestinian women as prominent participants in so many aspects of their society. Women appeared in the photos from all classes, in rural and urban areas, at home and in public, as veiled shoppers in urban markets and as un-veiled Bedouin women with children on their backs, as beggars and lep-ers, and as exquisitely dressed townswomen in traditional dress posed in studios.

Graham-Brown's photo-essay extended our vision of Palestinian women in history and society by presenting women in all manner of agricultural work. Photos showed them weeding, planting, caring for livestock with babies hung in slings on hooks, harvesting alongside men, picking olives with men, working with children to extract olive oil, and sleeping on the threshing floor to protect their crops. Druze women were shown carrying stones when road building was compulsory in Ottoman times. Urban women could be seen using sewing machines, processing food grown in urban gardens, grinding wheat between millstones, baking bread in communal ovens, collecting water from the neighborhood well, and drying manure for fuel. They embroidered in groups at the Arab

Women's Union in Ramallah, crushed clay and threw pottery, and separated tobacco leaves for drying at the Nazareth Arab Cigarette and Tobacco Company, though it was rare to use women as cheap unskilled labor in industry.

Other works that contribute to the historical portrait of Palestinian women include Judith Tucker's investigation of the *sharia* (Islamic law) court records during Ottoman times.[29] Hamida Kazi and Julie Peteet revealed some of the early political work of Palestinian women in a section of an article and chapter, respectively, on Palestinian women's lives before 1948.[30] They described opportunities such as charitable organizations founded by middle- and upper-class women during the British Mandate period through which the women contributed to the national cause. Annelies Moors researched the relationship of women to property and inheritance in a study that extended back to the 1920s based on interviews with older women.[31]

Some studies of Palestinian women that are not historical nonetheless further our understanding of their roles in this early period. Rachel Taqqu and Kathryn March, for example, challenged conventional notions of public and political involvement among Palestinian women in women's informal associations.[32] The authors exposed the ways that Palestinian women had impact on their society but were generally hidden from view by the limits of Western notions of power, authority, and the public/private dichotomy. Ibrahim Muhawi and Sharif Kanaana confirmed generally unacknowledged realms of women's power, especially old women's power, in their introductory essay to their Palestinian folktales collection. Palestinian women exercised more power and authority as "other" in Palestinian society through the communication of ideas and values by the elderly women who relayed the *hikayat 'ajayiz*, the old women's tales. Muhawi and Kanaana argued that modernity itself destroyed women's traditional forms of authority, power, and networking, challenging the conventional view that tradition restricted them.[33]

In the late 1970s and early 1980s there began to emerge a new literature on the history and situation of Jewish women in Palestine, critiquing the Zionist claim of the liberated woman. Scholars began to argue that rather than liberating women according to the nationalist myth, Zionism actually limited their experience and subordinated their demands for equality. Lesley Hazelton wrote a path–breaking book in English, published in 1977, which raised new questions about women in Zionism and began to deconstruct Zionism's gendered rhetoric. Hazelton discussed women's early historical exclusion from the kibbutz, agricultural schools, defense organizations, and anything else outside the narrow definition of women's place based on centuries of Jewish tradition, European double standards, and patriarchal socialism. She analyzed formative institutions such as the kibbutz, army, Judaic concepts of gender that informed nationalism, cults of fertility in the demographic contest between Jews and Arabs in Palestine, and Zionist formulations of manhood.[34]

Some of the work on pre-1948 Israeli women focused on their experience of the kibbutz as a dramatic experiment in social change. Men wrote most studies on the kibbutz and asked why such experiments had failed to liberate women. As late as 1976, Tiger and Shepher employed the sociobiological argument that blamed the failure on women themselves. Women's so-called natural preference for closeness with their children and other essentialist female differences undermined social and economic equality.[35] Almost twenty years later, Marilyn Safir refuted these theories, locating failure of social equality in the system itself. In her article "The Kibbutz: An Experiment in Social and Sexual Equality?" she highlighted the difficulty women had in even joining the kibbutz. Once members, they struggled against the notion of work defined in male terms and against the undervaluation of female work.[36]

In fact, far from advancing the liberation of women, some argued that the kibbutz actually weakened the multiple bases of women's power. The kibbutz institutionalized disregard for the values of traditional female work and relegated women to the most menial tasks. Safir went back to the beginning of settlements in Israel in which there existed, at best, "one-way equality" that allowed women to do men's work but prevented men from doing household, educational, or service work. As the kibbutz developed in response to economic and military needs, traditional forms of respect and security for women, such as marriage, were rejected as reactionary, and a threat to group solidarity and the new economy. Nonfamilistic divisions of labor reduced women's engagement in the social services and drew them into production efforts. Women attempted to adopt male values and appearance in a continual battle to be included in the work designated by men as "nation-building."

Hidden in the egalitarian ideals of labor Zionism itself were the seeds of inequality. Dafna Izraeli pointed out that although the labor Zionists were committed to social equality within a socialist framework, they saw it as a by-product of an economic revolution. By defining "the problem of Jewish existence as the fundamental and overriding social issue to which all efforts had to be directed," Zionists reinforced the marginality of women's struggles.[37] Deborah Bernstein's work asked why

the struggle for gender equality remain[ed] a marginal episode throughout the period of social experimentation among Jewish settlers in Palestine, despite the fact that it was ideologically consistent with the general Zionist and especially Socialist-Zionist goals of creating an egalitarian society.[38]

Bernstein found many ways that inequality between men and women were reproduced despite the fact of an ideologically supportive labor movement and an active women worker's movement. Reasons for the inequality were numerous, including patriarchal Jewish society and a consensus that national liberation goals were more urgent than women's liberation. Even the most radical women saw fit to subordinate their needs as women to the needs of the new nation.[39]

Yuval-Davis pointed to the patriarchal side of Zionism that promulgated the role of the Jewish mother as one of national reproduction. She was important in the demographic race between Jews and Arabs and in the central question of who was considered a Jew, a question synonymous with who was a legitimate citizen of the state.[40] Yet despite the predominance of the patriarchal sides of Zionism and the exaggeration of the emancipation myth, Israeli women still had unprecedented opportunities in the work world. This was due in part to socialist underpinnings and in part to the victories of women's own battles against the limits on their lives in the Yishuv (Jewish society in Palestine).

Keepers of the History by Elise Young is one of the few studies that attempt to address both Arab and Jewish women's histories and relationships in Palestine and Israel. Young linked the perpetuation of Jewish women's oppression to the exploitation of Palestinian Arabs and the land itself. She attributed the failure of the struggles for women's equal rights to Jewish women's allegiance to Zionist goals that gave them political and economic dominance over Palestinians.[41] Simona Sharoni studied Arab and Jewish women since the first *Intifada*. Her book, *Gender and the Israeli-Palestinian Conflict*, challenged paradigms of conflict resolution and traced some of the radical political actions jointly taken by Israeli and Palestinian women.[42] The studies of Young and Sharoni are exceptions in a field which, for the most part, has not undertaken joint studies of Jewish and Arab women for all the reasons outlined above.

In a way, Deniz Kandiyoti summed up the impact of these works on women and gender in Middle Eastern political processes. She wrote that the kinds of knowledge feminist scholarship on the Middle East has produced contains a new "gender-aware focus on social institutions . . . [as] the site of power relations and political processes through which gender hierarchies are both created and contested."[43] Yet despite these breakthroughs, there are still very few books on Palestinian and Israeli women and gender of any time period that examine complex interdependencies of their histories.

The exploration of these questions relies on an analysis of narratives created by women and men who envisioned new national communities for Jews and Arabs in Palestine. These discourses were organically anchored in shared historical contexts. The next two chapters provide a glimpse of these historical contexts through a chronological study of Arabs' and Jews' political identities in Palestine that gave rise to the texts that will be deconstructed in subsequent chapters for their hidden and not so hidden assumptions about gender.

Historicizing Narratives I

Under the Ottomans

As with all forms of intellectual production, the writing of history
is organically linked to and affected by the ideological environment and historical context of the author, often shedding more
light on the times of the author than on the intended subject.
Beshara Doumani, "Rediscovering Ottoman Palestine"

The writing of history in the next two chapters attempts to sift the narrative out of what Doumani refers to above as "the ideological environment." It traces the evolution of both peoples' national identities in Palestine. How did specific subgroups of Arabs and Jews come to think of
themselves as members of a modern nation centered in Palestine? Both
were responding to inner dynamics of their own societies and to external
elements beyond their control. Each side's claims and rejection of the
other's claims were part of the groups' intertwined histories.

The following two chapters of historical chronology contextualize the
literature used for discourse analysis later in the remainder of the study.
They look at some of the social, economic, and political changes that
shaped the dialectical processes in which history produced texts and texts
produced history. These two chapters delineate historical contexts, first
under Ottoman rule and then under British rule, that gave rise to the
cacophony of voices of new national consciousness in the two movements in Palestine.

Following these two historical chapters, parts II, III, and IV lift the
texts produced during this period out of context and splice them themati-
cally to expose a panorama of gender-nation connections. These two
chapters, therefore, attempt to recontextualize them. They ask what happened in Palestine to produce these texts and identities. What were the

changing conditions that generated new interpretations of human reality in nationalist terms?

The telling of the histories of two peoples in Palestine has been intimately linked to the politics and agendas of the movements themselves.[1] Histories of Israel have often focused on the internal dynamics of Jewish society in and out of Palestine, not mentioning Arabs except when they were impossible to ignore, primarily when they attacked Jews or threatened Zionist goals. Early histories of Palestinians, often written by Jews, were the opposite. They focused on the ways Palestinian identity evolved based on their reaction to Zionism. Both histories omitted crucial aspects of each people's evolution as a nation.

Over the past two decades, the telling has changed. For the Palestinians, the focus has shifted more towards the internal dynamics of Palestinian society, economy, and political leadership. For the Israelis, it has shifted to the ways that interaction with Arabs and Arab society was central to the evolution of Jewish nationalism. These two chapters incorporate some of the recent revisionist perspectives on internal and external dynamics of both peoples, attempting to create a portrait of national identity that is neither mythic nor monolithic.

Nineteenth-Century Collective Identities in Flux

Although Zionists held their first national congresses in the 1890s and Palestinians in the 1920s, Jewish and Palestinian Arab identities went through many changes long before these dramatic official acts. Ordinary people responded to imperatives of political, economic, and social changes that bombarded them long before newly emerging leaders articulated actual national movements. Historical change planted seeds of Palestinian Arab and Jewish modern political identity as early as the eighteenth century.

Palestinian Arabs and Jews lived in a multiethnic, multilingual, multireligious Ottoman Empire in which the official ruling class was of Turkish origin. But the major identification of the ruling class, of the empire as a whole, and of its subjects, including the vast majority of Palestinians, was Islamic. Ottomans organized religious minorities such as Greek Orthodox Christians, Armenian Christians, and Jews into *millets* which were autonomous groups with their own languages, schooling, religious worship, and legal institutions. The Ottomans gradually lost territories in wars with Europe and Russia so that throughout the nineteenth century ethnic, national, and religious diversity decreased.

The Ottomans implemented administrative and economic changes throughout the nineteenth century in an attempt to consolidate power in the face of internal threats from local rulers or separatist national groups, and external threats from wars that whittled away imperial domains. Arabs who lived in Palestine responded to these changes in ways that began to shape a new sense of themselves as a people with experience distinct from that of surrounding Arabs. While retaining their identification as Ottoman subjects, as inhabitants of different subregions, and as members of disparate *hamulas* (clans), factions, classes, cities, or villages, Arabs in Palestine began to interpret their experience in unique ways and to take action as a distinct people.

Beshara Doumani attributes the origins of this new sense of collectivity to changes in relationship between merchants, peasants, and the Ottoman government occurring as early as the eighteenth century.[2] Gershon Shafir sees the period of Egyptian rule with Muhammad 'Ali and his son Ibrahim Pasha in Palestine from 1831 to 1840 as a catalyst for changes that intensified after the new Land Codes of 1858.[3] Alexander Scholch focuses on changes beginning with the Crimean War period, from 1856 to 1882, associated with Palestine's integration into the world market economy.[4] During these periods, Ottoman or Egyptian authorities introduced reforms. Foreign powers introduced changes in trade, communications, banking, diplomatic, and missionary activities. Palestinian Arabs introduced changes as landlords, farmers, and merchants.

This sense of Palestinian-ness developed despite obstacles unique to Palestinians that didn't exist for other Arabs in the empire. For most of the Ottoman period, for example, Palestine was not a contiguous political unit. It was reorganized several times but most often existed divided between Damascus and Sidon. Despite these divisions, the Palestinians united for the first time in a revolt in 1834. When Muhammad 'Ali wrested control of Palestine from the Ottomans and sent his son Ibrahim Pasha to rule Palestine in the 1830s, new laws angered Palestinians, including tough military conscription and new rights for non-Muslims. The rulers ignited further resentment among Muslim Palestinians when Ibrahim allowed Christian Palestinians to trade in grain and livestock, areas that had been closed to them under Ottoman law. Kimmerling and Migdal posited that the revolt of 1834 brought together "dispersed

Bedouin, rural *shaykhs* [officials or leaders], urban notables, mountain *fallahin* [peasants], and Jerusalem religious figures against a common enemy. It was these groups who would later constitute the Palestinian people."[5]

Later nineteenth–century administrative innovations furthered this sense of collectivity. Rearrangements of the *sanjaks* of Jerusalem, Nablus, and Acre separated them from Syria and Lebanon. In 1872, a reorganization promulgated by the Ottoman legal proclamations of *Kudus-i Serif* incorporated all of Palestine for a few months.[6] But for two generations, until World War I, Jerusalem, including southern and central Palestine, was an independent district linked directly to the imperial center in Istanbul, independent from Syria, and this, in part, contributed to the formation of a Palestinian identity distinct from Syria. Butrus Abu-Mannah argued that "the existence of the *sanjak* of Jerusalem for almost two generations as a separate entity from the other regions of Syria was tremendously important for the emergence of Palestine about fifty years later."[7] It provided a clearer sense of Palestine's boundaries. Abu-Mannah claimed that it empowered the wealthier Jerusalem families in ways that would have a major effect on the nature of Palestinian national leadership in the first part of the twentieth century.

Doumani focused on the absence of a coherent administrative unit in Palestine to explain the dearth of references to a place called "Palestine" in Arabic literature. Most Arab writers referred to *Bilad al-Sham*, or Greater Syria, rather than to "Palestine." This was a source of political fragmentation that slowed development of a cohesive Palestinian intelligentsia. "Palestine" nevertheless existed in the consciousness of the native population that had local roots, shared collective memories, and economic, social, and kinship networks as merchants, religious leaders, tax farmers, or political elites.[8]

A number of the changes introduced by the Ottoman rulers in an effort to strengthen their central government supported the development of a distinctive Palestinian elite. For example, the Ottomans established nondemocratic representative groups that privileged urban Palestinian leaders over rural or nomadic ones and created opportunities for them to work with each other.[9] The *Tanzimat* Ottoman reforms destroyed the power of local *shaykhs* and chieftains and helped to establish the domination of the cities. This enhanced the power of local urban notables. Muhammad Muslih located the social basis of Palestinian collective awareness among elements of the nineteenth–century ruling elite or "office holding notables."[10]

Changes in the land tenure system in the late nineteenth century further bolstered the development of a Palestinian elite and had far-reaching economic, social, and political repercussions for Palestine. In an area dominated by agriculture, there had been no private property. Instead lands were for the most part "*miri*," state-owned lands, and "*iltizam*," tax farms. After the Crimean War, there was an economic boom coupled with repressive taxes, debts, and climatic traumas that led to the privatization of some lands.[11] One important aspect of the *Tanzimat* reforms was that the Ottomans implemented a land law in 1858 that made previous changes official and introduced new laws in land ownership.

The 1858 Ottoman Land Code permitted the purchase of land for private and foreign ownership, made large land ownership possible, and allowed Palestinian property to pass into the hands of Lebanese and Palestinian families who eventually sold some of it to Zionists.[12] Doumani explained that the rise of a land market began in the 1830s and that these changes had already introduced a new class of urban-based landowners.[13] In fact the first land purchase made by Jews in Palestine occurred in 1855 outside Jerusalem.[14] The Palestinians who worked the lands owned by urban notables comprised a rural labor force settled on the land, rooted in village life, but not owning the land. Greenstein noted that the results were "growing capital and income inequalities in Palestinian Arab society and increasing social differentiation in villages between those who profited from economic changes and those who were crushed or displaced off land."[15]

An overemphasis, however, on the emergence of prominent urban landowning families in Palestine as the basis of Palestinian national consciousness obscures the importance of nonelite Palestinians in this process. Donna Robinson Divine argued rather that it was in the interaction between Ottoman political developments and local Palestinian Arab responses that new realities emerged. Imperial policies and Ottomans' increasing ability to mobilize resources combined with the actions of ordinary Palestinian people to forge new perceptions and necessities of collective identity. Creative survival under changing conditions imposed by the Ottomans meant that Palestinian Arabs of "various classes and from a variety of cities and towns" faced tensions between old and new economies, marriage patterns, and family relations and values. "Palestinian Arabs had to change their outlooks, behavior and their relationships" to meet changing circumstances, and these changes were different depending on class differences, regional disparities, and how different parts of Palestine were affected by the world market economy.[16]

The rising influence of Europeans in the Ottoman Empire exerted changes in Palestinians' lives. European powers established consulates that acted as centers of influence offering "protection" to a growing number of Ottoman subjects. This had significant impact on small Palestinian Christian minorities including the Greek Orthodox, Russian Orthodox, and Syrian Orthodox, as well as Armenians, Roman Catholics, Melkites, and Maronites. At first only specific Ottoman Christian sects were the main beneficiaries. As early as the sixteenth century, for example, the Capitulations gave France the right to protect European Catholics in Ottoman territory. France then extended its protection by the nineteenth century to include Ottoman Catholics and European missionaries working among them.[17] In the eighteenth century, Russia wrested from the Ottomans the right to protect the largest Christian communities in the empire, the Orthodox Christians. Foreign protection gave Christian Palestinians political advantages that led to their growing wealth, culture, and influence. Individual Palestinians went to study in Europe and brought back ideas of the Enlightenment, opened schools, and formed new associations.[18]

Palestinian Jews were also experiencing political, economic, and social changes. Jews, like other non-Muslim minorities in the Ottoman Empire, were organized into "*millets*," in charge of their own schools, internal taxation, and religious and legal institutions. Like the Christian minorities, Jews had lived in Palestine for centuries experiencing periods of cultural advance and decline. After "the great flowering" of the sixteenth century, the Jewish communities grew weak and poor because of instability in political security and natural catastrophes such as plagues, earthquakes, and droughts.[19]

In the eighteenth century the Ottomans attempted to consolidate the Jewish communities in Jerusalem, whereas immigration of Jews from Izmir, Morocco, and Italy were responsible for increasing populations in Tiberias and the Galilee. The majority of the Jewish communities of Palestine (the "Old Yishuv") were Sephardi or Mizrachi Arabic-speaking Jews (from the Middle East), with very few Ashkenazis Jews (from Europe). No Ashkenazis lived in Jerusalem, where the Ottomans enforced restrictions on numbers of Jews permitted to live there. At the end of the eighteenth century, a group of Hasidic Ashkenazis (a religious branch) immigrated from Lithuania, mostly to Tiberias, and became the first group to keep connections to their European communities of origin that supported them materially and spiritually.[20]

By the nineteenth century, waves of immigration and consolidation of Jewish communities in Jerusalem, Safed, Tiberias, Hebron, and Acre numbered Palestinian Jews at only several thousand. They were dependent on the will and fortune of local rulers. By 1824, Ottomans permitted Ashkenazi Jews to live in Jerusalem again, where they rebuilt old synagogues. While the number of Jews in Safed and Tiberias grew, many were killed in the great earthquake of 1837.[21]

When Muhammad 'Ali conquered parts of the Ottoman Empire and sent his son, Ibrahim Pasha, to rule over Palestine in the 1830s, there were about seven thousand Jews. Some were merchants, property owners, and pensioners. Others were rabbis and scholars who were "chronically destitute." Sephardi Arabic-speaking Jews made up the largest group, which included artisans, craftsmen, small businessmen, shopkeepers, and day laborers.[22] Muhammad 'Ali created laws that introduced concepts of religious equality. He welcomed Christians and Jews of all nations and guaranteed their rights and commercial activities.[23]

Yet this was a time of growing insecurity for the non-Muslim minorities. When Palestinians revolted in 1834 against Muhammad 'Ali and Ibrahim Pasha, they also attacked Jews and Christians. In Jerusalem, peasants looted Jewish and Christian houses and raped women. The following month, Muslims made fierce attacks on the Jewish and Christian families in Tiberias.[24] In 1839, Sir Moses Montefiore, an English Jew knighted by Queen Victoria, negotiated with Muhammad 'Ali to obtain a charter for Jewish settlement in Palestine. But Muhammad 'Ali was defeated in 1840 and Ottoman restoration put an end to Montefiore's plan. Instead he joined with Baron de Rothschild, another prominent English Jew, to build a modern hospital in Jerusalem.[25]

When the Ottomans regained control over Palestine, security for minorities once again increased, causing the Jewish population of Palestine to double over the next four decades.[26] During these forty years between

Ottoman restoration and the first Zionist settlement in the 1880s, Jewish communities in Palestine established their own leadership patterns. When the Ottomans made Jerusalem a district capital, they designated the chief rabbi as a *hakham bashi*, a recognized authority. His authority was limited to the communities of Sephardi Jews who were Ottoman subjects. By this time most of the Ashkenazis were foreign nationals under protection of different foreign consuls depending on their places of origin. During and after the Crimean War, as the power of the foreign consuls increased, the Ashkenazi communities remained divided in different groups, dependent on the charitable contributions of their European brethren. Sephardi communities, united under Ottoman administrative dictates, received some of these funds and distributed them to scholars and notables, increasing the gap between rich and poor in their communities and enforcing class divisions.[27]

Some Ashkenazis began to seek common ground with Sephardis in the 1860s with the publication of the first Hebrew-language journal. *Halevanon* was published in 1863, followed by *Havatzellet* in 1870.[28] These Ashkenazi-based journals began to emphasize a common identity among Arabic-speaking and Yiddish-speaking Jews. Despite huge cultural differences between Sephardic and Ashkenazi Jews in Palestine, Sephardic Jews began to respond to Ashkenazi outreach in part because other Arabic-speaking Muslims and Christians did not accept them.

Ashkenazi influence increased in the 1870s with the activities of the new French-based Jewish organization, the *Alliance Israelite Universelle*. The group founded the first agricultural school in Palestine, *Mikveh Yisrael*.[29] In 1878 another agricultural settlement, *Petah Tikva* (Gateway of Hope) was founded by a group of Rumanian Jews near present-day Tel Aviv. The settlement was abandoned because of malaria and then resettled again by Russian Jews in the 1880s.[30] By 1880, Orthodox religious Jewish communities were increasing their numbers in Jerusalem, Safed, Tiberias, Hebron, Jaffa, Acre, Nablus, and Haifa. Ashkenazis challenged Sephardic hegemony and became the majority by 1880.

European Jews outside Palestine experienced political, economic, and social changes that would eventually have a profound impact on the history of Arabs and Jews in Palestine. As eighteenth–century Enlightenment ideas of individual rights, citizenship, and religious equality became politically embodied in the French Revolution and spread through Napoleon's conquest of Europe, radically new opportunities opened for Jews.

Restrictions on their lives eased; they could become citizens in France and Germany; intermarriage was no longer illegal; assimilation into Christian society became a possibility. These breakthroughs met with organized, official and unofficial, nonviolent and violent resistance by non-Jews in Europe, in the last decades of the nineteenth century.

This backlash of anti-Semitism evoked three kinds of responses from European Jews. One was to leave Europe for the United States, where it seemed possible to live as Jews without being attacked. The second response was to work for reform and revolution in Europe, to broaden democratic participation to secure freedom and rights, or to work for socialist revolutions that would create classless societies where Jews could function as ordinary human beings without constraints or threats. The third response was the national solution. The idea of returning to Zion was not new. Religious Jews had prayed for a return to Jerusalem as an official part of their liturgy for two thousand years. But religious Zionism depended on the appearance of the Messiah. Those wishing to assimilate were pressured by European authorities to remove that prayer, to renounce their ties to Zion, and to prove their loyalty to France or Germany.

The new modern Zionists saw a return to Zion as a political solution to political problems that did not depend on the Messiah but rather on ordinary people. Jews of Europe had watched the nationalist movements in the Balkans and the unification of Germany and Italy. Some began to envision that Enlightenment principles of equality and freedom could only be attained through national autonomy. Adherents to nationalism thought it was the only way that being a Jew could become a natural human phenomenon rather than an indignity, liability, or something to hide. A handful of Jews articulated a vision of the Jewish people as constituting a nation in their ancestral land of Israel, unified by common history, religion, culture, and language.

In the United States in the 1840s, Mordecai Noah proposed establishing a Jewish state near New York and then changed his mind to Palestine. Rabbi Zevi Kalischer and Rabbi Yehuda Alkalai in Europe saw Jews' return to Zion as a beginning of redemption. In the 1850s Rabbi David Gordon wrote *Hamaggid* with ideas about a return to Zion. In the 1860s Dr. Chaim Lurie founded Frankfurt-on-Oder to encourage settlement in Palestine. Following the unification of Italy, Moses Hess, a German socialist and friend of Marx, wrote *Rome and Jerusalem* (1862), in which he advocated a Jewish political revival in Palestine that would be a social and spiritual example to the world. Perez Smolenskin wrote a journal, *Hashahar* (The Dawn), which discussed the spiritual foundation of Jewish nationalism. Eliezar Ben-Yehuda wrote that Palestine was the physical basis of the spiritual renaissance of the Jewish people.[31] None of these ideas met with any significant response until the pogroms of 1881 in Russia.

1880–1908: New Responses to New Problems

The birth of nationalism among Jews and Palestinians contained an implicit paradox. By the last decades of the nineteenth century, European power and expansion posed a threat to both Arab and Jewish lives. The rise of modern anti-Semitism in Europe and of European colonialism in the Middle East, and Ottoman attempts to stay alive in the face of European encroachment, provoked a search by both peoples for action that would preserve their identities in new, more viable collectivities. During these decades before and during World War I, a small but growing number of Arabs and Jews turned to nationalism. This direction was paradoxical in the sense that the very effort to preserve themselves as a distinct people transformed them into something they had never been before, a modern nation.

Pogroms in Russia catalyzed waves of Jewish emigration. Most of the Jews who left Russia at this time went to the United States but a few hundred went to Palestine under the auspices of two new groups, *Hovevei Tzion* (Lovers of Zion) and BILU (an acronym for "House of Jacob, come and let us go," from Isaiah 2:5).[32] From 1882, this "first aliya," immigration wave, created different kinds of agricultural communities in Rishon Letzion, Zichron Yaacov, Rosh Pina, Rehovot, and Hadera. The settlers did not want to become a traditional colonialist planter class and so organized *moshavot*, cooperative agricultural settlements. But the *moshavot* floundered and were put under the support of Baron Edmond de Rothschild, who turned them into colonial plantation farms dependent on Arab labor.[33]

Nationalist ideas were expressed in the writings of Moses Leib Lilienblum, a convert from socialism to Jewish nationalism, who argued that nationalism was the only remedy for anti-Semitism and for the alienation of Jews from host countries. In 1890 Lilienblum wrote the first

Hebrew play performed in Rehovot.[34] In 1882, Dr. Leon Pinsker, who had been an advocate of integration into Russian life, changed direction in "Auto-Emancipation," where he theorized that hatred of Jews was rooted in the fact that Jews led abnormally rootless lives. Nationalism was the only thing that could ever afford them the possibility of a normal existence.

Theodor Herzl was an assimilated Viennese Jewish journalist and playwright horrified by the upsurge of anti-Semitism surrounding the Dreyfus trial in France, a country he had assumed to be emancipated. By 1895 he was pursuing a plan to evacuate European Jews to a country of their own and by 1896 published his ideas in "The Jewish State."[35] He disapproved of Hovevei Tzion and insisted that settlement in Palestine must be obtained through official international political guarantees. He went to visit the sultan of the Ottoman Empire to propose a solution to the Ottomans' financial difficulties in exchange for granting Jews an independent state in Palestine. The sultan refused to see him.

By 1897, Herzl had convened the first international Zionist Congress in Basle, Switzerland, with two hundred delegates. The program of the First Zionist Congress stated that "Zionism aimed at the creation of a home for the Jewish people in Palestine to be secured by public law."[36] Max Nordau, a German-speaking Hungarian, played a major role at Basle. The Zionist Organization promoted Jewish immigration to and acquisition of land in Palestine. In 1899, the Jewish Colonial Trust based in London became the first bank of the Zionist Organization, supported by many Jews with a small number of shares. In 1901, the Fifth Zionist Congress created *Karen Kayemet* (the Jewish National Fund) to purchase land and support settlements through voluntary contributions and a small annual tax.[37]

The Zionist Organization nearly collapsed at this stage not only from lack of funding but also from factionalism. Ahad Ha'am (Asher Ginzberg) had in the early 1890s criticized the practical Zionism of Hovevei Tzion and now attacked Herzl's political Zionism. In his 1891 essay, "The Truth from Eretz Yisrael," he warned that Zionist colonists would become despots if they relied on Arab labor.[38] He was one of the few to recognize that Arabs had densely settled Palestine and that they would struggle to hold onto their land.[39] In 1897, he wrote that it was not enough to meet the physical needs of people by creating a state in Palestine: it was more important for the community to be infused with Jewish ethical values in a "national spiritual center."[40] The 1901 Zionist Congress witnessed stormy debates over cultural, practical, diplomatic, and legalistic approaches.[41]

Herzl further developed his ideas in his utopian novel, *Altneuland* (1902), in which he envisioned a European-like society twenty years in the future where Jews could fully participate in sovereignty, economy, and culture. Upper-class, cultured, and literate Arabs would appreciate, flourish, and live freely in Jewish society. In reality, Herzl gave up on negotiations with the Ottoman sultan and turned to Great Britain, bringing to the Sixth Zionist Congress in 1903 that government's proposal for a Jewish state in Uganda. Nordau defended the plan but opposition was massive. By 1904 Herzl had reiterated his loyalty to Palestine; he died that year.

The split between those who thought there should be a homeland no matter where and those who remained fused to Palestine continued through the Seventh Zionist Congress in 1905.[42] While the Zionist Organization did not disintegrate after Herzl's death, it did not accomplish much. The Young Turk Revolution in 1908 stirred hopes that the new Ottoman leaders would negotiate with political Zionists for territory in the Ottoman Empire.[43] The new government's narrowing focus on Turkish nationalism not only dashed that possibility but also eventually constricted the rights of non-Turkish people in the empire, including Jews and Arabs.

Despite the diplomatic dramas roiling among leaders outside Palestine, Zionist settlements continued to grow in Palestine. Baron Edmond de Rothschild had discontinued his support of the *moshavot* by 1900 because they were not financially feasible. Instead the settlements became part of the Jewish Colonization Association. In 1903, the second aliya brought a wave of young, idealistic Jews without property who entered the labor market with little experience and lots of desire for a higher standard of living than their Arab competitors. By 1905, the socialist ideals of the immigrants urged them to live by their own labor and not to exploit Arab workers. This met with resistance from previous Jewish settlers, who refused to hire Jewish workers at higher wages than were given their Arab counterparts. The tension resulted in a new policy known as "conquest of labor," which insisted that Jews hire only Jewish laborers.

In 1909, immigrants' attempts to find viable means for survival led them to create a new socialist experiment in communal living. Jewish settlers founded the first kibbutz in Degania, a collective agricultural settlement with no private property or class divisions. Such collectives were the only way these settlers with minimal agricultural experience and no funds could survive. Cooperative settlements built on national lands became the foundation of a new national identity centered on Ashkenazi labor, exclusion of Arab labor, and use of Sephardi or Mizrachi Jews in lower-status positions. The workers also founded associations that would become the backbone of national socialist programs such as workers' kitchens, labor exchanges, and a medical insurance program, *Kupat Holim*, which included both a national workers' sick fund and clinics.

Whatever the ideals, the practical result of these developments was to exclude Arab laborers and maintain higher wages for Jewish workers. Jews went to Yemen to convince several thousand Yemenite Jews to emigrate to Palestine, where they worked for "Arab" wages and lived at lower standards, helping to maintain the policy of "Jewish-only" labor.[44] Whereas in other colonial ventures the indigenous peoples' grievance focused on exploitation by the colonizers, Palestinian Arabs focused instead on their exclusion from the labor market, a situation created in part by the new Zionist settlers and in part by Palestine's continuing integration into the world economy.[45]

The centrality of the Jewish worker found voice in Nahman Syrkin's "The Jewish Problem and the Socialist-Jewish State" (1898).[46] Syrkin's ideas laid the basis for the ethical, utopian socialist-democratic orientation of labor Zionism. Ber Borochov urged a more rigorous Marxist approach in "The National Question and the Class Struggle" (1905), in which he argued that class struggle for Jewish workers would only be possible in a state of their own.[47] A. D. Gordon articulated his theory that the regeneration of the Jewish people depended on Jews' physical labor to regenerate the land of Palestine. The transformation of *Eretz Yisrael*, the land of Israel, was synonymous with transformation of the Jewish people by turning them into physically strong and healthy laborers.[48] Before World War I, Zionists formed the early socialist political parties that included *Hapo'el Hatza'ir* (The Young Worker Party) and *Po'alei Tzion* (The Workers of Zion).[49]

There were individual Jews who criticized Zionist separatism from Arabs. They studied Arabic culture, translated Arabic literature, and even supported Arab political goals. A Palestinian-born Arabic-speaking Jew, educated in Cairo, argued that Jews must embrace Arab culture and that it would be destructive to introduce European culture. A minority of Jews held the opposite position that complete separation was the best strategy. Moshe Smilansky warned parents that their children would become like *fallahin* if they couldn't keep them away from the Arab peasants. Vladamir Jabotinsky, the eventual leader of the right-wing revisionist Zionists, saw separatism as an important Zionist tactic.[50]

Any attempts to bridge the gap between Jews and Arabs were subordinated to the Zionist goal of national sovereignty. Mainstream Zionists, right-wing revisionists, or left-wing socialists privileged Jewish rule in Palestine over all other considerations, whether for fair treatment and close relations to Arabs, or for class equality and worker unity. This prioritization of goals led, in the decade before World War I, to an expanded Jewish presence in old and new cities and in new cultural institutions. New immigrants founded the city of Tel Aviv near the Arab settlement of Jaffa, expanded their settlement in Haifa, and made the first attempts to use Hebrew in place of European languages. They founded the first Hebrew theater, *Habimah,* the first art school, *Bezalel,* the first technical college, the *Technion,* two Hebrew high schools in Jaffa and Jerusalem, and a teachers' seminary.

Jews, however, were not alone in privileging the goal of national autonomy in Palestine. They were not unaware of the growth of national consciousness in the Ottoman Empire's Arab population. Nationalism was a new offshoot of an old desire for long-established Arab societies to survive. The multilayered processes that gave rise to a Palestinian Arab national identity before the Great War involved the erection of boundaries between Turks and Arabs, a breakdown in boundaries between Muslim and Christian Arabs, and the creation of boundaries between Palestinians and other Arabs. These were not separate or linear processes and so a general pan-Arab identity continued to develop at the same time that a separate Palestinian consciousness emerged.[51]

An important factor in the growing sense of collectivity among Palestinians was the emergence in the late nineteenth century of a political elite. Arab families were empowered by Ottoman administrative changes introduced during that time that put leadership in the hands of prominent families. These included the Husaynis, Nashashibis, 'Alamis, and Khalidis in Jerusalem, the 'Abd al-Hadis and Tuqans in Nablus, the Sa'ids, Dajanis, and Bitars in Jaffa, and the Shukris, Tahas, Khayats, Khalils, and Mahadis in Haifa. Ties among the families were furthered in part by the increasing numbers of their children who went abroad to study. This led to an enhancement of networks among the returning graduates.

Jerusalem's great Muslim families did not have the commercial wealth of the notables of Jaffa or Haifa, or the connection to an agricultural hinterland like the families of Nablus. But when the Ottomans created the municipality of Jerusalem as a legal entity in the 1860s, the civil service and municipal council acted as a leadership training ground for the sons of these families who had acquired significant responsibilities by the 1880s. In most parts of the country the Sunni Muslim majority had little contact with Christians or Jews. But in Jerusalem, Christian and Muslim notables shared the experience of leadership on the municipal council that influenced the growth of Palestinian awareness as a cross-religious identity. The municipal council maintained roads and water systems; banned the dumping of waste in public areas, which decreased Jerusalem's stench; established fire and police departments; and collected taxes. Ottomans were careful not to allow any one family among the Khalidis, 'Alamis, and Nashashibis to gain too much power.[52]

Palestinian notables had held religious positions of importance for a long time. But by the last decades of the nineteenth century, authority derived more from secular positions of political and administrative leadership than religious ones. In Jerusalem the proportions of Muslims, Christians, and Jews would change dramatically over the next few decades but the Muslims maintained their majority on the municipal council. This kept notable families loyal to the Ottomans, at least until the Young Turk Revolution changed the nature of the political game within the empire. But it also meant that members of these families gained leadership experience that prepared them to lead a separate Palestinian nationalist movement after the empire's demise.

Ordinary Palestinians forged new connections as well. One age-old factor was the presence of the *Qays* and *Yaman* factions. These ancient divisions among the Palestinians and Arabs generally fanned divisive hostilities but also ironically succeeded in bringing Christians and Muslims together in ways that crossed confessional boundaries and forged Christian-Muslim ties.[53]

More important, structural economic changes in Palestine throughout the nineteenth century produced new connections among Palestinians. Muslims and Christians, landowners and tenants became linked to each other in new ways through their ties to networks of merchants, shippers, bankers, insurance agents, and those who directed the resources of Palestine to Great Britain. Haifa and Jaffa grew in population and prosperity with expanding construction of buildings, railroads, ports, shops, investments, mosques, commercial buildings, imports and exports, industry, consumption, and tourism.[54] Palestinians became more connected to each other through the creation of technologies inside Palestine intended to connect them to Europe via railroads, shipping lines, and a telegraph network. From 1880 to 1918 the population of six main Palestinian cities grew. Palestinians acted as middlemen between European traders and Palestinian growers, causing a reorganization of agriculture.[55]

The peasant population also grew. As some family members moved to coastal cities there was a movement of population between inland mountains and coastal plains that created connections between previously disparate populations. Peasants as "debtors, taxpayers, titleholders, and migrants" became more tied to urban life but experienced a growing gap between themselves and the urban elite.[56]

Palestinians were influenced not only by internal developments but also by pan-Arab nationalism emerging throughout the Ottoman Empire. Christian Arabs were aware that a modern Arab identity could take a pan-Muslim direction that would leave them outside the boundaries of the new collectivity. This spurred them into advocacy of a nationalism that stressed secular Arab-ness over religious identification. Najib 'Azuri, for example, was a French-educated Christian Syrian who founded the *Ligue de patrie arabe* in 1904, briefly published *L'independence arabe* from Paris in 1907 and 1908, but mainly influenced the growth of nationalist expression with his 1905 book *Le Réveil de la nation arabe*. 'Azuri advocated an Arab nation independent of the Turks, whom he blamed for the ruin of an Arab civilization that included Christians and Muslims.[57]

Palestinians continued to experience conditions unlike those of their fellow Arabs. They began specifically to feel the impact of a Jewish nationalist presence in Palestine. Some Palestinian leaders expressed openness to Zionism. Some praised Jewish settlers for their attitudes, technologies, and organization; others admired the Zionists' renaissance of the Hebrew language. Much of the early anti-Zionism came from urban notables, with Christian attacks out of proportion to their numbers in Palestine. In Jerusalem, Husayn al-Husayni continued to help the Zionists until 1914, when he began to favor restrictions on them.[58] Although

Muslim notables on the whole opposed Zionism, some believed like Asad Shuqayr that Zionism would encourage desired development of the country.[59]

It is significant to note that, at this stage, Jews, Muslims, and Christians still worked together. All three groups had representatives on the Jerusalem municipal council under Ottoman auspices. The last municipal council that met before the empire fell had six Muslim, two Christian, and two Jewish representatives.[60] In the rural regions of Palestine, early Zionist settlers and Palestinian peasants for the most part enjoyed generally close and good relations, especially when Zionist colonies employed five to ten times as many Arabs as Jews.[61]

The peasants felt the impact of new Jewish settlements most directly when absentee Arab landowners sold land to Zionists on which peasants had rights to cultivate. Ottomans also confiscated lands from peasants in debt to sell to the settlers. Tensions accrued over land dispossession, water resources, grazing rights, boundaries, defense of settlement property violations, and blood revenge, causing a rise in consciousness of shared experience among some Palestinians.[62]

Relations in the cities were even more vexed. Palestinian notables opposed Jewish immigration and land purchases in defense against economic competition and extension of special privileges to foreigners.[63] In 1891, Palestinian merchants from Jerusalem complained to Ottoman authorities about Jewish land acquisition and the Jews' potential to form monopolies.[64] In 1901, Arab notables in Jerusalem petitioned to protest new Ottoman regulations giving foreigners the right to buy land.[65] According to Neville Mandel's work on Arab relations to Zionism before World War I, it was not until the Young Turk Revolution in 1908 that the discomfort felt by Palestinian Arabs over Jewish settlement coalesced into overt anti-Zionism.[66] Thus in 1914 when Raghib Nashashibi, a Muslim landowning Jerusalem notable, ran for the Ottoman parliament, he promised: "If I am elected as a representative, I shall devote all my strength day and night to doing away with the damage and threat of Zionists and Zionism."[67]

The growth of anti-Zionist ideology went hand in hand with the growth of Palestinian Arab identity. Both unfurled in the new writings, periodicals, newspapers, and organizations founded by and for an increasingly literate populace. Competing voices of a distinct Palestinian identity emerged in discussions of local news, anti-Zionism, and even pan-

Arabism. New Arabic-language journals included *al-Quds* in Jerusalem, *al-Asma'i* in Jaffa, *al-Karmil* by Greek Orthodox Najib Nassar, and *al-Najjah* and *Filastin* by Yusuf and 'Isa Daud al-'Isa, who were Christians from Jaffa. In 1911 Najib Nassar wrote the first Arabic book on Zionism, *Al-Sahyuniyya*, dealing with its history, objectives, and importance.

The news media emphasized the need to organize as Palestinians rather than as Ottomans or as Arabs to oppose Jewish settlements. Palestinians participated in local organizations including the Palestinian Patriotic Party, the Orthodox Renaissance Society, the Ottoman Patriotic Society, the Economic and Commercial Company, and the Literary Club founded by Najib Nassar.[68] Yet at this point Palestinian identity was not seen as conflicting with Ottoman or Arab identity.

1908–1920: Shattering the Old Imperial Paradigm

The Young Turk Revolution of 1908 changed the political framework for Arabs within the Ottoman Empire. The Young Turks restored the 1876 constitution, promising for a brief time greater freedom and wider participation for all Ottoman subjects. Palestinians sent delegates to Istanbul as representatives to Congress, including Ali Nashashibi from Jerusalem, Salim 'Abd al-Hadi from Jenin, and Hafiz al-Sa'id from Jaffa. The Arab Literary Club formed in Istanbul and included Jamal al-Husayni from Jerusalem.[69] But by 1910, the Committee of Union and Progress had taken over the government and ended the trends towards democracy and decentralization. Turkish nationalism burgeoned as a response to mounting pressures from Europe, a breakdown of Ottoman ideals, and the secession of Christian peoples (Serbs in 1830 and Greeks in 1833) that left the empire a Turco-Arab state. Attempts to emphasize the "paramountcy of the Turkish element" led to increasing separation from and subordination of Arabs.[70]

Donna Robinson Divine challenges the conventional view that Turkification of the empire had brutal effects on Palestinians. She argues instead that despite threats to Arabic language and culture, the Young Turk Revolution ushered in a period of freer exchange for Palestinians. Younger men and women embraced new political ideas and participated in a new level of discourse about social and political changes. The surge in newspapers helped develop a discourse of reform.[71] "Newspaper articles that called for a rethinking of family and of the position of women . . . could have chosen no signal more subversive of tradition."[72]

The consequent search for a better position within the empire led Arabs to demand support for their own language and for elements of national autonomy. One of the Arab responses to the repressive measures was to join secret societies. Palestinians such as 'Awni 'Abd al-Hadi from Jerusalem and Rafiq Taimimi from Nablus attended *al-Fatat*, a secret society in Paris and Syria. Palestinians also formed the Nablus Youth Society in which about one hundred students promulgated a Syrian, Palestinian, anti-Zionist, and Arab nationalist program.[73]

Then in 1913 Palestinians supported the Arab Congress in Paris, appealing to Ottoman authorities for more freedom and representation for the empire's Arab subjects. The congress also appealed to European nations for help in this process of becoming more independent.[74] Among those Arabs who participated in the 1913 Arab Congress were advocates of a pan-Syrian nationalism that would include Palestine.[75] Other groups advocated Lebanese independence, but all these groups and individuals shared the common ground of desire to change Ottoman government policies and increase the independence of the empire's Arab subjects. By 1913, the newspaper *Filastin* had begun to refer to "Palestine," rather than the *sanjak* of Jerusalem, as a *"watan,"* or *"bilad,"* homeland.[76]

World War I ushered in a period of dramatic change for the Palestinians. Kimmerling and Migdal observed that "the 'war to end all wars' must have seemed nearly as apocalyptic to those in Palestine as to the subjects of the European frontline states." Everyone in Palestine suffered intense hardships and the population declined. In a final attempt to resist destruction, the Ottomans denuded the landscape by cutting down the trees of Palestine for fuel, confiscated farm animals and grain, conscripted thousands of *fallahin* to fight in the losing imperial army, and left the women, children, and elderly to manage survival.[77]

The war hurt the Palestinian leadership as well, severing their links to Europe. The emigration of consuls and missionaries increased insecurity among families who had come to depend on them. Those Palestinian delegates who had participated in the short-lived Ottoman Parliament of 1908–9— 'Ali Nashashibi from Jerusalem, Salim 'Abd al-Hadi from Jenin, and Hafiz al-Sa'id from Jaffa—were now hanged by the Turks for treason.[78] Yet the war created opportunities and made certain decisions necessary in view of the possible end of the Ottomans, beginning of independence, or imposition of new foreign control. Some Arab nationalists entered into negotiations with specific European powers to further their chances of gaining political sovereignty after the war.

The Yishuv (Jewish settlement in Palestine) suffered during the war, cut off from its immigrant and financial sources. The Turks abolished the capitulations and with them the legal status of most Jews in the empire. When the empire joined the war on Germany's side it exiled many "enemy" subjects including Jews. Matters got worse when Jamal Pasha, the governor of Syria and Arabia, initiated harsh persecution of Zionists after uncovering an espionage network of young Jews working for the British. The Jewish population of Palestine was significantly reduced (from eighty-five thousand to fifty-six thousand) but agricultural and organizational structures survived.[79]

When the Ottomans joined the war on Germany's side, Britain sought support from populations within the empire. European powers made three fateful promises during the war that affected the future of Jews and Arabs in Palestine. In a 1915–16 correspondence between Husayn Ibn 'Ali, the sharif of Mecca, and the British high commissioner in Cairo, Sir Henry McMahon, Britain promised that if Arabs within the empire revolted against the Ottomans, Britain would support the creation of an independent Arab state after the war. This independent Arab kingdom had unspecified boundaries, and although Palestine was not mentioned by name, after the war Arabs assumed that it was included. Later in the 1930s, McMahon officially denied it.[80] Indeed there was an Arab revolt against the Ottomans, and Arabs awaited the fulfillment of the promise.

The second promise that the British made to Ottoman subjects to further weaken the empire was to the Jews in Palestine. In an attempt to garner support from Jews within and beyond the empire, Lord Balfour wrote a letter to the British Jewish leader Lord Rothschild promising British support for a Jewish home in Palestine. The Balfour Declaration of 1917 stated that "His Majesty's Government view with favor the establishment of a national home for the Jewish people . . . [as long as] nothing shall be done which may prejudice the civil and religious rights of existing non-Jewish communities in Palestine . . . "[81] But a third promise, between Britain and France, took precedence over the other two promises. In 1916, British Sir Mark Sykes and French Charles Georges-

Picot signed a secret agreement to divide the Arab lands of the Ottoman Empire between Britain and France.[82]

When the war ended in 1918 the economy of Palestine was in ruins. The Ottoman Empire no longer existed. Britain and France indeed divided the Arab lands of the empire between them. Yet Jews and Arabs took initiatives now to implement the contradictory promises that Britain had made to them during the war and executed plans for national self-determination. Arabs and Jews adhered to two different nationalist movements. Ran Greenstein observed that "the growing consolidation of common identity *within* each community became detrimental to the prospects of constructing an identity shared *between* communities."[83]

The first bold step was to implement Arab independence. Faisal, the son of Husayn of Mecca, led an Arab military force into Damascus in 1918 and became king of an independent Arab state. In Palestine, six patriotic and religious societies and one hundred individuals proclaimed loyalty to the Arab government of Faisal in November 1918. They also denounced the Balfour Declaration.[84] For two years Palestinian activists pressed for unity within an independent Syria. "*Wataniyya*," or Palestinian Arab patriotic nationalism, competed with and was embedded in "*qawmiyya*," pan-Arab nationalism; as Greenstein noted, these "were not mutually exclusive organizing principles."[85] Faisal went to the Paris peace talks in January 1919 as the Arab representative and met with Chaim Weizmann, the Zionist representative. In January, Weizmann and Faisal reached a secret agreement: Faisal said he would support a Zionist presence in Palestine if Zionists supported Arab independence.

Meanwhile, in the wake of Ottoman collapse, Palestinians founded thirty to forty clubs; three became politically significant. The Muslim-Christian Association was composed of older political notables. They opposed Zionism and advocated the creation of self-government in Palestine within a Syrian independent state. The Literary Society and the Arab Club were composed of younger educated Muslim activists mobilized by emerging ideologies. They were active in Arab schools, organized intellectual, athletic, and cultural events, opposed Zionism, and wanted Palestine to be ruled by Faisal.[86]

In February 1919, Jerusalem and Jaffa Muslim and Christian societies met as the First Palestinian National Congress. Thirty politically active men from around the country voiced support for becoming part of

Faisal's independent Arab nation and rejected the Balfour Declaration.[87] The Palestinian Arab Congress sent delegates to Paris and to Damascus but the British refused to let them leave for Paris. So the congress authorized Faisal to represent the delegates in Paris.[88] Palestinians helped organize the first General Syrian Congress in July 1919. In March 1920 they called for Syrian independence uniting Syria and Palestine. Younger Palestinian leaders expressed more enthusiasm than did older notables.[89] Palestinians organized and carried out anti-Jewish riots in April 1920. The British blamed the riots on Hajj Amin Husayni, who fled to Damascus. In May 1920, Palestinians in Syria formed the Palestinian Arab Society.

The British and French dismantled Faisal's government, declared Iraq a British mandate, and installed Faisal as king of Iraq. Faisal argued that his agreement with the Zionists was tied to the Allied war pledges for an independent Arab nation. So the plan's failure rendered the agreement nonbinding, and he withdrew support for an independent Jewish state in Palestine. Faisal's defeat was pivotal for the Palestinians who returned home from Syria and in December 1920 organized the Third Arab Congress, which dealt for the first time with Palestinian Arab affairs instead of general Arab ones. It called for a national government in Palestine with a representative council elected by Arabic-speaking people living in Palestine since 1914 and it rejected the Balfour Declaration.[90] The Nashashibi family boycotted the congress, which appointed an Arab Executive Committee led by Musa Kazim al-Husayni. The committee met to formulate policy in between the annual Palestinian congresses.[91]

With the collapse of the Ottoman Empire and the defeat of Faisal's government, Palestinian Arabs embarked on a new future freighted with the triple challenge of articulating identities (1) separate from old Ottoman and Arab ties, (2) within the mandate of foreign British rule, and (3) against the constraints of growing Zionist political and economic presence. For Jews, the exchange of Ottoman for British masters meant acquiring rulers who would actually negotiate with them, sometimes in their favor and sometimes against them. The next chapter examines the development of both peoples' national communities under a new imperial paradigm, British rule.

4

Historicizing Narratives II

Under the British

[Nationalism arises from] . . . a set of complicated and measured socioeconomic and politico-cultural processes which have forged a new identity and novel interpretation of the human reality.

Ilan Pappe, *The Israel/Palestine Question*

Britain's and France's victory in World War I extended their imperial rule over the Middle East. The British took Palestine as a mandate in 1920 under the auspices of the League of Nations.[1] During the almost thirty years of British rule that followed, Palestinian Arabs and Jews consolidated independent societies, expanded their economies, developed their collective identities, and struggled to gain control over the country while deepening the separation between them. Both peoples developed national institutions and leadership but faced great obstacles to achieving independence.

British rule supported Zionist and Palestinian national growth in several ways. For Jews, British rule was more supportive than Ottoman rule in terms of the growth of their institutions and autonomy. For Palestinians, British rule furthered Palestinian goals because, for the first time in centuries, Palestine was ruled as one political unit. The Jewish Palestinian communities increased their numbers sevenfold. Palestinian Arab populations also increased at one of the fastest rates in the world but their overall proportion fell from 90 to 66 percent. Jewish immigration and land purchases increased Yishuv (Jewish communities) size and self-sufficiency. Palestinian activism mobilized people at all levels of society to recognize and act as a collectivity in unprecedented ways. While neither community was ever homogenous, each emerged under British rule with a stronger sense of unity as a modern nation.[2]

The period of British rule also imposed innumerable obstacles on both sides. Britain recognized Palestinian opposition to Jewish land purchase and immigration and repeatedly set limits on Zionist expansion. Ottoman politics had not prepared Palestinians for political dealings under British terms. Divine observed that "the difference between the cultural legacy of their past and political context established under British domination . . . [that was hostile to it] gave rise to enormous confusion and disarray."[3] Perhaps the most difficult aspect of British rule to accommodate was the obliteration of four hundred years of Ottoman privilege for Muslim society. The British granted Jews and Christians status equal to that of Muslims.

The 1920s: Negotiating a New Imperial Paradigm

British imperial policy in Palestine arose out of the tension between at least two forces within the British ruling establishment. Local British rulers and English visitors who came to investigate violence between Jews and Arabs in Palestine tended to sympathize with Palestinian Arabs. The more distant British government tended to express an awareness and support for Jewish needs.[4] Herbert Samuel, the first British high commissioner in Palestine, attempted the elusive balancing act between honoring the Balfour Declaration by making it possible for Palestinian Jews to organize while at the same time safeguarding Palestinian Arabs' civil and economic rights.

During the first years of British rule, thousands of Jewish immigrants entered Palestine on the third aliya. They were primarily young, poor, and socialist, and dedicated to building a Jewish nation. Their presence sparked new protests from various segments of the Arab community. For example, when a struggle erupted on a May Day parade in 1921 in Tel Aviv between communist and socialist Jewish workers, Arabs attacked Jews there and in other places. In August 1921, Palestinian Arabs went to London to protest Jewish immigration to Palestine. Samuel sought to quell these tensions with a constitution in 1922 that called for a legislative body representative of Muslim, Christian, and Jewish communities.

But Muslims and Christians boycotted elections because the council would have provided them with no power to make decisions about the Jewish communities and thus no ability to redress their main grievances: Jewish immigration, land purchase, and labor policies. This meant that

Palestinians excluded themselves from representation in the mandatory administration. Escalating violence by Palestinian Arabs against expanding Zionist presence precipitated the Churchill "white paper" of 1922 that sought to curb Zionist immigration.[5]

In these first years of the Mandate, the Yishuv founded many new institutions that would become essential to their growth as a national community. They formed the Haganah defense force in 1920 after Arab attacks. The 1920 Histadrut was a general union of Jewish workers whose aim was to create a workers' society in Palestine. A three-part educational system developed with left-wing schools affiliated with the Histadrut, right-wing schools affiliated with "General Zionists," and religious schools affiliated with the Orthodox communities. A banking system began to evolve and agricultural collectives developed. A Jewish Agency advised and cooperated with British authorities and became the representative in Palestine of the Zionist Organization, which continued to acquire land, tax its members, and hold international congresses to set goals. The Zionist Organization created a constitution in 1921.[6] A university was established in the 1920s that some criticized as bourgeois but others defended as a necessary component of national rejuvenation.[7]

The Assembly of Delegates became a forerunner to the Knesset, with 314 representatives from both religious and secular communities. Above the assembly was the thirty-six-member Va'ad Leumi, or National Council. The legislature was ideologically heterogeneous, with many different factions that basically divided into three camps. The Socialist Labor Zionists were led by Syrkin, Borochov, and Gordon and included parties like Po'alei Tzion, led by David Ben-Gurion, which supported settlement on the land but focused more on workers in the cities. Hapo'el Hatza'ir, inspired by David Gordon, emphasized collective settlement on the land as the most fundamental building block of the new nation. Other leftist parties included Ahdut Ha'avoda, MAPAI, the Palestine Communist Party, Hashomer Hatza'ir, and MAPAM. The religious factions included Mizrachi Torah, Hapo'el Hamizrachi, Agudat Yisrael, and Po'alei Aguda. At the center and right were the General Zionists, who were more middle class and led by Chaim Weizmann. Jabotinsky led the Revisionists, who were territorial and political maximalists.[8]

Arab Palestinians remained the overwhelming majority throughout the Mandate period. Whereas traditional forms of social organization persisted in dividing Palestinian Arabs, changes conspired to increase a sense of collectivity as a people. Around 90 percent of the Palestinians were Muslims, most identifying as Sunni but also including Druze and Shiites. Ten percent were Christians—half Greek Orthodox and the other half divided amongst Roman Catholic, Greek Catholic Melkites, and Maronites. Each community had its own administration, educational institutions, and living quarters. Each community was divided along rural/ urban lines, but the majority were fallahin and 10 percent were semi-nomadic Bedouins. Rival hamulas dominated small towns and villages led by rival mukhtars (leaders).[9]

During the Mandate, educational and economic development continued. More children attended schools, literacy rates rose, and educational growth was significant. There was an emergence of Arab working classes and an expansion of Arab middle classes. Arab loss of land turned peasants into workers who found employment on British construction sites of ports, railroads, and roads and contributed to a rising cash economy. New factories further expanded the proletariat classes. Middle classes that had been predominantly Christian now grew with Muslims and these new middle classes challenged the authority of the landed gentry. They developed new organizations such as chambers of commerce, a Palestinian Bar Association, and new women's societies for educational, cultural, and charitable purposes. Professional classes continued to grow.[10]

The British appointed Hajj Amin al-Husayni to the powerful position of mufti of Jerusalem. Al-Husayni, educated in Islamic Reformism and trained as an Ottoman officer in World War I, became a young activist opposed to Zionism. After the war he founded *al-Nadi al-'Arabi*, the Arab Club, for pan-Syrian unity. Early in the Mandate, al-Husayni became president of the Supreme Muslim Council that advocated support for Palestinian nationalism throughout the Arab world. From the same family, Musa Kazim al-Husayni, who had been in the Ottoman administration, headed the Arab Executive Committee. Muslim-Christian Associations established branches throughout the country. In Nablus they changed their name to Arab Nationalist Association to de-emphasize sectarian issues.[11] But the traditional sectarian framework also meant a conflation of anti-Zionist sentiment with anti-Jewish sentiment. This was true in part because all Zionists were Jews even if all Jews weren't Zionists, and in part because wherever Europeans ruled they imported their brand of modern anti-Semitism. The Middle East was no exception.

The Husaynis became the focal point not only of Palestinian national-ist and anti-Zionist activities but also of intra-Palestinian rivalries. The Nashashibis moved somewhat closer to the British, whereas the Husaynis distanced themselves. In 1923 the Nashashibis formed the Pal-estinian Arab National Party; by 1925 they began to openly declare their preference for Arab participation on the administration's legislative council. In 1924 and 1925 the Muslim-Christian Association split into warring factions and there was an overall decline in political institutions, in part because more Jews were leaving the country than arriving in the economic slump of the mid-1920s. The 1928 Seventh Palestinian Arab Congress attempted to heal these rifts, which would again resurface in the 1930s.[12]

During the first decade of the Mandate, the issue of land was central to both Arab and Jewish aspirations for sovereignty in Palestine.[13] Land purchase was a centerpiece of Zionist policy: once land was owned by the Jewish National Fund it was inalienable and could be worked on by Jews only, although in practice Arabs continued to be hired. Most of the land in Palestine was owned and worked by Arabs, but most of the peasants who worked the land didn't own it. Lands of the plains and valley regions had been held by the villages under *musha'*, or collective village owner-ship, while lands in hill country had been under private ownership. But in the 1920s musha' land continued to change hands to absentee landlords mostly because of peasant indebtedness that had accelerated during the war.

Peasants retained "rights" of cultivation but not in legal terms, and many of their plots were smaller than what was necessary for subsistence survival.[14] These factors made it possible for Jews to purchase land from Arabs living outside Palestine and from Palestinian notables, many of whom were prominent in the national movement, and who sold 50 per-cent of the properties bought by Jews.[15] So as Jewish land purchases in-creased, Palestinians who worked the land were forced to leave, many without compensation because they didn't legally qualify as tenants, al-though some had the option to stay on a portion of these lands. There are wildly conflicting estimates of how many peasants were actually dispos-sessed. By 1935, more than three thousand claimed to be. Britain's Land-less Arab Inquiry recognized and compensated nine hundred claims. Some say the number was as high as eight thousand.[16]

In 1929 the first major outbreak of Arab violence towards Jews since

1921 occurred. Jews had prayed for centuries at the Western Wall that was the remains of the ancient Jerusalem Temple and one of their holiest sites. On top of the Jews' holiest site, conquering Muslim Arabs built a mosque in the seventh century to commemorate Muhammad's ascension to heaven on a night journey. In 1928, after many failed attempts, Orthodox Jewish women demanded a *mehitza*, or dividing curtain, so they could pray at the wall, and they finally got one. Jewish resistance to the removal of the mehitza sparked the mufti to form a committee to defend the wall and eventually to build around it. He used anti-Semitic French literature to show that Jews were taking over holy places.[17]

In response to Muslim threats to Jewish holy places, revisionist Zionists formed their own defense committee. In 1929, when Jews sang patriotic songs and raised a flag at the wall, Palestinians came from in and out of Jerusalem to defend the Haram al-Sharif, their holy site. Muslim violence towards Jews spread beyond Jerusalem, aimed ironically at religious Jews who were mainly non-Zionist, but only the Zionist groups were prepared to carry out retaliations. British reinforcements quelled the violence and Hajj Amin al-Husayni emerged more powerful than ever. Thus religious symbols were turned into national symbols.

The 1930s: Threats to Survival and Violent Responses

From 1929 onward, each community responded to mounting threats to its survival in increasingly militarized ways. Britain's 1930 Shaw Report confirmed that Jewish land purchase and immigration posed a threat to Arabs in Palestine. It sought to suspend Jewish immigration and land purchase, help Arab farmers, and resettle landless peasants. The Hope-Simpson Report further attributed Arab anger to Jewish-only labor policies. These reports shaped the Passfield White Paper of 1930, which demanded that Zionists not exclude Arabs from their economy, that Arabs accept Zionist presence in Palestine, and that Arabs and Jews represent their own demands on a legislative council.

A combination of Zionist, Palestinian Arab, and British opposition scuttled the council. Then the election of Hitler in Germany in 1933 set into motion events that had profound repercussions for both Jewish and Palestinian national movements. Hitler's anti-Jewish policies precipitated immigration from Germany and Poland that doubled the Jewish population in Palestine in the Fifth Aliya throughout the 1930s and rendered the White Paper impotent.

The failure of the White Paper to redress Palestinian grievances and subsequent burgeoning of the Jewish communities were some factors that led to a major Arab revolt. Zionist land sales, tenant dispossession, and unemployment were elements of a plethora of economic problems that faced rural Arabs. Zionist presence exacerbated Palestinian insecurity already on the increase due to peasants' inability to gain access to land, debt burdens, growing inequalities amongst the peasantry, market pressures, and the inadequacy of subsistence farming.[18] Not only did absentee landlords continue to sell land to Jews, but now small Palestinian Arab farmers also sold their lands directly to Jews in response to a crisis of subsistence farming.

A younger generation of educated Arabs responded to these threats with greater defiance of British authority. Palestinian Arabs created youth groups such as Boy Scouts and Young Men's Muslim Associations. In 1932 Muslims held a youth congress that eventually coordinated with Christian groups. In 1933 youth groups held illegal demonstrations and leaders were arrested. In 1934 youth groups patrolled the coast to prevent Jewish immigration.[19]

New Arab political parties formed, such as the Istiqlal in 1932, which advocated pan-Arab unity. Raghib al-Nashashibi founded the National Defense Party in 1934 with the Dajani family. Husayn al-Khalidi, from another prominent Jerusalem family, formed the Reform Party. The parties claimed to transcend divisions between the Nashashibis and Husaynis. In 1936, the Husayni forces attempted to reassert control by forming the Palestine Arab Party; it was more militant and capable of organizing youth in its Boy Scouts. But rivalries and antagonisms continued between the leading family factions that led to verbal attacks and occasional violent confrontations between Palestinians.

Secret societies also came into being, such as The Holy War, founded by 'Abd al-Qadir al-Husayni (Musa Kazim's son), which bought arms for violent resistance. 'Izz al-Din al-Qassam formed a group that advocated rejection of modernity and adherence to strict Muslim ideals as a mode of resistance to the British. His funeral in 1936 became a militant nationalist event. At the same time, demonstrations in Egypt and Syria led to negotiations with the Mandate powers for new treaties granting greater autonomy. These phenomena exemplified to Palestinians the limits on their own situation and the power of resistance.

The Great Arab Revolt was the most important and sustained opposition to British rule and Zionist settlement. The spark that ignited the revolt in April 1936 was an attack by Arabs that killed two Jews. Mayors of eighteen towns and hundreds of petitioners endorsed the call for a general strike by all Palestinian Arab workers and a boycott of Jewish goods and of sales to Jews.[20] Fighting erupted in the countryside where armed bands disrupted transportation. Arabs from outside Palestine, such as Fawzi al-Qawuqji, a Lebanese-born Iraqi army officer who led attacks on British forces, joined them. It took twenty thousand British troops to stem the violence.

The British Royal Commission conducted an investigation into the violence that led to the banning of political parties and the arrest and exile of leaders such as Hajj Amin al-Husayni. Its report by the Peel Commission recognized that Jewish and Arab goals were irreconcilable. Zionists demanded unlimited immigration and land purchase. Hajj Amin al-Husayni demanded that Palestine be declared a state minus the four-hundred thousand Jews who had immigrated since World War I. So the British Royal Commission concluded in 1937 that the Mandate was unsustainable and recommended partition of Palestine into an independent Arab state in eighty percent of the land and a Jewish state in the remaining parts.[21] Arabs immediately rejected partition. Zionists were divided but finally expressed a conditional acceptance of partition based on enlarged borders.

Palestinian resistance erupted again, this time in a more sustained and violent revolt from 1937 to 1939, with attacks not only on British leaders and Zionists but on other Palestinian Arabs as well. Arabs fought Arabs along multiple rifts within Palestinian society: between the great family factions, between peasants and upper classes, between clans within villages, along sectarian lines (killing of Christians and Druze), and between rural and urban dwellers, in a concatenation of class struggle, old feuds, and civil war.[22] The British responded with increasingly brutal force, including suspension of civil rule and imposition of harsh military government, demolition of houses, taking of prisoners, exile, and killing. They basically eradicated Palestinian leadership through arrests, exile, and execution.

The revolt had profound political ramifications for Arabs, Jews, and Great Britain. The British stopped negotiating with Palestinian Arabs and turned to Arab leaders in other countries. The Arab general strike and boycott strengthened the self-sufficiency of the Yishuv, and Arab attacks pushed Zionists to higher levels of militarization. Kimmerling and Migdal observed that the revolt "mobilized thousands of Arabs from every stratum of society, all over the country, heralding the emergence of a national movement in ways that isolated incidents and formal delegations simply could not accomplish."[23] It marked the end of the old notables' power linked to Ottoman and then British power and ushered in new leadership. From then on leaders would either have bases of support and influence in specific regions of the country or else would claim to speak for all Palestinians but live beyond its borders.[24] The revolt thus "helped to create a nation—even while crippling its social and political basis."[25]

One of the achievements of the revolt was the 1939 White Paper in which Britain acceded to Arab demands to halt Jewish immigration, curtail land purchase, and eventually establish an independent Palestinian state where the Palestinian majority would have authority over the Jewish minority.[26] In an effort to gain Arab support on the eve of World War II, Britain repudiated both the Balfour Declaration and the partition plan. This time it was the exiled Arab leaders who claimed to speak for all Palestinians at home who rejected the 1939 White Paper. For Jews, the White Paper signaled defeat of their aspirations for a homeland at the precise moment of their greatest need.[27] David Ben-Gurion, chairman of the Jewish Agency Executive, vowed to fight on the side of the British against the Nazis as if there were no White Paper, and to fight the White Paper as if there were no war.

The 1940s: Victories and Catastrophes

The outbreak of World War II found the two national communities in Palestine more self-aware, larger, and more separate than ever before. Although Palestine was not an arena for combat, it became a rear base for British operations in North Africa. Unprecedented construction projects produced a boom in Palestine's economy. Britain needed Arab support, but despite British attempts to halt Jewish land purchases, Arabs continued to sell land and Jews doubled their landholdings. Illegal Jewish immigration into Palestine increased as thousands of Jews fled Europe. Britain's fight against illegal immigration, including sending Jewish refugees to internment camps, led to a "war within a war" and to the catastrophic sinking of two ships, the Patria and the Struma, killing hundreds of Jews who were fleeing Hitler.

Recognition of the loss of British support for Zionism led to Zionists' increasing desire for independence from British rule. Jews engaged in arms smuggling in preparation for fighting the British. They increased their military experience by fighting under British command as individuals. Out of a population of about 550,000 Palestinian Jews, 119,000 registered for military service in the first month of the war. By the end of 1942, nineteen thousand Palestinian Jews were in active service, 10 percent of them women, and the numbers increased to thirty-two thousand by the end of the war.[28] They also eventually fought in their own brigade under Jewish officers.

As the atrocities of the Nazis became known, Jews in Palestine became more militantly anti-British and anti-Arab. The 1942 Biltmore Conference galvanized American Zionists, gathering six hundred leaders in New York. It called for the opening of Palestine to Jewish immigration under the authority of the Jewish Agency, and after the war, the creation of a Jewish state "integrated in the structure of the new democratic world."[29] The heightened sense of urgency amplified the rifts among Zionists, deepening divisions between Ben-Gurion's direct-action, expansionist, U.S.-oriented faction and Weizmann's diplomatic, gradualist, British-oriented faction. Within Palestine the rifts further widened when Menachem Begin entered the country in 1942. He unilaterally abrogated the wartime moratorium on opposition to the British. The Irgun and a smaller, more radical LEHI or Stern Gang carried out assassinations, bombings, and terrorist acts against the British in Palestine.

With the collapse of the Arab Higher Committee at the end of the Arab Revolt in 1939, Palestinian Arabs entered the war with their leadership in disarray. Hajj Amin al-Husayni went to live in Germany and supported the Nazis to defeat the British. Hitler promised al-Husayni that when the Nazis entered Palestine they would destroy the Jews. Other leaders returned from exile to Palestine in exchange for promising the British they would not engage in political activity. They gave measured support to the 1939 White Paper and distanced themselves from the mufti and Nazi propaganda beamed to Palestine. Leaders such as Fakhri al-Nashashibi encouraged Palestinians to enlist in the British armed forces; about nine thousand signed up directly, with another fourteen thousand joining the Transjordanian Arab Legion under Allied command. Many Arabs in Palestine believed that time was on their side and that after the war the promises of the 1939 White Paper would result in their political independence.[30]

Returning leaders of the Istiqlal party challenged the Husayni faction and the overall hegemony of Jerusalem notables. They were able to do this in part because of a war-generated economic boom that enlarged the middle classes and expanded the prosperity of peasants. Leaders of the Istiqlal party such as Ahmad Hilmi, 'Awni 'Abd al-Hadi, and Rashid Ibrahim acquired the Arab National Bank and took over the Arab National Fund to purchase land. Muslims began to use government educational systems in unprecedented numbers owing to increasing peasant interest. Professional groups emerged including a Palestine Arab Medical Association and growing numbers of Palestinian women who entered medical and legal professions.[31]

The fact that the Istiqlal was not tied to local factions but rather had a broad base of support in middle and peasant classes meant that the major clans of Jerusalem opposed it. Husayn's supporters and those who favored a Nazi victory formed the New Arab Palestine Party, and by the end of the war the Husayn-based Arab Palestine party was again the most powerful voice.[32] But by the end of the war decisions about Palestine were increasingly in the hands of other Arab leaders. Newly independent Arab states held a conference in 1944 and when Palestinians couldn't agree on a representative, the other Arab leaders chose Musa 'Alami. The Arab League, formed in 1945 and based in Cairo, appointed the Arab Higher Executive for Palestine, favoring the Husayni faction. The league was often at odds with Palestinian leaders and simply subordinated them.

By the end of the war, it was the Jews' turn to revolt in Palestine. They were absorbing information about the worst atrocities in their history and concluding that their survival as a people was at stake. In 1946 a quarter of a million Jewish refugees were packed into displaced persons' refugee camps in the West, where many lived for years and from which many tried to get to Palestine. Britain ordered the blockade of thousands of Jewish refugees seeking asylum in Palestine. The Irgun and the Stern

Gang intensified their terrorist campaign aimed at getting rid of the British in Palestine. There were attacks, kidnappings, and assassinations. This time the British sent eighty thousand troops to try to quell the violence and imposed martial law in parts of the country. The Anglo-American Committee of Inquiry found that Jewish displaced persons wanted to go to Palestine and called for the immediate acceptance of one-hundred thousand refugees. There was growing U.S. pressure under President Truman for Jewish refugees to be allowed to enter Palestine. This pressure was matched by growing British determination to refuse them entry and to reinforce British command over Palestine.[33]

By 1947, newspaper headlines were full of the plight of Jewish refugees and violence in Palestine. Great Britain referred the Palestine problem to the United Nations, a new force in this drama. The Special Committee on Palestine (UNSCOP) witnessed the war between the Jews and the British, including the turning back of 4,500 Jewish refugees aboard the ship Exodus. The refugees ended up back in displaced persons camps. UNSCOP's report in August unanimously called for the partition of Palestine into independent Arab and Jewish states. On November 29, 1947, the United Nations General Assembly voted to partition Palestine. It was one of the only times during the Cold War that the United States and the Soviet Union cooperated to support the partition of Palestine and that the Soviets supported Israel. Jews in Palestine rejoiced in wild celebrations and Arabs prepared for war.

A few days later, from the beginning of December until the British left in May 1948, Palestinian Arabs and Jews fought each other in a civil war. Palestinians led by the Arab Higher Committee and Hajj Amin al-Husayni rejected partition, called for a general strike, set fire to the Jewish areas, and organized military forces to attack and rid the country of Jews. A Liberation Army was organized in neighboring Arab states by the Arab League. The British administration wanted nothing to do with the unfurling violence and took a hands-off approach. In the first months of fighting, Palestinians seemed to have the upper hand establishing the pace and kind of warfare. The Jewish forces were not prepared for combat. Furthermore the Palestinian population was double that of the Jews, whose fighting forces were outnumbered.

From December to March, Palestinians appeared victorious. Hajj Amin al-Husayni moved to Cairo and then to Lebanon to direct the fighting carried out by the *shabab*, young Palestinian men at home. By

March 1948, Palestinian confidence soared while Zionists faced a bleak situation. The United States withdrew support for partition. The Arabs cut off Jerusalem from the rest of the Jewish settlement, laying siege to the Etzion Bloc and other settlements, and Arab states were ready to invade when Britain departed in two months. Jewish Haganah forces were mostly composed of part-time soldiers. In the war of the cities and the war of the roads, Palestinian victories were evident.

Despite these apparent victories, Palestinians, at first in Haifa and Jaffa and then elsewhere, began to leave their homes within a week after the fighting began in December.[34] As the fighting intensified, two waves of movement developed. The more prosperous classes, including leading notables with a high proportion of Christians, found refuge in Lebanon, Egypt, and Jordan. Middle classes and villagers left Jerusalem and coastal areas and landed in home villages or in Nazareth and Nablus. By March there were between thirty thousand and seventy-five thousand displaced Palestinians, or 2 to 6 percent of the population, including the mass exodus of entire families.[35]

Divisions among the Arab leadership made it difficult for Arabs to maintain their victory over Jewish forces. Hajj Amin and the Arab Higher Committee did not have a broad base of institutional ties and had a hard time coordinating the logistics of war from outside the country. King Abdullah decided the Arab part of Palestine should be included in Jordan. The Arab League blocked the formation of an independent Palestinian government and made decisions without consulting the Arab Higher Committee. On the battlefield fighting forces were divided into those loyal to the Husaynis and those who were not. In addition, Arab League forces of Syrian volunteers led by Fawzi al-Qawaqji favored a pan-Arab solution to Zionist challenges instead of a Palestinian national one. To counter these pressures and lead Palestinian units, the Arab Higher Committee turned to 'Abd al-Qadir al-Husayni, son of Musa Kazim al-Husayni, who had fought in the Arab Revolt and gained more military experience under the Nazis in the Wehrmacht.[36]

By April 1948 'Abd al-Qadir al-Husayni was martyred in battle and the British prediction that the Jews would be defeated by the Arabs lost its certainty. The Haganah shifted from the use of part-time soldiers to reliance on full-time soldiers and from defensive strategies reacting to Arab initiatives to offensive strategies. In April the Haganah committed atrocities in a massacre of Palestinians in the village of Deir Yasin, violating a non-belligerency pact with local Jewish forces. Arabs retaliated, killing seventy doctors and nurses in a medical convoy near Jerusalem. Palestinian military plans counted on the defeat of Jewish urban society in brutal street-to-street fighting. Instead Jews won Jaffa and Haifa. The Arab military command and city officials left Haifa, precipitating the flight of fifty thousand Palestinians. Altogether two-hundred thousand to three-hundred thousand Palestinians left their homes between April and June.[37] When the British officially withdrew in May, Jewish forces had won control of the lands promised them by the partition plan minus the Negev.

On May 14, 1948, Ben-Gurion, as head of the provisional government, gave the Declaration of Independence for the State of Israel. Truman recognized the state, and the Soviet Union immediately followed suit. On May 15, Egypt, Lebanon, Jordan, Iraq, and Syria invaded Israel, turning guerrilla warfare and civil war into conventional warfare and international war. Ben-Gurion beseeched the settlements to defend themselves until the Israeli army arrived, which had the effect of mobilizing every man, woman, and child. In the first weeks after independence, the Israelis began moving Jewish refugees out of the displaced persons camps in Europe, giving priority to men and women of military age.

In one period of ten days in July, Israeli forces drove out more than one-hundred thousand Arabs beyond its borders into other parts of Palestine. In October's offensive against the Arab Liberation Army and Egyptian forces, another one-hundred thousand to one-hundred fifty thousand Palestinians became refugees. Through the remainder of the war and into 1949, Israeli forces destroyed 350 abandoned Arab villages, allocated Arab lands to Jews, and built 130 new Jewish settlements. Some Jews were refugees who had survived the Holocaust, but many were Arab Jews, turned into refugees when their Arab hosts attacked them in reaction to the emergence of Israel. Overnight, the newspaper headlines in the West shifted from the tragic plight of Jewish refugees to the tragic plight of Arab refugees. Some Palestinians poured into towns like Nablus, but most moved into refugee camps throughout the West Bank under Jordanian control or into the Gaza Strip under Egyptian control. Others moved to Lebanon, Syria, Jordan proper, Egypt, and Iraq.

By the time it accepted a cease-fire at the end of 1948, Israel had doubled its meager partition-plan borders, incorporating the Galilee and Negev.

Where there had been catastrophe for Jews in the slaughter of the Holocaust and a refugee problem in the years following the war, there was now victory in the state of Israel. Where there had been a victory for Arabs in the White Paper's defeat of Zionism and promise of independence, there was now the catastrophic loss of Palestine to Israel, Jordan, and Egypt, and a Palestinian refugee problem. The catastrophes and victories of the 1940s were the culmination of more than a century of the evolution of national consciousness and new political and cultural institutions. They laid the foundation for the rest of the twentieth century: a struggle between a state and a stateless people.

For Jews, national development would occur within a sovereign nation-state. For Palestinians who remained in the country, national development would occur under the rule of Israel, Jordan, or Egypt. Those who left would be under the control of Arab countries not particularly interested in helping to birth another Arab nation despite rhetorical support for Palestinians. Rashid Khalidi noted the poignant irony that "the defeats, the dislocations, the dispossession, the flight, and the expulsions" were the very things that finally "resulted in the universalization of a uniform Palestinian identity" beyond class, religious, regional, and factional divisions.[38]

II

Imagining Communities

Politicizing Masculinities

Shahada and *Haganah*

I will guard my land with my sword so that all will know that I am a man.

> 'Abd al-Rahim Mahmud

A man without land is not a man.

> Jewish sages, quoted by Dr. Zerah Warhaftig

Gender became a site of conflict and contestation in emerging national communities throughout the Middle East, in part through explicit and implicit assumptions about "real" men and "new" women. Some of these references can be found in the literature of the latter half of the nineteenth and first half of the twentieth centuries, when Western-educated elites wrote about "catching up" to the West. Much has been written about the importance of the "new woman" in this process.[1] She embodied the best or worst of modernization depending on one's point of view. Debates about "the woman question" strategized how much to emancipate woman, how much and what kind of education to give her, how many aspects of traditional confinement to eliminate or retain. One of the first "feminists" of Egypt was, not surprisingly, a man.[2] Qassim Amin wrote *The Liberation of Woman* and *The New Woman,* partially in response to Western attitudes that accused the Middle East of being stagnant and its women of being symbols of backwardness.[3]

But when men fashioned images of modern womanhood, they were not really talking about women but about themselves. Debates about the new woman represented notions of manhood and modernity that had implications for political development and power. In this way, nationalist writings politicized masculinities. The politicization of masculinities was one piece of a broad set of processes by which gender shaped and was shaped by nationalism.

Men on each side of the conflict wrote that life was not worth living without control over their own destiny, without sovereignty in their own land. The development of new political identities in Palestine rested in part on what it meant to be a man. Nationalism demanded that men make the ultimate sacrifice. They had to give their lives to a new political entity, the nation, which was synonymous with life itself. Palestinian men spoke about the sacrifice of their lives to the nation as *shahada*, or martyrdom. Jewish men described the sacrifice of their lives as *haganah*, or defense. *Shahada* and *haganah* were means to attain freedom from rule by other men, by attaining or preserving a land base. Texts written almost entirely by Arab and Jewish men in and out of Palestine between the 1840s and 1940s imagined two new political communities as primarily masculine.

On Becoming Real Men

It was men as primary leaders and propagandists who defined problems and solutions in ways that linked nationalism to manhood. 'Abd al-Rahim Mahmud, for example, was a Palestinian poet and martyr who proclaimed in a poem that "I will guard my land with my sword so that all will know that I am a man!"[4] Benjamin, a fictional Jewish teenage Holocaust survivor, declared in a film that "God needed earth to make a man, and I need earth to become a man!"[5] Proof or achievement of manhood became a subtext of nationalist narratives.

The bronzed, muscular farmer/soldier "new man" was a Zionist alternative to the stooped and victimized diaspora predecessor. Jews associated *galut* (diaspora) with traits deemed derogatorily feminine, such as passivity or vulnerability. In a sense Jewish men felt relegated to being metaphorical women, subjected to degradation by other men of dominant cultures. The new man of Jewish nationalism was supposed to overturn the powerlessness of two thousand years by taking a physical stand to defend himself, his women, and his children. Zionism was an "apotheosis of the masculine" in which men crossed from unmanly passivity to manly action, from feminine acceptance of oppression to masculine assertion of independence.[6] National liberation for Jews included a "reassertion of manhood [which] restored potency after a seemingly endless and depressing impotence."[7]

In 1898, Max Nordau forged a remedy for the stereotype of the weak Jewish male, stooped by dusty devotion to the Torah, when at the Second Zionist Congress he urged a program of physical fitness for Jewish youth. Athletic clubs came into existence in Jewish communities throughout Europe. In "Jewry of Muscle," Nordau wrote:

> Our new muscle-Jews have not yet regained the heroism of our forefathers who . . . pit[ted] themselves against the highly trained Hellenistic athletes. . . . But morally, even now the new muscle-Jews surpass their ancestors, for the ancient Jewish circus fighters were ashamed of their Judaism and tried to conceal the sign of the Covenant by means of a surgical operation . . . while the members of the 'Bar Kochba' club loudly and proudly affirm their national loyalty."[8]

The Palestinian Arab man was supposed to be able to defend *ard* and '*ird*, or land and women's sexual honor. Social status was linked to one's relation to land. Palestinian men expressed their rage at dispossession that would narrow access to a sustaining land base. They expressed a sense of betrayal by Jews, Britons, Arabs, and most bitterly, land-selling Palestinians who severed themselves from an authentic past and viable future. They fought to acquire material possession, control, and defense of land and women as underpinnings of national consciousness and male self-respect.

What follows is an examination of three ways certain Jewish and Arab nationalists politicized masculinities in Palestine. First, they imagined "the people" of the nation to be men and the nation to be a community of men. Second, they linked redemption of manhood to a national liberation that defined sacrifice as *shahada* and *haganah*. Finally, they forged their relation to the nation in rebellion against or in continuity with their fathers.

Communities of Men

Nationalism was a project of omission and boundary making. Texts implicitly posed questions like: Who are the people and who are not? Who are "we" and who are "they"? By groping for the boundaries of peoplehood, nationalism both empowered and disempowered certain groups of people within its borders. Nationalist narratives, for example, gave voice to certain men and silenced most women. Use of the generic word "man" bolstered notions of nation as a community of men. The term "man" connoted a universality that masked many hierarchical power relations contained in the nation. In the 1920s, for example, Golda Meir expressed preference for the politics of "high" diplomacy over "women's" politics because the former stood for universal values central to all mankind, whereas the latter was bound to limited, even petty, concerns of women.[9] "Man" as a category signified international relations and the realm of the public arena where important actions had impact on all people, whereas "woman" as a category signified smaller spheres of domesticity where actions affected the few.

Using masculinized terminology generated ambiguities of meaning regarding women's place in nationalism or omitted them completely. It was often unclear whether "man" meant man and woman, or actually men. When Ahad Ha'am wrote in 1904 about "the influence of great men on the history of the human race," did he mean great men and women, or was he expressing the assumption that historical influence was primarily a male domain?[10] The near total silence of women in the texts spoke loudly not about their actual absence in national movements but about attitudes towards them and towards politics in general.

Zionist texts abound with designations of the Jewish people as men. In an essay written in 1881, Peretz Smolenskin referred to fellow nationals as brothers and sons: "For four thousand years we have been brothers . . . of one people. . . . Even in frequent exiles, Jews were not lonely, for everywhere they found brothers—the sons of their people—in whose homes they were welcome."[11] Herzl's vision of the state was a means by which Jewish men became "real men." Zionism was the "manly stance," the foundation for a "new man."[12] The American Zionist, Louis Brandeis, referred to "Our Jewish Pilgrim Fathers [who] have laid the foundation" in Palestine. Brandeis envisioned a vibrant society in which deeds of male settlers were lauded, achievements of women ignored, and resistance by Arab neighbors dismissed as banditry:

> In the Jewish colonies of Palestine there are no Jewish criminals; because everyone, old and young alike, is led to feel the glory of his people and his obligation to carry forward its ideals. The new Palestinian Jewry produces instead of criminals, scientists like Aaron Aaronson, the discoverer of wild wheat; pedagogues like David

Yellin; craftsmen like Boris Schatz, the founder of the Bezalel; intrepid *shomrim*, the guards of peace, who watch in the night against marauders and doers of violent deeds.[13]

Arab nationalists outside Palestine also evoked the people of the nation as men. 'Abd al-Rahman 'Azzam, an Egyptian who wrote about Arab unity in Palestine in the 1930s, referred to the Arab person as a man and equality as something achievable between some men and other men, who were sons of the original man, Adam:

> The Arab is a man who is prepared to hold back at any time and who accepts peace whenever it is offered him, without insisting on the complete defeat of his enemy, and with no arrogance on his own part. . . . For the Arab, all men are created equal; they are descended from Adam. . . . Men live by their opinions and ideas.[14]

Nationalists further masculinized peoplehood by describing the land as father. Arab nationalists philosophized about the nature of national love which men cultivated for a "father" land: "The member of the nation loves the fatherland because he loves it. . . . The Arab loves his fatherland and its different regions with a pure love because it is the fatherland."[15] Jewish men portrayed Palestine as a fatherland to distinguish it from the natal motherland of the *galut*. Hess obliterated females from his narratives when he referred to God as "Lord," the land as "our lost fatherland," and every Jew as a "man, . . . whether he wishes it or not, bound unbreakably to the entire nation." Hess envisioned in 1866 that "the Jewish people . . . will have the courage to dare claim its ancient fatherland, not only from [the male] God in its prayers, as hitherto, but also from men."[16] British Zionist Norman Bentwich proclaimed that "Zionism is as old as the captivity of the Jewish people, when the Temple was destroyed by Nebuchadnezzar . . . the Jewish people have been attached more devotedly, perhaps, than any other to their Fatherland."[17]

Another way that Palestinian and Jewish writers masculinized the nation was in their references to an ancient past dominated by men. While both peoples constructed predominantly secular movements, they nevertheless felt free to invoke old religious moments to deepen the sense of shared nationalist history. This evocation of the past to affirm a distinctively modern political vision was common to all national movements. Palestinians and Zionists rummaged through their historical luggage for

examples of Jewish kings' rule over Zion from around the tenth century
B.C.E. and Arab Caliphs' rule over the Middle East by the late seventh
century C.E. to justify acquisition of power in the twentieth century.

Ancient religious texts were sources of heroic models who legitimized
modern secular movements. Although all the ancient sources contained
powerful women, nationalists selected imagery that represented the
people as men born of fathers, from an original father, Adam, and the
great Father, God. In the 1840s, Alkalai articulated political claim to modern Palestine by citing Jacob's biblical journey to Shechem, where he purchased ground in Palestine, and the conquest led by Joshua of the land of
Canaan. In 1882, Emma Lazarus elevated biblical heroes to modern symbols of hope in her poem "The Banner of the Jews": "With Moses' law
and David's lyre/ Your ancient strength remains unbent/ Let such an era
rise anew/ To lift the 'Banner of the Jews.'"[18]

During the Mandate period, Arab nationalists inside and outside Palestine reached back to early Islamic history to authenticate a modern
secular mission. *Fatat 'Adnan wa-Shahamat al-'Arab* (The Daughter of
'Adnan and Arab Chivalry), the title of a play presented in 1918 by a
literary Muslim group to the Rashidiyya school club in Jerusalem, refers
to the ancient ancestors of the northern Arabs.[19] Palestinian writer 'Ajaj
Nuwiyhid in the 1930s evoked heroes of Arab conquest and sovereignty
in his poem *"Kul shabab"* to confer legitimacy on modern patriots: "Palestine, this is your day. You must rejoice for you have men like Khalid
and Yazid."[20]

Redemption of Manhood through Nationalism

An implicit goal of Jewish and Palestinian national movements was the
salvaging of manhood wounded by violence and degradation. Economic
dependence, defenselessness, landlessness, exile, dispossession, and murder affected both men and women. Yet nationalists often grappled with
these issues only as they affected men. Zionist and British colonization in
Palestine and anti-Semitism in Europe affected everyone, but the national movements that arose in response to these threats sought to redress injustices by augmenting the power of certain groups of Palestinian
and Jewish men.

One way that official anti-Semitism undermined manhood was by restricting the means by which Jewish men earned their living. Herzl reacted to the promulgation of official anti-Semitic laws in Europe that limited social and professional opportunities, barring young men from full participation in culture and work. After the false accusation and exile of Dreyfus, he wrote *The Jewish State* (1896) from "one man to other men." He surmised that "perhaps our ambitious young men, to whom every road of progress is now closed . . . will ensure the propagation of the [national] idea."[21] He hoped that the frustration of these young men would energize the building of a new Jewish society. The new land meant unlimited opportunities for men: "Every man need think only of himself, and the movement will become an overwhelming one. . . . We shall live at last as free men on our own soil, and in our own homes peacefully die."[22]

Palestinian men voiced awareness of growing economic competition as the project of Jewish nation building intensified. They experienced Jewish immigration as a personal calamity for men, threatening bread-winning capacities. In a study of pre-1948 Palestine, Naji 'Alush acknowledged some men's complaints that despite the development of industry and agriculture since the arrival of Jews, Jewish laborers still earned twice as much as Arab laborers and Jewish peasants earned more than Arab peasants. 'Alush expressed the perception of high competition between the two communities that threatened Arab men's ability to earn livelihoods.[23]

But threat of deprivation of livelihood paled against the danger of dispossession. The notion that men could not live normal lives if they were not sovereign in their own land was central to nationalism. For Jewish and Palestinian nationalists, exile was a weapon aimed against manhood. Severance from a land base and from the means of defense resulted in a profound devaluation and impotence of Jewish and Palestinian men.

For Jewish men, exile signified disgrace and futility. In "Auto-Emancipation," early Zionist Leon Pinsker argued that the dishonor of Jewish men stemmed from the fact that "our fatherland is the other man's country."[24] For Jews, the word *galut*, or exile, came to capture an entire "*mentaliut*," or existential frame of mind, which accommodated oppression. Pinsker wrestled with the impenetrable barriers that separated Jewish men, no matter how smart or energetic, from life's fulfillment in the *galut*:

It is true that our loving protectors have always taken good care that we should never get out of breath and recover our self-respect. . . . Single-handedly each separate individual [Jew] had to waste his genius and his energy for a little oxygen and a morsel of bread. . . . We waged the most glorious of partisan struggles with all the peoples of the earth. . . . But the war we waged . . . has not been for a fatherland, but for wretched maintenance of millions of 'Jew peddlers.'[25]

French Zionist Bernard Lazare believed like many of his compatriots that Jewish nationalism was the only alternative to remaining the object of other men's contempt: "For a Jew, the word nationalism should mean freedom. A Jew who today may declare 'I am a nationalist . . . ' will be saying 'I want to be a man fully free, I want to escape the . . . outrage, to escape the scorn with which men seek to overwhelm me.'"[26]

Palestinian men sounded an alarm in the face of encroaching Zionist power that could rob them of respect and even survival on their lands. Texts railed against Jews, Britons, Palestinians, and other Arabs whose betrayal led to dispossession.

In *Mudhakkirat Dajajah* (Recollections of a Hen), Ishaq Musa al-Husayni wrote a fictional story that compared Palestinian men to a female hen.[27] The hen could at first run free, master of her own fate. Next she was fenced in. Then she was sold to shopkeepers who forced her to share her coop with more sophisticated hens, which multiplied rapidly with the intention of kicking out the old hen. In this way, al-Husayni captured men's anxiety about their ability to determine their futures in their own land in light of continued Jewish immigration. Using the metaphor of a hen, he asserted that lack of sovereignty led to emasculation or feminine powerlessness.

Nationalism inspired Palestinian Arabs to articulate the notion that sacrificing their lives was the highest expression of love for the nation.[28] Arab men who became nationalists constructed ideologies of national sacrifice from their disappointment, anger, and hope. The drive to prevent dispossession and the powerlessness to prevent it fueled the pull towards martyrdom. In the discourse of martyrdom, death was the noblest act. A letter from three Palestinians who received the death penalty in the British court system illustrated the honor accorded martyrdom. The condemned men wrote to all Palestinians on the day before their execution in 1929:

> We ask all the Arabs in Palestine not to forget our blood and spirits which are flying in the sky of this lovely land. With pleasure, we sacrifice ourselves in order to become the basis of independence and freedom for our people.[29]

In the 1930s, Ibrahim Tuqan, the prominent Palestinian poet from Nablus, wrote "*al-Shahid*" (The Martyr), in which he described the full honor accorded a man who was strong and unafraid of danger, pain, or death. Tuqan wrote that even if no one knew about the way a man had died, if nobody cried at his death, or if no one knew the location of his grave, the matter of his body was unimportant because his name would be everywhere. "O how joyous was his face when he was passing to death; singing to the whole world: could I but sacrifice myself for God and my country."[30]

'Abd al-Rahim Mahmud, poet and martyr, reasoned that real men had two choices: to live with honor or to die fighting for it. Honor was linked to the power to rule oneself in one's own land, rather than be ruled by others, and to demonstrate "courage and noble self-denial in defense of honor and country."[31] As a rebel in the 1936 revolt, he forged images of heroic manhood through action and poetry. His poem "*al-Shahid*" highlighted two aspects of his commander:

> In my hand I will bear my soul,
>> ready to throw it into the abyss of death.
> A man should live with honor and dignity,
>> otherwise he should die gloriously.
> The soul of the noble man has but two aims:
>> either to die or to attain glory.
> I swear I can see my fate, but I quicken my steps towards it.
> The only desire I have is to fall defending my usurped
>> rights, and my country.[32]

"Usurped rights" were not the rights of women for freedom of movement, choice, or sexuality but the particular rights of men to remain in charge of their own fate, dignified masters over the resources of their land and women. Women were supposed to proudly sacrifice the blood of sons, husbands, fathers, and brothers. The Quran teaches that those who die "on the path of Allah" enter Paradise and immortality. Sura 3:161 states: "Consider not those slain on God's path to be dead, nay, alive with God, they are cared for."

Jewish men who became nationalists sought to end landlessness and exile by gaining access to the means of defense. *Haganah*, or defense, whether of land or women, was new for Jewish men, whose key condition in exile was their lack of the right to bear arms. Zionist writings stressed the possibility of resisting the indignities of *galut* existence by ending centuries of enforced disarmament. The inability to come to their own defense in host nations of the diaspora drove men and women to endure disease, starvation, and death in Palestine. The crucial difference was that access to the means of defense on settlements in Palestine transformed these hardships, including the opposition of Arab neighbors and British overlords, into worthy challenges.

In *Reinventing the Jewish Past*, Myers points to a "narrative divide between Jewish victims and heroes." "Jewish passivity" had "fatal consequences while Jewish self-defense and resistence" were "virtuous expressions of national vitality."[33] Anything was better than dying defenseless in countries that prohibited attempts at self-defense. Rabbi Zvi Hirsch Kalischer asked as early as 1866: "Why do the people . . . of other countries sacrifice their lives for the land of their fathers, while we, like men bereft of strength and courage, do nothing?"[34] The ideal nation then was "a country for which men are prepared to die."[35] Zionism would be an antidote to *galut* "heroism of despair" by making possible *haganah* of women and land. Nationalism would restore the means of defense to men's hands but not necessarily to women's.

Rebellion and Continuity: Fathers and Sons

Palestinian and Jewish men co-opted their respective pasts in different ways to imagine their futures. For Arab men, already in their own land, continuity with the past was empowering. The family represented unbroken Arab presence in Palestine. British interests, Zionist interests, and modernization threatened continuity of this family. Ability to defend the family depended on acquiring influence over policy and the means to fight. Dispossession divided families and rendered fathers helpless to be models worthy of sons' respect. During the Palestinian rebellion of the 1930s, Abu Salma likened the separation of Arabs from land to severing sons from a father and generations from each other. Exile created orphans and widows, prisoners and homeless people, who constituted a lost citizenry:

Arise, see the citizen lost
between promise and threat;
Some cast into prison, some homeless in exile;
Here an orphan and wailing widow, there a man lost!
Arise, see the fatherland slain ear to ear!
Generations throng round the graves,
their footprints bloody.[36]

Isaak Diqs recalled an idyllic Bedouin childhood in Palestine. His family lived in an area where they could stay without seasonal migration because the climate was nurturing. He perceived this place of his youth to be mercifully isolated from the outside world except for market day on Thursday at the neighboring village. On this land shepherds of both sexes could meet in the cover of dusk as lovers while their animals grazed. Diqs remembers his father's simmering regret over separation from these lands. On his deathbed, the father soothed his sons with reassurances: you will "go back and find the vines have been waiting for you."[37] A father's power lay in his ability to pass on a means of sustenance to his sons.

Zionist men had no such luxury of an idyllic past. Instead, to achieve self-respect they had to leave birthplaces that emasculated them, to go to a completely foreign land. They made a severe break with their past, with their families, with their fathers' way of life to construct lives of dignity that would eventually have some future continuity. Zionists' emigration to Palestine constituted a dramatic break with, and even rejection of, their fathers' lives. The modernizing project in general disdained old, fixed ways of life, and for Zionists the old life was synonymous with ultimate powerlessness. Diaspora existence strained families, divided them arbitrarily because of external political exigencies, or made them islands of resistance or accommodation. To build a society where they could achieve the continuity expressed by Palestinian men, they would first have to bid farewell to family, natal land, tradition, and mother tongue.

Preservation or redemption of manhood in nationalism lay in the ability of men to hold onto or gain access to land and to protect it from rival interests of other men. Nationalism would free men and women from domination by non-Jews or non-Arabs. This kind of "independence" never fully included women or even all groups of men. Some women took advantage of the notion of individual rights in modern nationalism to forge their own interpretive frameworks and to challenge men's conventional expectations of them. Yet Zionist women who founded agricultural collectives or became carpenters and Palestinian women who organized public gatherings, petitions, and charitable organizations remained the exceptions. As a daughter of modernity and nationalism, the "new woman" remained linked to men's agendas.

Men wrote about being at the helm of nations that would themselves be a new kind of family. In some ways the Syrian Arab nationalist and founder of the Ba'th Party described this well. In 1940 Michel 'Aflaq wrote an essay titled "Nationalism and Revolution," in which he compared love of country with love of family. 'Aflaq sought to elicit a declaration of national love by placing it on the same level with the marriage vow:

The nationalism for which we call is love before everything else. It is the very same feeling that binds the individual to his family, because the fatherland is only a large household, and the nation a large family. Nationalism, like every kind of love, fills the heart with joy and spreads hope in the soul; he who feels it would wish to share with all people this joy which raises him above narrow egoism, draws him nearer to goodness and perfection.... It is ... the best way to a true humanity ... and as love is always found linked to sacrifice, so is nationalism. Sacrifice for the sake of the nation leads to heroism.[38]

Thus men could become lovers and heroes. Sacrifice entailed *haganah*, opportunity to defend the new family/nation, or *shahada*, the imperative to die for a family/nation that was not yet free. Independence, the meaning of homeland, and access to the means of violence could be interpreted in so many ways. Yet nationalists interpreted the nation to be a place in which (at least certain) men could consider themselves at home. Dignity at home would be unassailable or, if assailed, defended by brothers. Nationalism became a male affair through masculinized definitions of national community, freedom, dignity, economic opportunity, and security. Although the threat of dispossession or life in *galut*, exile, obviously had profound repercussions for both men and women, it was primarily men who got to define the hermeneutics of sacrificial heroism through discourses that included *shahada* and *haganah*.

Feminizing Lands

'Ird and Ard, Adam and Adama

> We have asked to become engaged to a girl
> Her bride price is very expensive.
>
> 'Ajaj Nuwiyhid

> Whoever separates . . . [the lover] from his beloved deprives him
> of life.
>
> A. D. Gordon

Pal███s not just the father(land) but also mother, lover, and bride. Bo███b and Jewish nationalist writers described *Filastin* (Palestine) or *Eretz Yisrael* (the land of Israel) as a mother capable of birthing real men, or a lover for whom one sacrificed everything. Writers designated women and land as two of the most precious commodities of emerging peoplehood. Palestinian nationalists expressed some of these concerns with use of the Arabic terms "'*ird*," which connoted honor based on protection of women's sexuality, and "*ard*," land. Zionists expressed some of these ideas with the Hebrew word for man, "*adam*," and its feminized form, "*adama*," which doesn't mean "woman" but, in fact, "land." In this chapter we examine why and how Palestinian and Jewish nationalists created the illusion of land as female, and conflated women and land. In the next chapter we explore their illusions and expectations of women.

Ard and 'Ird: Possession of Land and Women

Arab poets and theorists articulated men's reverence for land and women as part of a modern Palestinian male identity. Muhammad Is'af al-Nashashibi alluded to these images in a poem he wrote in the last years of Ottoman rule. The poem contained one of the early warnings of Zionism's threat to Arab possession of land. There was ambiguity about whether he was addressing the women of Palestine to underscore a dread of losing land or whether Palestine itself was perceived to be female. Nashashibi introduced a theme that would be repeated by others: the imperative of shedding blood to protect the female land and the women:

O young woman of our homeland!
Shed blood instead of tears if you want to cry.
Sister of exaltedness!
Palestine is lost;
nothing but blood is left now.
You will suffer and weep with blood,
when weeping tears becomes of no avail.[1]

With the defeat of the Ottomans and the subsequent takeover by the British, poets began to construct a land of Palestine as superseding all other love, including the love of actual women. In fact, faithfulness to the land was sometimes opposed to the actual love of real women. Poetic verses hung in 1918 under the Rashidiyya school club's map of Palestine read: "Palestine, the blessed land, is the land of the Bani Ya'rub (Sons of the Arabs). Oh, best land of all! Do not despair. You are the only love we have."[2] Men pledged themselves to love the female land, and sacrifice for her, even if that meant renouncing love of real women. Men had to leave actual women behind to sacrifice themselves for the female land.[3]

Iskandar al-Khuri al-Baytjali in the 1920s elaborated on the metaphor of Palestine as a young woman. In his poetry, she was the land and the people. At first, she was a weak, thin girl—from the reign of the Ottomans until the Empire's defeat in 1918. British occupation served to revive her, to wake her from lethargy, infusing her with youthful energy and activity. This activity evoked an image of the Arabs' conquest so many centuries ago, when they imagined Palestine to shine:

Strength has spread through her body and penetrated deeply into
    her bosom.
She was revivified after being weak and thin.
This is Palestine, who until recently was at a loss and humiliated
    by the Turks.
She has become languid, while she was bright at the time of the
    Arabs.[4]

After more than a decade of rule by the British, Palestinian poets embellished their images with metaphors of marriage as a way to express the enduring and sacred connection to land despite colonial rule. 'Ajaj Nuwiyhid, for example, portrayed Palestine in the 1930s as the bride of Arab men, a bride who had to be won at the highest cost, with the blood of the groom. Dying for the beloved would become a way to demonstrate men's unquestionable love for and loyalty to land. Full manhood became entangled with blood and death in the context of a brotherhood of martyrs:

We have asked to become engaged to a girl
Her bride price is very expensive
But she deserves it
Here is our answer:
We will fight for the sake of your eyes
Death is our aim
and we have many men.[5]

Reverence for land could be opposed to love for woman, transcendent of it, or just like it. Both land and women were represented as objects of desire and inspiration. The poet Abu Salma ('Abd al-Karim al-Karmi) wrote poetry about Palestine in the 1930s. One scholar described him as a man whose "love for women mixes . . . with his love for his country. The woman is often seen to be his country-woman, but she has no real identity. She seems to be the same heroine of classical poetry for whom the poet weeps at the remains of a deserted camp."[6]

The prominent Palestinian poet Ibrahim Tuqan embroidered the metaphors of land and woman. His first major theme was nation and his second, woman. His descriptions of women's beauty sometimes reached an intensity similar to the passion for land and nation when he wrote, for example, "I move away in awe, longing to kneel at her feet. My soul is torn between reverence and burning love."[7] Salma Jayyusi, collector and translator of Palestinian poetry, observed how Tuqan's "mischievous spirit in his pornographic poems and the ardor of his nationalistic poetry with their critical candor, acted as a catharsis for a people suffering from both political suppression and emotional and sexual repression."[8] But for male nationalists the end of political suppression did not mean the end of sexual repression. In fact, it was the opposite: nationalism depended on continued control of women's sexuality.

When Jerusalem historian 'Arif al-'Arif composed a treatise on Bedouin life in the 1940s, he highlighted the juxtaposition of women and land in Bedouin cosmology. He observed that the hierarchy of meaning in the life of a Bedouin man isolated women and land as necessary ingredients for fulfilling manhood: "If you were to ask a Badawi (Bedouin) what is the most important material factor in his life, his answer probably would be Land. If you asked him what is the second in importance, he would answer Woman."[9]

Fawaz Turki was only a child in Palestine when al-'Arif wrote his history towards the end of the British Mandate period. But forty years later, long after the British were gone, he summarized this epistemology of love for woman and land. Turki asserted that "to Palestinians, no phrase is more familiar—perhaps one should call it a metaphrase—than "*ardi-'irdi.*" Translated literally this phrase means "My land is my womenfolk." As understood by Palestinians, the phrase means "My land is my nobility . . . my being what I am."[10]

Here was a play on words associated with the two kinds of honor that were supposed to be the building blocks of a man's life. *Sharaf* was nonsexual, flexible, and acquirable honor based on the deeds of a man. 'Ird was honor that could only come through control of women's sexuality. It was a more rigid aspect of honor that could not be augmented, but only lost. Popular proverbs acknowledged that the tensions that arose within Arab communities often arose around *ard* and '*ird*.[11]

Adam and *Adama*: Marriage of Man and Land

Leon Pinsker, in "Auto-Emancipation," likened the Jewish people to children and the Land of Zion to their mother. Jews could be illegitimate children in other peoples' lands or legitimate children in the motherland. Implicit in Pinsker's analogy is the compassionate, accepting mother with whom her children can finally feel at home and loved, in contrast with the cruelty of host countries of the Jewish *galut*. The metaphor for life in the diaspora was that of Cinderella. *Galut* Jews were conceived not only as childlike but also as poor, outcast, unprotected.

> The Jew is . . . nowhere regarded as a native, he remains an alien everywhere. That he himself and his forefathers as well are born in the country does not alter this fact in the least. In the great majority

of cases, he is treated as stepchild, as a Cinderella; in the most favorable cases he is regarded as an adopted child whose rights may be questioned; *never* is he considered a legitimate child of the fatherland.[12]

A life-giving motherland could bestow on men an indigenousness, a way to root themselves to a land they could belong to and tend. The motherland image turned the native land into a womb that brought forth new-born sons. But when Jews created a new reality of life and work in Palestine, the symbol shifted from mother to lover, as the emerging male hero reclaimed his lost bride, the land. In 1909, on the commune of Bittania, the charismatic leader Me'ir Ya'ari sanctified the land as a metaphorically mixed mother and bride: the people were thus her sons and the

> bridegroom who abandons himself in his bride's bosom. . . . Yes, thus we abandon ourselves to the motherly womb of sanctifying earth. . . . In this last hour before our wedding night, we bring as holy sacrifice to you, earth of our fulfillment, these our very lives, our daily lives in the Land of Israel; our parents, children, brothers, our poverty and wealth.[13]

When the Jewish people exchanged passive waiting-to-be-saved for a more aggressive shaping-their-own-destiny, they could no longer be portrayed as downtrodden females. Female sexuality was thought to be passive. With the notion of an aggressive female sexuality as too threatening, the Jewish people turn into the active male making his way back to the lover. For A. D. Gordon, this transformation from passive female people to active male lover was a logical one. In 1910, he discarded scripture for a new interpretation of the cosmos and Jewish man's relation to it. He compared the relationship of the Jews to Palestine with a man burning for his lover. Life in Palestine meant a life of poverty compared with the middle-class life some Jews had achieved in the *galut*. Yet "the lover prefers a dry morsel of bread in a poor cottage in the company of his beloved to a life of luxury without her. . . . Whoever separates him from his beloved deprives him of life."[14]

In the rebirth of men there is an intersection between mother and lover. The mother gives physical birth, the lover gives spiritual, emotional, or sexual birth. To come alive one must have the mother; to stay alive, to make life worth living, or to propagate life, one must have the lover. The presence of a female, even if passive, is vital to a successful enterprise. The inability to live without possession of female love through mother and lover is turned into the equivalent of death without land:

> We are engaged in a creative endeavor the like of which is not to be found in the whole history of mankind: the rebirth and rehabilitation of a people that has been uprooted and scattered to the winds. ... Palestine is the force attracting all the scattered cells of the people to unite into one national organism. .... We seek the rebirth of our national self, the manifestation of our loftiest spirit.[15]

We cannot assume that the rebirth of Jewish women's national self turned them into lesbians united with the female land. The bride/lover metaphor functioned to exclude women from nationalist imagery. The gendered core of certain aspects of Jewish tradition left women out of the process of rebirth. Their lack of covenant through Brit Milah, circumcision, reduced them to incomplete Jews, just as the epiphany at Sinai reduced them to objects to be avoided in spiritual preparation for meeting God.[16]

In 1927, Edmond Fleg, a leader in the Parisian Jewish community, wrote "Pourquoi je suis Juif" in which he captured the sense that for a Jew to be fully alive "he" must have contact with the female spirit of Eretz Yisrael. As usual "Jew" really meant "Jewish man," for it was not a woman who was imagined saved by union with a female spirit. For Fleg the female land of Israel was a lodestone with the power to enliven: "I am a Jew because, born of Israel and having lost her, I have felt her live again in me, more living than myself."[17] Thus for men who had been degraded or emasculated in the diaspora, feeling the female spirit set them on a trajectory towards freedom and wholeness.

The marriage analogy reinforced the notion of the Jewish bond with the land as spiritual and sexual. In the 1930s, philosopher, theologian, and Socialist Zionist Martin Buber emboldened the marriage analogy with a Hebrew play on words. Adam, the name for the first human being in the Bible, is also the Hebrew word for "man." *"Ben adam,"* or son of Adam, thus became the word for "human" and *"b'nai adam,"* sons of Adam, the word for "mankind." *Adama,* the female form of *adam,* is not the word for woman, but rather the Hebrew word for "land." Thus Buber described Zionism as "the great marriage between adam and adama."[18]

In 1939, Buber wrote about a mutual liberation between land and man when he referred to a female land of Palestine:

> I am told, the desert is willing to wait for the work of her children: she no longer recognizes us, burdened with civilization, as her children. . . . Our settlers do not come here as do the colonists from the Occident to have natives do their work for them; they themselves set their shoulder to the plow and spend their strength and their blood to make the land fruitful.[19]

Zionists also saw marriage as a symbol of normalization and respectability. Through the marriage between Jews and land, they imagined they could gain the respect of non-Jews and achieve "normalcy." In Koestler's 1940s fictional *Thieves in the Night*, for example, there is a passage that posits a difference between Jews and other peoples in the way they relate to land. The bride/land of Israel was paradise lost. Alternatives to reunion with the lost bride were fruitless ventures fraught with illusion and failure. Only marriage to the land of Palestine would permit the Jewish people to live "normal" lives:

> Our nationalism is homesickness for normality. . . . This earth means something different to us than Croatia means to the Croats or America to the Americans. They are married to their countries; we are searching for a lost bride. We are homesick for a Canaan which was never truly ours. That is why we are always foremost in the race for utopias and messianic revolutions, always chasing after a lost Paradise.[20]

Fertilizing with Blood and Sweat

Dam and *damiyya* are Hebrew and Arabic words for blood. The image of a land in need of blood to become "fruitful" recurred in the writings of both Palestinians and Zionists. On both sides, there were men who wrote about their land as "barren." For Palestinian men, a barren land was one that had lost its ability to sustain and nurture its people. Only by fertilization of the land could it renew its capacity to bear a vigorous people. The semen that would impregnate the female earth, fertilizing it to reproduce future generations, was the blood of men who died for it. Martyrs' blood would water the land, making it able to nurture its people again. As women's blood gave life to actual human beings, men's blood would give life to a nation. As women's blood birthed individuals who would live and die for the nation, men's blood would birth the abstract community of the people.

In Palestinian poetry there is a kind of pagan quality to the images of blood bestowing fertility on the land and giving birth to life in the nation.[21] Through the shedding of blood, Palestinian men could resuscitate land desiccated by centuries of Ottoman rule, British colonialism, and Zionist occupation. Palestine was to give birth to men who could sufficiently sacrifice for it. When it failed to bear these kinds of men, nationalists accused the land of sterility. A fertile land was one that gave birth to men capable of leading the people against its enemies. Palestinian poet Sulayman al-Taji al-Faruqi lamented after the Tenth Zionist Congress in Basle in 1912:

O Palestine! This situation has lasted too long.
Woe unto my people,
are there no more men among them?
Our enemies have gone too far in their iniquity . . .
Palestine!
Your children have been unfaithful to you.
Living in you has become blameworthy.
I wonder, have heaven and earth become sterile?
If not, why do they not give birth to great men?[22]

The fertile land was imagined to bear anything beneficial for the Arab people. Abu Salma wrote a poem titled "*Filastin*" in 1938 in which the land appeared to be the "mother" of Arab political consciousness. This mother was instructed to "smile" because her sons had died fighting for her freedom:

To the mother of all Arabism,
you should smile because today
we are all your good sons.
We sprinkle our hearts over death
to cause our independence to germinate.[23]

Egyptian poets also praised Palestinian men who gave their blood to fertilize the land. The poet Ilyas Farhat wrote that the grass in Palestine was higher than trees because of the blood shed by Palestinian men that had watered the soil: "That blood shed on your soil sanctifies it and fills it with the *al-Malab* scent. On your land grass has become higher than the cedar trees, which tower up to the clouds."[24] 'Umar Abu Risha compared the blood of Arabs who died fighting for Palestine with rain that let life spring from the land: "You are the tears of the sky, O blood!/ when the fields become thirsty,/ when the ears of wheat and the chamomiles become dry."[25]

Ahmad Muharram wrote: "They are watering what they planted with blood. In fertile land which, without running blood, would be barren."[26] 'Ali Mahmud Taha wrote his famous poem *"Nida al-Fida"* on the eve of the Arab armies' invasion of Israel in 1948. He cried, "Brother! . . . if fighting flares up and swords are crazed with killing; if her soil runs with my blood and my hand grasps tightly some pebbles of that soil; if I am dead, find me."[27]

"Ummuna al-ard," or "our mother the earth," was a phrase sprinkled throughout the discourse on Arab identity. The Iraqi poet Muhammad Mahdi al-Jawahiri urged all Palestinians to see how "generous" they could be with their blood shed for their land and mother.[28] But out of the desperation for possession of the land, poets went beyond blood to another image, fire. As men drenched the land with their blood, they would seek revenge for other men's transgressions through fire. The fire of revenge was another means by which the people could root themselves in their lands. Harun Hashim Rashid employed the metaphor of fire in a poem he wrote in honor of a martyr. Fire became the means of scouring the land of British and Zionist poisons and making the fields accessible to Palestinians:

Can we forget the martyr of Palestine?
Can we forget the way he extended his hands to take revenge?
From his eyes he threw fire that came from his chest.
Palestine this is the battle of revenge so be strong.
In spite of all the tears and the pain we will bring you hope.
Tomorrow we will come back to our glory, to our fields and our
     homes.
We will plant our trees in the fields tomorrow.[29]

Other Palestinian poets used fire to symbolize a cleansing cataclysmic break with the current spiral of defeat and impending loss. Ibrahim

Tuqan, for example, wrote: "by high endeavor and nobler than all its elements: flame and tempests. . . . It stems from the nature of sacrifice, from the essence of noble giving, a torch of justice whose scorching heat, many times has set nations free."[30] Ahmad Makhrum dealt with the struggle of Palestinian men to be heard and recognized by others through metaphors of volcanic eruptions:

The other volcanic mountains rested but yours could not
The Arab people shouted from its bottom but the sound blew
    away to the moon
People shouted from their land,
for their patience was at an end
for all the sleepy people,
theirs is a country of disaster, a damaged nation.[31]

Transformation of Land and Men

The theme of barrenness can also be found in the writings of Jewish men. The blood and sweat of men were important to increase the capacity of the land to sustain its people. The process of expanding the land's capacity would also expand men's capacity to be men. In Zionist discourse, there are references to the "barren" female land in need of fertilization. It would take men's imagination, labor, and sacrifice to bring the potential of the land to realization, whereas the process of making the land (pro)creative would in turn create real men. Impotence and marginality would cease through contact with Eretz Yisrael.

Focus on the barrenness of the land justified the need for the labors of Jewish men to improve the land. These were literal and figurative fields upon which Jewish men proved themselves. The blood and sweat of Jewish men engaged in productive labor and self-defense became the symbolic semen that fertilized land, bringing it back to life as it renewed their own. The offspring of the match between the female land and Jewish men's sweat and blood would be a free Jewish people.

From the earliest phases, Zionist writings were rife with sentiment about the land's power to heal the Jewish people and turn out new men. At the turn of the century, Max Nordau, for example, wrote "Zionism" in which he described the transformative power of a return to the land for the Jewish people as a whole. The Jews he visualized were men:

Never has the attempt been made to transform millions of physically degenerate proletarians, without trade or profession, into
farmers and herdsman; to bring town bred hucksters and trades-
men, clerks and men of sedentary occupation, into contact again
with the plough and with mother earth.[32]

A few years later, the Marxist Zionist Ber Borochov elaborated theories of hard physical labor as salvation of another kind. The Jewish people
had lost their productivity, according to Borochov, living for centuries
with severe limitations on the kinds of work the rulers and laws of host
countries permitted them to do. Only through the creation of a Jewish
homeland could a "Jewish proletariat" be restored and its "productivity"
ensured. Through the "workers' toil" and "production" the Jewish people
would become part of the world revolution against class society.[33] Was
the productivity of women in question here? Was reproductivity synonymous with productivity? By definition, this Marxist "productivity"
included predominantly "male" forms of work that produced material
commodities and ignored or belittled domestic products of women and
children. Women had the choice to remain on the sidelines or become
"men."

By 1910, A. D. Gordon had formulated a philosophy of man's redemption through land that would become the "religion" of the Second Aliya.
He wrote, "When, O man, you will return to Nature—on that day your
eyes will open, you will gaze straight into the eyes of Nature, and in its
mirror you will see your own image."[34] The Jewish man, as constructed
by Gordon, would only stand erect, free of oppression, when he returned
to his own soil and his roots in nature. Nations, in his view, were cosmic
phenomena born of man's interaction with nature in a particular patch of
earth:

What are we seeking in Palestine? Is it not that which we can never
find elsewhere—the fresh milk of a healthy people's culture? What
we seek to create here is life—our own life—in our own spirit and in
our own way. . . . We must ourselves do all the work.[35]

These images were portrayed in the early Palestinian film *Sabra*, produced in the 1930s. In the film, Jewish men work the land with newly
burgeoning muscles, going out from their tents with tools slung over
their shoulders to make the land fertile by their labor. Backbreaking work

consists of carrying heavy rocks to turn infertile rocky hillsides into fertile oases. Images in the movie convey a country regaining life through Jewish men's sweat and Jewish men regaining life through hard labor on the land.[36]

The belief that work on the land was the "real" work of "real" men was illustrated by the anecdote of a New York rabbi turned Palestinian farmer. The rabbi, a young man who had left his congregation to settle in Palestine, was proud of his reputation as a good farmer: "I would like to have a picture taken of myself milking this cow. I would like to send a copy to each of my former parishioners in the Bronx: let them see how a *real* man should live."[37]

The 1952 film *Tomorrow Is a Wonderful Day* captures images of postwar and pre-1948 hope for mutual transformation that took on greater poignancy for young Holocaust survivors. The teenager Benjamin arrives in Palestine fresh from the displaced-person camps of Europe. His spirit has been broken by Nazi abuse and he is angry, withdrawn, and uncooperative. We see him march out to the steamy, stony fields of his new home in a youth village in Palestine. With other young Jewish men he starts work on a wall that will demarcate the village from surrounding lands (read: Arab lands). The wall forces him to recall the walls of the concentration camps and in a dreamlike sequence, he wrestles free of the terrifying and degrading memories of his childhood in Europe.

In the backbreaking labor of building the stone wall, which he at first resisted, Benjamin found a way to rebuild himself. He thus became a symbol of Jewish men's struggle with the parched earth and the parched self: the earth restored him to wholeness as he restored it to productivity. As the camera scanned young men cutting wheat in the field, laboring to produce enough bread to nourish the people, the voice-over stated: "A young boy becomes a man in one afternoon." Like God's creation of Adam from the dust of the earth in Genesis, Zionists created men from *adama*, the soil of Palestine.

When nationalists imagined the sacred connections of men to land, they feminized the land as mother, lover, and bride. Both Palestinian and Jewish men imagined a female land and a barren land, in need of their blood and sweat to become productive. As a (male) people became wedded to the (female) land, sacrifice of individual men's lives morphed into rebirth of an entire people.

Marriage analogies symbolized a new relationship between people and land imagined to be somehow monolithic and mythical. Palestinian and Jewish nationalists grafted patriarchal images of male possession onto modern political identities by co-opting old commodifications of women and land as signifiers of a new nationalism. Thus both peoples reconstituted well-worn notions of '*ird* and *ard, adam* and *adama* to fuel modern conflict and identity in Palestine.

Imagining Women

Umma and *Um*, *'Am* and *Imma*

A woman must first prove her success inside the house by raising
her children to love their country. She must strengthen their national feeling and nurse them with the milk of nationalism.
Muhammad al-Bindari

The women's enthusiasm lent wings to the men's courage.
Theodor Herzl

If the work of "real" men was to fertilize a land imagined to be female to
give birth to a new community, then what was the work of women?
Women were not supposed to participate in *haganah*, defense, of their
land or their men, or to fertilize a female land as farmers or builders, or to
sacrifice their lives in *shahada*, martyrdom. Instead, nationalists carved
out for woman both a high moral niche and a low drudging role. Woman
became a symbol of the immutable and eternal national qualities of an
ancient people, the daily producer of an authentic national culture, the
reproducer of new citizens, and the way to measure progress, modernity,
and legitimacy.

This chapter interrogates texts for the ways men imagined women's
bodies and souls to occupy the new community of the nation. *Umma* is
the Arabic word for community and *um* is mother; *'am* is the Hebrew
word for people or nation and *imma* is mother. One of the most important expectations for women was as mothers. They were prized as child
bearers, for their ability to reproduce and to instill national feelings in
their new citizen-children. Women also inhabited nationalist texts in
debates among men about equality for women and how much this
would gird or undermine the strength of the nation. The first section
of this chapter explores some of the ways nationalists constructed

motherhood as paramount to the survival of the people and nation. The second section examines the debates over equal rights that were sometimes seen as a direct threat to the maintenance of women as mothers in a strictly domestic sphere.

Wives and Mothers

Men assessed women's worth according to their usefulness to the nationalist project. Women were noted as obstacles or supports to men's projects. When actual women appeared in nationalist texts at all, it was primarily as wives and mothers of a male leader. For some Palestinian Arab men, the views, beliefs, or stature of their wives were important measures of their own development of national commitment and consciousness. Others elevated marriage to a nationalist act.

One author of a study of Palestine during the Mandate period saw marriage as central to the emergence of national community. It provided a way to forge links across a community riven by class and ideological differences. To achieve a new sense of community, some degree of identification across class boundaries and patronage lines was necessary. Women and marriage could facilitate this transcendence. Townsfolk's disdain for peasants weakened fledgling national identity that was supposed to link people across the boundaries of class. The esteem of a community for its peasants' labors could in part be bestowed and certainly symbolized by marriage between the classes at least theoretically.[1]

In another study of Palestinian history, the author used his own wife as a model in his critique of Arab nations' support for Palestine. Imil al-Ghuri castigated Arab leaders for withholding arms and money, Arab landowners for selling land to Jews, and Palestinians for refusing to participate in the 1936 strike. He contrasted these reprehensible actions with the example of his unnamed wife. She exemplified a good nationalist because she contributed her own money to the cause. He explained that this was a reason he chose her for a wife. She loved her country and proved this by giving so much of her own money to defend it.[2]

In a history of the 1948 war, 'Arif al-'Arif interrupted a traditional chronicle of military battles in Palestine to pay homage to a wife. In the middle of a detailed account of battles, al-'Arif acknowledged the courage of 'Abd al-Qadir al-Husayni, a grand hero of the war, and then turned to the hero's wife. 'Abd al-Qadir's wife, who remained nameless in the text, was listed among al-Qadir's many achievements as a nationalist. Not only did he use his own money to buy weapons, not only did he lead men into combat, but he had a wife who was noted by the author to be a good nationalist from a good family. She helped the fighters by cooking for them and washing their clothes. Her mundane domestic chores were thus elevated to a new level of national service.[3]

Early leaders of the Yishuv praised or criticized wives, and in one case, a mistress, for being supporters of or obstacles to the cause. Rabbi Yehuda Alkalai's wife deserved mention for her role in disseminating his ideas. So fervently did she support the cause that she "sold her jewels" to enable Alkalai to publish his book about the idea of return to the land of Israel in the formative years of Zionism.[4] Moshe Lilienblum, on the other hand, received his main encouragement for his work on nationalism from his mistress: "his only moral support came from an 'enlightened' young woman in Vilkomir, with whom he became romantically involved. But that . . . complicated his situation for, as was the custom of the ghetto, he had been married since the age of sixteen."[5] Ahad Ha'am also married early to a woman who became quite sick. She was thus not able to help him and he considered her a burden, interfering with his work for the nation.[6]

The "father" of political Zionism, Theodor Herzl, seemed to evaluate the women in his life as good or bad for the movement. As the only son of a wealthy merchant, he had been profoundly influenced by his mother. One historian wrote: "his mother, who adored him and remained, until his death, the dominant influence on his personal life, raised him to dream of himself as meant for great things."[7] His mother received credit for introducing him to high German cultural heritage and cultivating in him a sense that he was special. His mother's "sense of form, of bearing, of tactfulness, and of simple grace" contributed to his abilities to function as the first statesman of Zionism.[8] His wife, unfortunately, was another story. According to biographers she was unhappy because of her husband's devotion both to Zionism and to his mother. She would have left him if not for their three children.[9]

But if the real women in Herzl's life were shadowy or absent, helpful or burdensome, it was the imagined women in a work of fiction who helped him articulate a vision of national community. His fantasies were elaborated in his sole novel and last published work, *Altneuland* (Old New Land), about a "new society" built by Jews in Palestine. His utopia eliminated crime and oppression so that women and men, rich and poor, Jew and Arab could live happily and productively together. *Altneuland* critiqued two social poles of Jewish existence in Europe, bourgeoisie and impoverished. Whereas in the old world of the outmoded European bourgeoisie the young protagonist's desire for the hand of a wealthy lady is thwarted by rigid class conventions, in the new society of Palestine he will have his pick of any woman he desires.

The material misery of Eastern European Jews was at least as repugnant to Herzl as the pretentious bourgeoisie. In *Altneuland* the mother of a poverty-stricken Viennese Jewish family from Galicia sacrifices her own food to feed her children, while a "whimpering baby lay at the woman's flabby breast."[10] The oldest son, David, takes care of the family and despite starvation and overwork becomes a learned young man determined to get his family to Palestine. His sister, Miriam, helps her mother and siblings amidst the squalor in "selfless devotion." When we meet David twenty years later in the New Society of Palestine, he is no longer a starving waif but a "tall vigorous man" with a "sunburnt face," and Miriam is still selflessly devoted.

David reassures us that his sister is not compelled to work for her livelihood. He is man enough to earn enough money to support her but she "has duties and performs them because she also has rights. In our New Society, women have equal rights with the men."[11] But there is clearly much ambivalence around this notion of equality for Herzl. He repeatedly contradicts himself, belying a tension between women's rights and duties to husband and children:

> "Don't imagine that our women are not devoted to their homes. My wife, for instance, never goes to meetings."
>
> Sara smiled, "But that's only because of [the baby] Fritzchen."
>
> "Yes," continued David," she nursed our little boy, and so forgot a bit about her inalienable rights. She used to belong to the radical opposition. This how I met her, as an opponent. Now she opposes me only at home, as loyally as you can imagine, however. . . . "
>
> "That's a damned good way of overcoming an opposition."[12]

This male fantasy in which a powerful and perhaps threatening woman is won over by love, sex, and babies is a familiar one. It is based on assumptions that if one fulfills a woman's "natural" or "primary" desires for marriage and motherhood, she won't have to sublimate these "true" desires in subversive political action or by asserting herself inconveniently into public spaces. In other words there is the presumption that women who enter politics or the professions do so because they are frustrated in areas of intimacy. In a categorical dismissal of women's place in the public sphere typical of the times, Herzl wrote:

Our women are too sensible to let public affairs interfere with their personal well being. It is a common human trait—not only a feminine one—not to concern ourselves with things we already possess. The way was paved for our women during the last century. In some countries women had been granted the suffrage both active and passive, in representative local bodies and professional organizations. They showed themselves clever and able.[13]

One of the most outrageous fantasies of women's purpose in the nationalist cause had to do with unmarried women. In Europe, unmarried women were seen as burdens to their families or as parasites on society. *Altneuland* instead imagined single women mobilized into productive service for the state where they would run the "philanthropic" wing of government. In this way "old maids," as Herzl referred to them, could actually save others even less fortunate than themselves by running "hospitals, infirmaries, orphan asylums, vacation camps, public kitchens" under a "unified administration." So when a doctor became president of the New Society, he turned over his medical practice to his daughter, who was an unmarried doctor:

She is a good example of how a sensible society uses old maids, the single women who used to be sneered at or looked upon as a burden. Here they find their own salvation and that of others. Our whole department of public charities is conducted by ladies of that type.[14]

Just as marriage or remaining single became political issues in a nationalist context, so did intermarriage. As procreators of national community, women became guardians or destroyers of national boundaries through their marriage choices. In Palestine, the intermarriage of Jews and Arabs would lead towards assimilation or the blurring of national boundaries that was tantamount to treason. A woman had to be confined to sexual relations and breeding with "her own kind," as part of the nationalization of sexuality. Women were silent generators of national identity by bearing children at the right place with the right men at the right time in history. As bearers and rearers of the people, women were the invisible heart of change.

From the earliest moments in Arab and Jewish nationalism, woman's highest sacrifice for the nation would be the giving up of her male children for the nation. One young man, for example, had not been permitted by his father to emigrate to Palestine, instead staying behind to help his mother run the family business, which supported the father in Palestine. Then one day the father received this letter from the son:

Dear father,

You will be surprised to hear I have joined up and am coming over. Mother was a bit upset at first, but she has come round to think with me that we Jews should all go forward and fight for a land of our own. Hard as it is for her, she knows her duty to her nation.[15]

According to nationalist narratives, the supreme sacrifice of women would remain the bearing and raising of young nationalists willing to die for the nation. When a young South African immigrant to Palestine died fighting the British, the "proper" reaction of the mother was to carry her grief with pride and dignity:

Her first reaction to the news of his death was to say quietly that if her son had to die in war, she was glad he had not given up his precious young life for others, but had died fighting for his own people. . . . A year later her broken heart gave up its struggle with sorrow and quietly ceased beating.[16]

Rhetorical Equality

One of the most radical aspects of nationalism was its attempt to redefine the relationship of the individual to the state. Under the old imperial paradigm, individuals were subjects of a ruler, property of the state. Under the new nationalist model, the state existed for the individual, whose relationship to it was as citizen. Nationalist identity was somehow supposed to transcend old class allegiance and outlaw privilege by birth in ways that emphasized the ideal of equality.[17]

In reality, nations were predicated on inequalities, either institutionalized or understood. As nations throughout the world emerged in the nineteenth and twentieth centuries, many of them, at least at first, excluded most of their men and all of their women from citizenship and equality. Yet the very concept of citizenship and the dialogue it precipitated on equality opened possibilities for women. In Palestine, both Arab and Jewish nationalists seized on discussions of the new national community to question the place of women.

One of the earliest texts that linked the status of women with the progress of the nation was by Qassim Amin of Egypt. He was one of the first advocates in the Middle East to argue that granting equality to women was strategic to increasing the power of Arab society as a whole. In his late-nineteenth-century treatises, *The Liberation of Woman* and *The New Woman*, he argued against Western accusations that Middle Eastern societies were static and unchanging. Instead of women being the guardians of traditions, he wrote that modernization and, in fact, power in the modern world depended on the equal participation of women in society.[18]

Yet no matter whether one argued for dramatic social change or for preservation of traditional values to benefit the nation, women's status in the new nation became an issue. It was complicated by the struggle throughout the region to come to terms with how to meet the challenges of Western hegemony. What women might want for themselves could be confused with giving in to pressures to adopt gender roles imported from the West that might undermine "authentic" Middle Eastern identities. Women were seldom consulted about their own choices to change or preserve the status quo, yet they found themselves the objects of national debates.

There was a wide range of responses by Arab men (and women; see chapter 11) to modernization in Palestine. Roles of women were contested in the debates on new medicine, concepts of hygiene, education, culture, and work. In daily newspapers, articles, and book-length treatises, men argued the question of women's rights in terms of advantages and disadvantages to society as a whole, considering the impact on relationships between men and women, and between East and West. The reaction of the women in their own writings is found in part IV. Here we examine Middle Eastern men's responses.

Men who identified themselves as defenders of tradition viewed their people on the edge of a precipice of change buffeted by values that threatened to destroy the very basis of life, order, and nature. Nature dictated essential and unalterable differences between men and women. In 1935, the Egyptian writer Mustafa Sabri published *Qawli fi al-Mar'a* (My Opinion about Women), in which he identified a division between Eastern and Western men based on their granting of women's rights. He considered there to be a certain hypocrisy in Western men's granting of rights to women for, he argued, Westerners gave rights to women to enhance men's enjoyment of their women's femininity. "Eastern men" should not learn this hypocrisy from the West. Like the Western man, the Eastern woman was also hypocritical because she wanted rights without paying the price that Western women had paid in their struggle for liberty.[19]

Men, who saw themselves as advocates of change, saw resistance to change as threatening to the new national community. In 1939, Lebanese Sa'id Himadeh completed a study of economic organization in Palestine. He compared Arab and European societies through statistics on working women. *Al-Nidham al-Iqtisadi fil-Filastin* (The Economic Organization of Palestine) cited a lower percentage of Arab working women than European women. In fact, during the British Mandate period women occupied 4 percent of industrial positions and almost 18 percent of the "free jobs." If one took only Muslim women into account, Himadeh reasoned the disparity would be even greater.[20] He used these statistics to measure and express his concern with how much Palestinian society had to "catch up" to the West. His assumption was that the position of women was a measure of Western-style development in Palestine that in turn would enable it to stand on parity with other nations.

In the 1940s debates about women's place and rights continued. An Egyptian writer, Ahmad Husayn, held out a vision of women in the nation that was based on unalterable social roles and innate natural differences. He argued that it was nature that made men strong and brave and made women emotional and soft. The author implored women to be satisfied with their place in this order, to be happy to have marriage as their main goal in life, to acknowledge that their own success depended on the success of their husbands. Because the man was naturally stronger, the woman should obey him and expect his protection and defense. Women could become "famous" or gain public attention as the wives or mothers of famous men. Husayn cited queens married to kings, Miryam, mother of Jesus, and Khadijah, married to Muhammad. Nature also dictated social order by social class: poor men should not marry rich women and educated people should not marry the unlettered.[21]

Another Egyptian writer, Al-Bahi al-Khuli, confirmed this belief that men were in a "higher" position because of their physical strength and the characteristics of women's bodies, which were built for pregnancy, delivery, and nursing. These essential differences made women incapable of protecting the house or the family. A man had to step outside the house as defender of his family. It was not necessary for women to have intelligence or intellectual power but rather passion and caring. The house was the "normal" place for women in society. Women could go outside the house only for necessities; otherwise the family would suffer a loss. Women's most important national contribution, therefore, was to raise children and support their husbands by providing love and care for the family. Al-Khuli countered modernist arguments by stressing that women could never participate in state policy making for they were "characterized by ignorance and incapable of handling their family let alone policies of their country."[22]

Some writers welcomed changes for women as harbingers of wider social change. These authors argued that there was intrinsic goodness in "modernization." Both "order" and "nature" determined women's just place. "Change" and "progress" became moral and practical guides. Socialization and education could overcome any "natural" inequality between the sexes.

In the Zionist community, issues of women's rights were embedded in discussion of universal human rights. Idealistic nationalist manifestos heralded new eras of equality, some of which included women. The Zionist Pittsburgh Platform, for example, captured this idealism in 1918. In a statement drafted by Horace Kallen and refined by Louis Brandeis, the Zionist Organization of America called for "political and civil equality" in Palestine, "irrespective of race, sex, or faith." Equality between men and women was not detailed but mentioned in broad strokes of nationalist "justice-for-all." Women's rights would drift quietly on the coattails of other radical social changes. They would include public ownership of land, natural resources, and public utilities, the application of "the cooperative principle . . . to all agricultural, industrial, commercial, and financial undertaking, [and] free public education. . . . "[23]

The equality of women in Jewish settlements of Palestine attained mythic proportions that obscured a reality of struggle. A minority of women engaged in intense struggles to overcome many obstacles they encountered when they attempted to act outside conventional gender roles. References to women's marvelous achievements of equality abound in nationalist narratives, especially after World War I. Writers assumed that the status of women had direct bearing on the level of civilization achieved by society. Nationalists portrayed Jewish women as having the highest status of any women in the world. Abraham Revusky was a Zionist writer during the interwar years who lauded the high degree of civilization in the new society of Palestine due to the equality of women. In his detailed book about contemporary life in Palestine, the only time he referred to women throughout hundreds of pages was when dealing with issues of equality.

Revusky expressed both pride in and dread for women's new roles, which he believed demonstrated unprecedented achievements of freedom. He expressed pride in woman's status on *kvutzot* (collectives) as "unique" for "she lives there on the basis of absolute equality. She is not only accorded an equal voice in all decisions of the *kvutza*, but she also participates to a considerable extent in all branches of agricultural activity."[24] This was a blatant distortion of reality for the women who were permitted to enter production in limited ways according to the needs articulated by men in power, and who fought to be heard in collective decision-making processes.[25]

Men debated women's equality not because of their concern for women but because of their concern for the nation. They argued about how women must advance, change, or preserve tradition in their major life decisions and in their ordinary everyday activities. In both Arab and Jewish communities of Palestine, the rhetoric of equal rights strained under the weight of social expectations for women to be mothers and wives. Equal rights were synonymous with progressive nation-building but suspect as a Western import and as threat to fulfillment of women's main political role as mothers.

Women's sacrifices for the nation were not working on the land, dying on battlefields, or being physical builders. Rather, the primary sacrifice of a woman for her nation was to become a national womb, a producer and rearer of citizens, and a nurturer of men and their goals.

Yet liberal nationalism, and its cousin, liberation nationalism, defined citizenship as encompassing the radical notion of equality. This would have impact on the personal lives of a growing number of Palestinian and Jewish women and on the evolution of their national communities, linking them to changes taking place beyond the borders of Palestine and Israel, and most significantly linking them to each other in unpredictable ways.

III

Hierarchies of Difference

8

Civilizing Women

Hygiene and Lace

I have worked hard to raise them a bit.
            Antoinette Khoury, *Daughters from Afar*

How different [were Arab homes]... even from the plainer and, in our opinion, rather shabby looking colony that was our home, but which was the abode of cleanliness and comfort.
            Hannah Trager, *Pioneers in Palestine*

Modernization held a prominent place in the nationalist paradigm. National independence offered the potential to develop the resources of one's own nation for the benefit of one's own people without parasitic interference from foreign or imperial control. Ideas about modernization lay at the intersection of nationalism and gender in significant ways. In discussions of barren wastelands and forsaken wilderness in need of development, or in debates about women's rights and girls' education, gender informed modern notions of "progress" and national purpose.

Women were seen as both agents and objects of civilization. They could civilize a nation or be in need of civilizing. They were a measure of how advanced or backward a culture was, and the propagators of the civilizing mission. Notions of progress and purpose contained explicit and implicit judgment on what was civilized, what was backward, and what constituted triumph and transformation. Ideas about women undergirded claims to Palestine based on who was more progressive and thus better equipped to contribute not only to Palestine but to the world at large.

The next three chapters look at some of the ways issues of women and gender shaped and were shaped by notions of modernization and progress. This chapter examines women's role in *mission civilatrice* in Palestine. Christian Arab Palestinians such as Antoinette Khoury (see above quote) wished to "raise" her Muslim sisters to a higher level of civilization, as her Jewish sisters hoped to do for Arab Jews and Palestinian Arabs. As some women tried to improve the lives of other women, they did so at a price. Acting within the civilizing mission implied a denigration of the culture and values of those being helped, which in turn deepened rifts between women.

Bearers of Science

The dichotomy between a civilized, rational, modern West and a primitive, irrational, stagnant East justified colonizing movements throughout the world in the nineteenth and twentieth centuries. Even within Europe itself, women and "lower" classes occupied lower rungs on this civilizational hierarchy than did higher-class male standard bearers. These dichotomies between the civilized and the primitive became incorporated into nationalist ideologies as well. So even as Jewish and Arab nationalists sought to rid Palestine of British, and in the case of Palestinians, Zionist colonization, they sought to "raise up" their own people and bring them into the "modern" world. Zionist leader Jacob Klatzkin, for example, conflated nationalism with the progress of civilization when he wrote in 1914 that "Zionism pins its hopes . . . on the general advance of civilization and its national faith is also a faith in man in general—faith in the power of the good and the beautiful."[1]

Those who embraced nationalism and modernization as the key to their future linked the process of advancing civilization with scientific achievement. No one who adopted modernization as a guideline for change seemed concerned that science profited some and not others in the nation. There was little critique within modern national movements about how technological change and the ideological changes implicit in scientific modernization affected power relations, sustenance of natural resources, or status of women. Many nationalists believed that "change" was unquestionably necessary, positive, and neutral; it was the only thing that could ward off the inimical "stagnation" and "ignorance" perceived through the lens of the modernist paradigm.

Modernizers believed that "the material resources of the earth should be exploited in the interest of a comfortable life."[2] Nationalist elites sought control of this process and a greater share of the comforts at least in part through control of women and land. They believed that "modern" was opposed to "traditional" in unproblematic categories. Yet these categories were steeped in subjective perceptions and value judgments of what the past held and the future would bring. Categories of "tradition" and "modernity" could affirm authority, justify means, and define ends.

Jamal al-Din al-Afghani, the late–nineteenth-century Islamic reformer, drew this distinction between "religious tradition" and "secular modernity" in seeking a synthesis of the two. In the 1880s, he wrote that Arabs must acquire science if they wanted to liberate themselves from Western domination: "In reality this usurpation, aggression, and conquest has not come from the French or English. Rather it is science that everywhere manifests its greatness and power."[3]

After World War I, Qustantin Zurayq, a Palestinian historian of the Arab world, said that the only way to remedy the danger of domination by Zionism would be for the Arabs to become wholly part of the world by adopting scientific technique and secularist thought. Ironically, that is exactly what Zionists believed they could contribute to Arab culture. Those men of the Arab elite in Palestine who saw their roles as modernizers targeted women as objects and agents of this process. The Palestinian leader Musa al-'Alami adopted the premise that modernization was invariably linked to nationalist success. He wrote that real unity among Palestinians could only come about with constitutional government, scientific administration, and rational policy.[4]

One major battlefield in the struggle over modernization was in the realm of health and medicine. In this realm, women's practices were often targeted as advancing or preventing progress. 'Alami, for example, spoke in a story about his own birth, critiquing women's traditional practices from a modernist perspective. He told about throngs of women who came to the home of his mother in labor, with the closest female relatives allowed into the birth chamber itself. Women gathered and mingled at this event without regard to class distinction. All women, young and old, poor and wealthy, listened to the moans of the laboring woman. The laboring woman sat in the center of the room on a special wooden birthing chair with a crescent-shaped hole in the seat and a large bowl of water beneath it. The midwife was a privileged figure in the community. Yet 'Alami denigrated her from a "modern" perspective for being "unscientific" and lacking the "training and precept" of Western scientific medicine.[5]

Zionist writers expressed the hope that scientific knowledge brought by Jews to Palestine would endear them to the Arab population. In *Altneuland*, Theodor Herzl's 1902 fictional account of the new Jewish society in Palestine, there is a woman who is responsible for spreading medical knowledge and benefits to the peoples of the Middle East. Dr. Sascha personifies the national impulse for progress through medical advances. This "young lady" is a doctor who studied eye disease in Palestine and found it prevalent where "everything is in ruins." Dr. Sascha helps to found and direct "the greatest eye clinic in the world."[6]

In Herzl's fantasy, this woman devotes her life and scientific training to helping the sick and poor and contributes to her people's welfare, not only by caring for them, but by caring for their Arab neighbors. Her work advances medical knowledge around the world and endears Jewish society in Palestine to the world community. Finally, she resolves eye disease in Palestine and neighboring Arab countries so that Arabs are grateful for the existence of Jewish society in their midst:

> Large numbers of people . . . have had their eyesight saved or restored there. You can imagine what a benefaction that clinic is for the Orient. People come to it from all over North Africa and Asia. The blessings bestowed by our medical institution have won us more friends in Palestine and the neighboring countries than all our industrial and technical progress.[7]

Decades later in Palestine there actually existed such a woman, mentioned without name in one of the old nationalist texts. She was a physician and eye specialist in the Tiberias region of Palestine, working for the Zionist women's organization Hadassah. She fought eye disease that was in fact prevalent among Arab children in Palestine and helped to wipe out trachoma, the most common and contagious eye disease among Palestinian children, bringing about a 35 percent drop in eye disease around Tiberias.[8] Hadassah raised funds for medical facilities, doctors, nurses, and research. It had as part of its mission the spread of medical knowledge, training, and services to the Jews and Arabs of Palestine.

Jewish women participated with men in the improvement of health in Palestine, and not only as doctors. For example, they labored to drain swamps that harbored disease organisms. One valley in particular had the Arabic name Wadi al-Mat (Valley of Death), for the deadly fever epidemics that killed off Arabs and the German Templars. It was a point of pride that Jewish men and women transformed the dangerous swamp into a "flourishing and healthy" valley.[9]

The civilizing mission was not merely a project of some positive ideal of improving life and the world, but a project of power as well. The Zionists' civilizing mission in Palestine was one more point of divide between Jews and Arabs. Despite the concrete and welcome improvements in health brought to Palestine by Jewish doctors and researchers, the project was mired in a paternalism that firmly placed the modernizer in a position of power over the "modernizee."

Uplifting the Downtrodden

As nationalists on both sides adopted the civilizing mission for their own people, it became a point of divide within each group. Some Arab women sought to uplift others, but their good works were complicated by the project of power implicit in civilizing efforts. Christian women sought to "uplift" their "downtrodden" Muslim sisters; upper-class women sought to civilize the lower classes; and all disparaged the untamed Bedouin women. In this way, women served as markers of differences in civilization levels among their own people.

One Syrian Arab nationalist manifesto declared that nomadism was a primitive social state, and blamed it for lowering national economic output and being an obstacle to progress, which could only be completed through sedentarization.[10] When a Palestinian Arab scholar researched education in Mandate Palestine, he used the treatment of women among Bedouins, agriculturalists, and townspeople to crystallize differences between them:

> The only substantial social difference that was to be noted between one type of Arab society and another, was the status and function of women. While women in rural areas did not enjoy equal social status with men, they shared the burdens of life with men and engaged with them in the usual work on the farms. Seclusion of women was only practiced in the towns and in limited numbers of families in the country.... Emancipated women in urban areas showed their influence in political activities and social service and even in the liberal professions.[11]

Christian Arabs used the status of women to judge themselves superior to Muslims. In reality, there were Christian women who were freer
to operate in the public sphere and who self-consciously sought to "bring
up" Muslim women with them.[12] One wealthy Christian woman, for example, explained that although she had worked hard with Arab women to
improve their condition, it was difficult to change the "Muslim character."[13] The autobiography of one Christian Arab man highlights some of
the internal divisions in Palestinian society, and the roles that women
played in these divisions. Atallah Mansour, a Palestinian Arab journalist
in Israel, lived in a small village until 1948. His parents were Greek Orthodox and the family lived in the Christian village of Jish.

Mansour is conscious of owing his life and outlook to the women in
his family. During the revolt of 1936, for example, he recounts his sister's
bravery in saving his life by covering his body with hers when the British
shot at their fields. Mansour's father went on raids to cut fences at the
border between Palestine and Lebanon. The British ordered the villagers
to leave their homes, blew up houses, and killed and arrested them. After
spending several weeks in jail, Mansour's father along with other villagers was forced to build barracks for the British in Jish, while his mother
with other village women was ordered to provide meals. During this time
the villagers wished for the victory of "Abu Ali," Hitler.[14]

Although Mansour's mother accepted his father's Muslim friends,
Mansour describes the prejudice she harbored against them. She re-
sented feeling like a second-class citizen among Muslims; she had grown
up with tales of the deaths of her relatives in the 1860 massacre of Christians by Muslims. Eighty years after the massacre, descendants of survivors still recounted the property they had lost and how much poorer they
were away from their land.[15] When he was ten years old, a Muslim gang
beat up Mansour when he purchased eye drops for his mother from a
pharmacy owned by Jews. They yelled, "the idiotic peasants are destroy-
ing the country" (by buying things from Jews). Mansour's mother responded by decrying the hypocrisy of Palestinian Muslim leaders who
made fortunes for themselves through their own commercial dealings
with and lands sales to Zionists.[16]

British colonialist and Zionist discourses privileged Christians as
more civilized than Muslims and encouraged these divisions among Arabs. The British gave higher allocations for education of Christians and

approved of the higher status of Christian women. Women become entangled in these divisions as markers of difference and hierarchy among the Palestinians. Nationalism influenced these divisions in contradictory ways. On one hand it sought to mitigate differences among "the people" in favor of an overarching national identity. On the other hand, it exacerbated differences by internalizing the *mission civilatrice.*

Keepers of Cleanliness

Like Arab women, Jewish women embraced ideas of modernization and progress with divisive results. They too believed that those who gained access to progress had a responsibility to enlighten those who did not. Some Jewish women were in need of uplift and others were active civilizers. Jewish women from Russia and Europe were supposed to bring a higher level of civilization to the "wild frontier" of Palestine. Those who accepted this burden uncritically could not help but perpetuate the denigration of Jews who came from parts of Eastern Europe or the Middle East, and, of course, of Arabs who already lived in Palestine.

Russian immigrant Hannah Trager incorporated these dilemmas explicitly and implicitly in her narratives about one of the early Zionist settlements, Petah Tikva. She criticized other white women who were obstacles to helping world progress because they were too attached to their "little luxuries" and so refused to accompany their husbands to the lands in need of development. Because of this selfish reluctance of European women to migrate to wilder places in need of uplift, she argued, "the native races have suffered."[17]

Settler women expressed dismay over the "primitive" conditions under which they had to live in Palestine. Yet by comparing themselves with Arab women they felt they had made some "progress." Trager's narratives of the early settlers are rife with these kinds of comparisons. In one instance, the Jewish women of Petah Tikva journeyed back to their settlement from a vineyard at Rishon Letzion (First in Zion). They reflected on how much more developed Rishon Letzion was compared with Petah Tikva, and thus how much nicer a place to live. They were discouraged by the comparison with their own settlement, which seemed less developed. One woman consoled herself over the primitive conditions in which she lived by comparing herself with Arabs living around her:

On the way home . . . we passed some Arab villages and were struck by the contrast to what we had just left. The mud hovels crowded together, more fitted for animals than human beings, the diseased and towzled children who ran after us crying out: *"Bakshish!"* [alms] The dirty, prowling dogs, the crippled beggars. How different from the simple but clean houses or the white-washed walls, red tiles and green shutters, the street lined with trees. How different even from the plainer and, in our opinion, rather shabby looking colony that was our home, but which was the abode of cleanliness and comfort.[18]

Cleanliness and comfort was the guard duty of these women on the civilizing mission. Their special role in the unfolding drama of civilization and nationalism was not as engineers, carpenters, or soldiers but rather as keepers of the "abode of cleanliness and comfort." One male colonist posed the rhetorical question to his female friend in this way: "What social welfare work indeed can be as great as the work these brave women of ours in Judea have been doing for so many years, making homes habitable for the men they love?"[19] Women's realms were house-cleaning, bodily cleanliness, the science of hygiene, nutrition, health care, and modern motherhood.

Women functioned in these ways not only on the domestic level but also on national and even international levels. On the domestic level, for example, one of the women of Petah Tikva commented that she and the others were most concerned with maintaining the neatness and cleanliness of their homes, "and that before sundown."[20] On national and international levels women founded organizations to spread knowledge about cleanliness and modern motherhood. Cleanliness was not so much for the purpose of aesthetics, even though lack of cleanliness was perceived as unsightly, but rather for the maintenance of health along scientific principles that included modern sanitary conditions.

To the European Jewish women who settled in Palestine or supported the settlements from afar, *mission civilatrice* meant that other Jewish and Arab women were seen as "human material" in need of "uplift." Central European women founded lace-making workshops "to replace 'idleness' with productive work" for poor Jewish women from Arab countries. The lace-making workshops would not only help these women to learn a skill and earn money but also bring them to places where they could learn

Hebrew and develop a "positivist national identification with Palestine." By 1913, four hundred Jewish women were in craft shops. Most of them had been born in Palestine or had immigrated from Arab parts of the Ottoman Empire or Yemen.[21]

European Jewish women also taught Palestinian Arab women modern hygiene in prenatal and postnatal care units that they founded and staffed. They took pride in the fact that Palestine was leading other countries in the elimination of orphan asylums: of four thousand orphans left homeless after World War I, three thousand had been placed into families. When one American Jewish woman visited Palestine in the early 1920s, she wrote of the "primitive native" as being the "material" for welfare work. She related that

> along the road to Jericho, I stopped at a picturesque spot to take a snap-shot of a couple of Bedouin girls who were carrying on their heads great earthenware vases filled with water. . . . The method has not changed in two thousand years except for the new pipe and spigot attached to the spring. . . . Fancy then what it would mean to try to do uplift work with such human material.[22]

Nathan Straus founded child welfare stations for Jewish and Arab women in the 1920s to teach them the "first rudiments of sanitation."[23] Straus's child welfare stations in the Old City of Jerusalem taught Arab mothers "to mix infant food properly." It was conceived as a place to which mothers would come with their children for "advice and instruction." Rothschild's Palestine Orphan Committee gave girls "systematic training in housework" so that they could become up-to-date "mother's helpers and farmers' wives."[24] A woman's auxiliary of the Zionist Organization founded by European women was devoted to infant welfare for both Jews and Arabs; the auxiliary founded welfare centers in Tel Aviv, a baby home in Jerusalem, and a center in Haifa.[25]

European women supported the Women's International Zionist Organization's Domestic Science School in Nachlat Yitzchak to train girls in modern hygiene, housekeeping, and nutrition.[26] Provision of medical services in Palestine was a way that settlers believed they could contribute to the technical and industrial progress of all the peoples of the region. Some envisioned that the raising of health standards would be a blow against anti-Semitism as appreciation of their efforts spread, and as Arab hostility diminished when Arab people's lives improved.

Various women initiated schemes that they hoped would advance civilization in their nation and in the region at large. Dr. Olga Pickman Feinberg, for example, left her "clean Chicago home" to live as the only Jewish woman in Arab Jericho, where she tended the sick, created a sanitarium, and received kings and other dignitaries. This same woman flew to Aden in 1946 to care for four thousand sick Yemenite Jews, organize a nursing school, set up a hospital, and operate a camp until the Yemenites flew to the newly created state of Israel.[27]

The place of Arab-Jewish woman in the dominant Zionist narratives was similar to that of non-Jewish Arab woman. When an immigrant woman from Bulgaria, for example, turned her attention to "other" immigrants less fortunate than she, she found Jewish women from Morocco and Turkey living in squalor. They had settled, she believed, "for lack of better housing," in Arab mud-hut villages a few miles away. She perceived their "standards of sanitation" to be "appalling." She watched them each day sitting "listlessly on their doorsteps for hours and even days at a time, not worrying about the flies on the baby, not interested in the dirt in the house and yard, not even caring about work."[28] This scene roused Mrs. Meyer to teach them to clean and work. Each day she went to their homes to teach sanitation and modern housekeeping.

Among the schemes of some Jewish women to "lift up" others was one that focused on Jewish children of Middle Eastern immigrants. They lived in overcrowded poor homes on the Tel Aviv-Jaffa border area but were dispersed to European Jewish homes in the suburbs for additional care. Doris Katz, a Russian–South African immigrant, agreed to care for one of these children and was assigned a three-year-old Jewish boy named Mordecai from Yemenite parents. She was horrified to observe that he had never been fully undressed to take a shower or bath. She referred to his "native stubbornness" and to his mother who also had "native pride." Katz's main job in her estimation was to clean the boy up and return him to his home. When she later paid him a visit, she found him living among ten families in one room with a mud floor. Mordecai had again become "unrecognizable" to her, caked with dirt, mud, and food.[29]

When American Zionist leader Mordecai Kaplan tried to convince American Jews to go to Palestine, he summed up the civilizing mission for Jewish women. He addressed his remarks to women as well as men: "Our Jewish men and women ought to be made to feel that their going to

Eretz Yisrael to serve their own people would be as legitimate and noble an adventure as for other Americans to serve peoples of the Far East in a missionary or cultural capacity."[30]

An important part of Arab and Jewish women's tasks to "raise up" Palestine was to clean it. Proper cleaning could possibly raise a nation out of squalor and stagnation. Soap and water furthered the *mission civilatrice* that in turn bolstered hierarchies of difference between European Jews and Middle Eastern Jews, between Zionists and Palestinians, and between Christian Arabs and Muslim Arabs. Some Jews articulated their reasons for coming to Palestine as not solely for their own survival but "for the good of all." The impulse to reach out to one's "sisters" felt altruistic and noble to the women involved and entailed moving beyond the walls of their own domestic spheres. But the modernizing frame of reference colored these acts with condescension. Women's actions, intended to help others, colluded with class and race hierarchies that bolstered particular power arrangements in Palestine and compromised the actual caring that underlay their idealism and good works.

Educating Girls

Reading and Revolution

Fathers! Let us serve our country with our education and knowledge.

Anonymous woman's letter to *Al-Difa'*

Even as we make visible the roles of women and gender in nationalism,
we ignore girls.[1] But in the early histories of two movements in Palestine,
girls occupied a distinct place in nationalist cosmology. Emerging Jewish
and Palestinian national elites sought to legitimize their leadership by
articulating a modern vision of community based in part on what happened to girls. Concern for girls' education became a lightning rod for
both imperialist and nationalist fears and hopes for the future. Every
group vying for power in Palestine, whether Ottoman, British, Arab, or
Jewish, had its own agenda for girls' education.

Education for Progress and Preservation

In her analysis of women in nationalist movements of developing countries, Kumari Jayawardena stated that "the status of women in society
was the popular barometer of 'civilization.'" Education, freedom of
movement for women, and monogamy became hallmarks of "civilization" or "modernity." The "new man" needed the "new woman" to be
presentable in colonialist circles, rather than secluded, veiled, or illiterate.
Modernization would bear no more bound feet or bound minds.[2]

Nationalists and foreign colonialists alike charted the march forward
into modernity with a map of who should be educated in what subjects.
Literacy and schooling became not only a measure of "civilization," but
of the state of the nation or empire. Benedict Anderson made a case for

the link between the development of nationalism, the printing press, and an expanding readership that could imagine the new national community.[3] In Palestine, the rise of the press in the late nineteenth century coincided with the (proto) nationalist agendas of Arabs and Jews and the growth of educational institutions that spawned an expanding body of readers. As girls became part of this growing readership of nationalist texts, their potential for participation in the body politic expanded.

The education of girls held nationalists' attention because it represented three aspects of evolving political identity. First, it was a measure of freedom. Freedom meant political and economic independence, an end to foreign domination, control over the means of violence and defense, and, to varying extents, equality, individual rights, and democracy. Second, it was a measure of preservation of traditions and authentic identity. Preservation meant nurturing or inventing institutions of religious and cultural significance. Independence was the means to preserve the unique nature of an "essential" historical religious/cultural character of the people. Finally, it was a measure of modernization. Modernization meant achieving scientific, technological, medical, and secular breakthroughs. This would fortify the nation to contend with Western hegemony and to "progress."

In the context of these three goals of independence, religious/cultural integrity, and progress, girls were a locus of concern. They held a key to contradictory outcomes and visions of the future. Depending on the nature and content of their education, girls could be indicators of a new nation's success or failure to attain freedom, authenticity, and modernization. As Arab and Jewish cultures creatively imagined their nation, education of girls came to exemplify or threaten whatever contending nationalists viewed as critical for modern peoplehood.

Elsewhere in the Middle East, strategies for reform had included the opening of schools for girls. In Egypt and Turkey, Qassim Amin (1899) and Ataturk (1923) argued the importance of girls' education in advancing the nation as a whole. Both Amin and Ataturk believed that a society could not advance that restricted half its population from participation in some social, economic, and political functions.[4]

In Palestine, competition between nationalist movements sharpened focus on the education of girls. Each side produced studies of education in Palestine that connected girls' education to the success of the nation and to the failure or threat of the other. A. L. Tibawi, a Palestinian Arab, and

Noah Nardi, a Palestinian Jew, believed that education was critical to the success of their respective movements. Tibawi published *Arab Education in Mandatory Palestine: A Study of Three Decades of British Administration* in 1956, eight years after the British left Palestine. Noah Nardi published *Education in Palestine 1920–1945* in 1945, three years before the end of the Mandate. Each book contains explicit data and implicit assumptions about girls, nationalism, and conflict. Tibawi's and Nardi's works are not only "objective" compilations of statistics about education, as their titles and prefaces profess, but active constructions of their national communities.

No educational institution in Palestine was free from some group's political agenda. In the nineteenth century, Ottoman schools had trained select male members of the Arab provinces to learn Turkish in order to assume intermediary positions in government. Protestant missionary schools provided education for a limited number of mostly Christian boys and some girls as Europeans sought to "protect" Christian minorities. After the Young Turk Revolution of 1908, there was some improvement in opportunities for Muslim girls in Palestine, but this was supposed to occur only in the Turkish language, not in their own language of Arabic.[5]

The Ottoman state system in 1914 operated ninety-five elementary schools and three secondary schools in Palestine. Two hundred thirty-four teachers taught 8,248 pupils, 1,480 of whom were girls. Private Muslim schools, or *kuttabs*, in Palestine included 379 schools with 417 teachers and 8,705 students; 131 students were girls.[6] Before World War I, Christian women had a literacy rate of 80 percent to men's 90 percent, whereas 5 percent of Muslim women and 10 percent of the men could read.[7] This disparity had grown throughout the late nineteenth and early twentieth centuries with the opening of European Christian missionary schools. Some Arab men obtained scholarships to attend institutions of higher learning outside Palestine, but higher education for women was extremely rare. Jewish and Christian minorities ignored state institutions open to them and were left alone by the Ottoman authorities to manage their own schools.

With the demise of the Ottoman Empire and the advent of the British Mandate, three groups manifested their political agendas in part through the creation of educational opportunities for girls. British, Arab, and Jewish interests held separate and often conflicting goals for Palestinian schools during the interwar years. Arab goals were often subordinated to British policies and practicalities because many Arab schools depended on the British administration for funding. An exploration of some of the assumptions, expectations, and outcomes for girls' education in each of these groups illuminates some ways in which gender informed developing national identities in Palestine.

British Education for Girls

When the British military administration replaced Ottoman rule, it replaced Turkish with Arabic as the language of instruction. The British administration opened two residential training colleges for teachers, one for men and one for women. Tibawi reported that "women teachers, trained or untrained, were almost impossible to find among the Muslim community and [there were] very few among the Christian communities."[8] The British also encouraged local education committees that had functioned sporadically under the Turks to resume activity.

Official British policy identified girls' instruction to be among the three most important areas of education along with agricultural and technical education. British officials immediately created the post of education inspectorate and filled it with one Englishwoman in the 1920s, two in the 1930s, and three by the 1940s as administrators of Muslim, Christian, and Jewish female education.[9] Yet education for girls remained problematic. Separate elementary schools existed in towns and some villages for girls and boys. In towns, most opportunities for girls' education remained under Christian auspices; in villages, the opening of girls' schools was neglected. Until the 1930s there were only a few secondary classes available for girls attached to their elementary schools.[10]

During the Mandate definite changes for girls, however small, took place in the area of training female professionals. These changes were brought about in training colleges for women established during this period. The Women's Training College opened in 1919 with seventeen Muslim and twenty-nine Christian women, although Muslims made up at least 80 percent of the population. By 1927, two-thirds of the sixty-six students were Muslim. In 1930 girls composed roughly 20 percent of the student population as the training of women teachers proceeded slowly. By 1934, there were ten government schools for girls in villages of Palestine. By 1935 this number increased to fourteen along with the opening of the Rural Women's Teacher Training Centre at Ramallah, which became the first institution for training rural women teachers.[11] The WTTC in Ramallah opened with twelve Muslim girls and expanded by 1946 to thirty-four girls in a three-year course, with thirteen graduates.

The director of education under the British Mandate government believed that this was the limit of possible change for rural Muslim women and that it wasn't feasible to expand female education in the villages any further. Bethlehem, however, was an example of a town in which the Muslim community made many requests for more education. It received only one teacher. Beit Jalla, a smaller nearby village that was predominantly Christian, received four teachers. Muslim Arab women in Palestine had no access to advanced education because of collusion between the government system and local custom that ultimately prevented their entry into the labor force.[12]

Westerners came to Palestine to study the situation of education and thereby assess progress and needs. Ruth Frances Woodsmall visited Palestine on a Rockefeller Foundation grant in 1935. Her research identified a drastic disproportion of opportunity between girls and boys, and between Muslim and Christian girls. Her statistics for the period 1932–33 identified a population of Palestine that was at least 70 percent Muslim, in which 21,202 boys attended the Arab public school system but only 5,489 girls. Taking into account the total number of girls attending Arab, Muslim, and Christian schools, Christian girls far outnumbered Muslim.[13] Furthermore, among female teachers, Christian women predominated.[14]

British High Commissioner Sir Herbert Samuel proclaimed in 1924 that "the aim of the administration has been to promote the elementary education of all children between the ages of seven and fourteen."[15] Indeed, Woodsmall's research showed that between 1920 and 1933 education for Muslim girls in "government" and "Arabic" schools doubled.[16] According to statistics of the Palestine Department of Education, Arab teachers were among the most important groups of professionals trained under the Mandate. Yet in the first decade of the Mandate, among those who got to school, fewer than half stayed four years. Village schools taught bare literacy.[17] The British liked to blame the slow rate of growth of Muslim girls' instruction on "Islam." "Islam" became the umbrella excuse by which colonialists dismissed an indigenous culture as unchanging, rigid, or fanatically religious. "Islam" implied a way of life that presented obstacles to "progress." The British also blamed slow change on lack of demand and small budgets.

Another major concern of both the administration and the populace was the actual content of education for girls. As far as British government policy on female education was concerned, "girls must be brought up to understand the value of a good home where cleanliness, sanitation and above all care of children are to be regarded as the aim of every woman."[18] Education was supposed to keep woman in her place in the home as well as make her a transmitter of the values and technology of "modern" living. Thus, schools required girls to study and take examinations only in areas of "domestic science."[19]

The British established the Rural Women's Teacher Training Centre in Ramallah "to improve conditions in Arab villages by spreading a knowledge of domestic science among women and girls."[20] Schools taught sewing and embroidery and took students on visits to infant welfare clinics.[21] Although "domestic science" contained elements of real information to help women in their appointed roles as housekeepers, feeders, and caregivers for their families, it denigrated the knowledge they did have.

British policy praised the efforts of missionary schools in educating females but criticized them for "cultivating too much the literary side of education and . . . neglecting almost entirely what may be termed the domestic side." Helen Ridler, principal of the Women's Training College and inspector of girls' schools in Palestine, insisted on teaching handiwork to future teachers who would have to "teach girls who lead a life of seclusion and have long hours of leisure."[22]

British interest in female education remained fraught with contradictions. On one hand, it was to the British advantage to appear to encourage girls' schooling. The very ideals of the Mandate dictated that British presence raise this so-called backward society up to a new level of civilization, with education of girls as a gauge. Yet in practice the British attained political and military power by maintaining the status quo, especially in the villages, in ways that inevitably impeded change and initiatives by the villagers.

Arab Education for Girls

Whereas the British presented themselves as advocates of girls' education and blamed Islam for interference, Arab nationalists blamed British policy for supporting the status quo and hindering educational opportunity. Tibawi warned against blaming low education figures for girls in the countryside on Muslim custom or prejudice. As a nationalist and modernizer, Tibawi sought to prove that "Islam" was an infinitely flexible system capable of providing context for change and progress.

Like other modernizers, Tibawi sought authority for change in tradition. He invoked Muhammad to prove that change for women was justifiable and consistent with ideals of Arab society. He asserted that there is no real Muslim religious prejudice against female education by paraphrasing the Prophet: Quest for learning is a sacred duty of every Muslim, male and female. Tibawi directed accusations at defective and inadequate British planning and budgeting. He also argued that social prejudice and inequality between men and women were a result of low education levels among men, and that increasing men's levels of education would lead to improved relations between men and women.[23]

In Palestine as elsewhere in the Middle East, new terms of relationships between men and women emerged that affected attitudes towards girls' education. In some cases, for example, marriage began to move away from arranged practical contracts and towards companionate relationships.[24] The notion of companionate marriage meant that in addition to domestic, sexual, and reproductive functions, intellectual satisfaction became one of the services a wife should provide. Some of the support for girls' education arose out of this changing vision of marriage.

So part of the importance of education for girls had to do with producing "better" or more modern wives for more educated men. As more men gained access to education, they desired companions who were more their equals but would still serve them. Although there was widening support for girls' education, there remained limits both on what girls should learn and on permission for them to seek work outside the home or compete for jobs.[25]

Both British administrators and Arab nationalists saw women's positions and society in general as pliable through the medium of education. Educating girls led to certain social changes. What kinds of education and for what kinds of change were not always consistent. The Egyptian writer Muhammad al-Bindari, for example, was among those outside Palestine who designated the education of girls as a requisite entrance fee into the modern world. Yet he stated explicit preference for curricula that inculcated "traditional" values and skills.[26]

For the first time "women's skills" such as cooking and child care, health and hygiene, sewing and embroidery, which had always been passed down inside the family, became legitimate material for instruction in schools. Education for girls took place only in the context of separate all-girl schools and the subject matter was not supposed to mimic that presented in the West. Girls' schools could teach "the Arab way of life" so girls would not forget their traditions.[27] The "Arab way of life" suddenly needed to be taught in an institution that paradoxically took girls out of their traditional places in the home.

The process of attending school was more radical than the content of study. The school functioned as a place for girls to meet outside the confines of their homes. It removed girls from their homes and organized them each day in unprecedented ways. This process came to symbolize "progress." Although self-appointed modernizers, British or Arab, perceived these changes as having a positive outcome, many others were apprehensive about the demise of what they saw as a way of life. Education for girls endangered "traditions" that seemed suddenly vulnerable. But by changing the way these traditions were communicated, in a school rather than at home, there was a hope that "progress" would proceed without completely disrupting the old way of life.

Regardless of educational content and process, the completion of an education, even a professional one, did not ensure expanded opportunities for a girl. On the contrary, it often led to confrontation with further obstacles. Girls who managed to receive education had a difficult time if they attempted to work in their fields. One Christian Palestinian woman from Jerusalem, for example, moved to Beirut to complete her education as a teacher. She expressed her interest in social work and spent summers volunteering in villages. Her teaching experience in the village of Abu Sinan illustrated some of the disparities and challenges that faced women who pursued untraditional goals. This woman viewed herself as an agent of modernization and sought ways to use her education to implement improvements for her own people.

My two years of unwavering energy and resolution here in Abu Sinan haven't resulted as I have wished them and dreamed them to be. You see, being tied up in school, it was rather difficult to do much in the village as a whole, because the teacher is criticized unmercifully in this region. . . . I want to find out if I can be of help in Palestine. I feel that our villagers need more attention perhaps than those of Syria.[28]

The woman transferred to Haifa but we do not know the outcome of her move. Another woman ran a girl's school in Tarshiha. That village registered complaints that the behavior of this teacher alienated the parents of the students: they felt that she interfered with their lives.[29]

Yishuv Education for Girls

In the Yishuv, Jewish nationalists regarded education for both girls and boys to be the hallmark of a civilized society. Before World War I, education took place in schools that taught many different languages including French, German, and Yiddish. The *Va'ad Hinuch,* Office of Education, was founded in 1914 to oversee and support three different educational systems in which most schools taught in Hebrew. *Mizrachi* schools were for the Orthodox religious community; labor schools were for the Histadrut; and the general schools were for the vast majority. The latter two were self-consciously crucibles for forging a new generation of Jewish people free from the constraints of diaspora mentality and aware of the importance of nationalism.

First and foremost these schools began to produce a more homogeneous group of Hebrew speakers from diverse immigrant tongues. Nardi remarked in his study of Jewish education during the Mandate that the kindergartens themselves "besides fulfilling their own educational function . . . serve the larger national cause by encouraging and implementing the use of Hebrew among the children of parents hailing from diverse countries."[30]

One of the most constructive elements of education for both Jewish and Arab nationalism was language. Language was a central element in the contest for the hearts and minds of Arab and Jewish girls and boys. Before 1920, schools whose languages of instruction were Arabic and Hebrew were rare. The language of instruction in Ottoman state schools was Turkish; that of missionary schools reflected the origins of their missionaries. Jewish immigrants taught their children in their own languages of origin, German, Yiddish, or French. After 1920, however, a dual system began to emerge which was "bi-national and bi-lingual" in character.[31] The emerging languages of instruction were primarily Arabic and Hebrew with English, rather than Arabic or Hebrew, as a second language for both groups. Education in Hebrew for Jews and in Arabic for Christians and Muslims further developed separate cultural identities and segregation.

Jewish nationalists were aware of the potency of education of girls and boys in furthering national goals. Noah Nardi complained that Arab education was becoming a "negative" force in Palestine for "the Arab school system maintained by the government has constantly inculcated in Arab children a hostile attitude to Jewish aspirations in Palestine."[32] Yet when education served the interests of Jewish national feeling, Nardi interpreted its effects as "constructive":

> The child must be imbued with a love for Palestine and a desire to live in it and be satisfied with whatever it can offer him. . . . He must acquire a strong nationalist consciousness and loyalty. . . . He must learn to understand and cooperate with his Arab neighbors.[33]

When the British administration took over Palestine, they expanded the policy that permitted any group to establish its own schools. This worked in favor of the fledgling Yishuv. Jews were determined not to depend on Britain's meager allocation of resources for education, so they sought and received funding from abroad. The budget for Hebrew language schools thus exceeded the budget of British government schools for Arabs.[34] Nardi commented that the Zionist Organization complained of British hindrance to "organized Jewry in Palestine . . . asserting its authority over educational matters even after responsibility . . . was transferred to Knesseth Israel from the Jewish Agency."[35] Education was an unequivocal priority for immigrants to Palestine, so Jewish institutions allocated a generous portion of funding to schools.

Early Jewish nationalists wanted to believe that there were equal opportunities for their young to receive education. This was a reflection of the broader Zionist ideal of equality between Jewish men and women in Palestine. The British Zionist Norman Bentwich observed in the 1920s that "the equal part of men and women in all vocations and professions is one of the outstanding features of Jewish social life [in Palestine]."[36] One need only read excerpts of women's writings of the 1920s to understand how much discrimination there was wherever they attempted to gain education outside of traditionally female vocations, such as in carpentry, construction, or farming.[37]

Women's organizations emerged to address these discrepancies. They took a special interest in setting up schools for girls to train them in agriculture, trades, and the teaching profession. The General Training School for Girls in Tel Aviv granted teaching degrees. Schools in Nahalal and Ayonoth sponsored by the Women's International Zionist Organization (WIZO) provided girls with agricultural training. Girls received "industrial education" at a dressmaking school created by the Mizrachi Women's Organization, at vocational centers set up by Hadassah, and at trade schools established by the Amalgamated Clothing Workers of America in Ramat Gan, through the Pioneer Women's Organization of America.[38]

Discrepancies existed, however, not only between girls and boys but between Ashkenazi and Mizrachi Jewish girls.[39] In practice there were more opportunities open to European Jewish women than for Arab Jewish women. Reaching girls who were not being educated was an expressed concern of the Jewish Palestinian educational authorities. Many Jewish girls and boys from Arab countries were prevented from full participation in the educational system because of conditions that existed for them and their families, including unlimited working hours, low pay, apprenticeships without opportunity for mastery, illiteracy, and child marriages among the girls.[40]

A large number of girls did not work or receive education because they had domestic roles in their own homes as well as in their extended families. Those who did obtain work did so as domestics in others' homes. One article in the *Women's Labor Magazine* in 1942 reported that out of 700 Jewish housemaids, 515 had no schooling, and 33 percent had less than three years.[41] About half these domestic workers who found jobs worked in all-Jewish Tel Aviv. Other Jewish girls served as maids for upper-class Arab families.

Nationalist leaders lamented that the public school system reached only two-thirds of the Jewish children of Palestine. Eleven percent of Jewish girls and 6 percent of Jewish boys in Jerusalem in 1940 were illiterate and received no schooling at all. Many of these girls and boys were

Jews who had immigrated from Middle Eastern countries.[42] It was also disturbing to nationalists that many Jewish children attended schools not supervised by the Education Department. One thousand Jewish children attended missionary schools. By 1944, fewer girls went into agricultural training programs (1,250 boys to 900 girls). Twice as many boys went into vocational training programs (7,625 boys to 3,925 girls). Overall, the number of girls who did not work or study was well more than double that of the boys (1,440 boys to 4,000 girls).[43] Yet in general more girls attended secondary and continuation classes than did boys (3,825 boys to 4,225 girls).

Changing economic and political conditions in Palestine during World War II turned the tide of concern for girls in education to a concern with the dearth of boys entering the teaching profession. There was difficulty providing enough resources for either women or men to achieve the desired standard of education as a result of the war and world economic conditions after a decade of depression. Nardi observed that

inadequate salaries and financial insecurity have naturally resulted in a serious shortage of male teachers. The great majority of school graduates entering the Teachers' Seminaries are now women. In the years between 1939 and 1945 hundreds of teachers answered the call of the national organizations and volunteered for military service. Many women teachers, too, either volunteered for the Army Auxiliary Services or were forced to leave their jobs for lack of domestic help.[44]

By the 1940s there were extracurricular youth activities, providing opportunities for girls and boys in extensive networks of informal education. Hano'ar Ha'oved, The Organization of Working Youth, an organ of the Histadrut, sought to improve working conditions for young people through the creation of evening schools, clubs, and study groups. Its magazine, Bama'aleh (Upward), explained the youth group to be

an important training ground for colonization activities, training for maintenance of security outposts, volunteering in Jewish units and the British army and the Jewish brigade, helping police, pioneering the fishing industry, stevedoring, settling on the land, bringing Oriental and Ashkenazi together.[45]

Some of the youth organizations based on socialist values were ve-
hicles for downward mobility that moved youth from lower, middle-
class, or urban families into the countryside to become farm laborers.
Machanot 'Olim (Camps of the Settlers), an organization of the Histadrut, sought "to draw academic youth away from pursuing higher and
professional education and to bring them closer to the idea of eventual
settlement on the land, preferably in a collective settlement."[46] During
World War II, children who were under age for military service but who
attended secondary schools had to do one year of national service. Six-
teen- to eighteen-year-old girls and boys worked on farms, in security,
and as guards. Fourteen- to sixteen-year-old girls and boys cut their
school year short to spend a long summer session with their teachers on
the land gathering crops.[47]

The national objectives for Jewish education in Palestine reflected
widespread assumptions about the power of public education for creating
political change. Leaders argued that public education that could reach
girls as well as boys produced a worthy citizenry for the nation. Education of girls then would produce a public that could understand a lofty
communal vision, and then sacrifice for it.

The growth of two national movements in Palestine depended in part
upon changing educational opportunities for girls. Educators, policy
makers, and nationalists fought over control and content of girls' education. At issue here were both the nature and desirability of change for
women, and the understanding that change for women was at the core of
broader social change. Should girls learn traditional skills or more academic subjects as defined in secular education? Should girls study an academic program or traditionally non-female skills? Social values and the
direction of change appeared to hang on girls' curricula of study.
Whether one agreed that women had to change for the nation to modernize or that women must stay the same to preserve the nation's unique
traditions, nationalists advocated education for girls. Girls' education
thus became an ingredient in the cauldron of evolving national identities.
What happened to girls further separated Arab and Jewish communities
in Palestine.

For Palestinian Arab girls, the curricula in schools were often weighted
towards studies that reinforced traditional values. More Jewish girls were
involved in a wider range of study, including non-traditional arenas such

as agriculture. Yet the ability of Arab girls to read and to leave their house to meet others in school opened new possibilities for them as well. At stake in the education of both Jewish and Arab girls were the power relations between Jews and Arabs, East and West, and contending visions of modernization.

The Arab debate over the education of its girls was in part a verdict on the Mandate system itself as either an idealized benevolent benefactor or a system of brute imperialism. The British, as self-appointed tutors of modernity, explicitly intended to foster girls' education and saw education as "an index of social priorities."[48] Jewish schools, youth movements, and women's organizations viewed the creation of educational opportunities for all Jewish children as top priority in fund-raising efforts and in distribution of funds. Yet the claim of equality often preceded the reality.

Girls became symbols and measures of progress or regress, cultural continuities and discontinuities. How much equality, how many individual rights, and how much opportunity for study or work did these nascent national communities need to extend to girls to bring about desired changes for society as a whole? In this period of history almost never were girls' opportunities driven by concerns for their own well-being or freedom. With girls' well-being subordinated to the demands of the emerging nation, real changes for girls and women would continue to lag. Nevertheless, education for girls made an impact on individual lives as well as on the imagined and actual character of the nation.

10

Essentializing Difference

Gendering the "Other"

Mystified and domesticated, [she is] a figure of 'otherness' which provokes an elaborate and ambiguous narrative response. Such images define the place of 'Woman' and the 'Orient,' moreover, in terms which seem to close off the very issue they raise: that of the relationship between self and other: male and female, West and East.

M. J. Harper, *Critical Matrix*

Attitudes about gender shaped perceptions and judgments about the "other." Gender became part of the conflict between Jews and Arabs in Palestine by inflecting each group's understanding of the other. Conflicting ideas about women contributed to a sense that there were irrevocable, irreconcilable, essential differences between the two groups. These perceived differences between men and women, Arabs and Jews, Middle Easterners and Europeans were one of the means by which each side legitimized its claims to Palestine and invalidated the other's.

Images of difference between "our women and theirs" appeared in fictional works by Arabs and Jews. In plays, stories, novels, and poems, women became symbols of growing fear, hatred, or contempt one side had for the other. Men's and women's stories evoked Palestinians' struggle against the British and Zionists, and Jewish settlers' search for power over their own lives. These writings give us a glimpse of how the development of Jewish ideas about Arabs and Arab ideas about Jews were based at least in part on assumptions about gender.

Gender in Jewish Attitudes towards Arabs

European Jews had ideas about Arabs before their own arrival on the eastern shores of the Mediterranean. They had internalized European notions of the inferiority of both Arabs and of Jews from Arab lands. Jews who had themselves been treated as essentially different and inferior by Europeans wasted no time in expressing a similar disdain towards non-Europeans. Colonialist ventures throughout the nineteenth century were bolstered by pseudoscientific theories of race in which European white men "proved" their superiority to their own women as well as to non-Europeans.[1] The birth of modern anti-Semitism in the nineteenth century turned "Semitic" from a linguistic category into "Semite," a pseudoracial one. At the same time, Jews imbibed from fellow Europeans modern notions of the "racial" inferiority of non-Europeans. As colonizers, Zionists brought these ideas with them to Palestine.

These European ideas about Arabs mingled with Jews' own experience of anti-Semitism to further complicate their attitudes. Being outnumbered by a non-Jewish majority in Palestine and in the Middle East, Jews conflated Arabs with other threatening majorities with whom they had lived. This made it difficult for most Zionists to understand the degree to which their presence constituted a threat to Palestinian Arabs. Instead Zionists saw themselves as the underdogs in an established Arab-majority society. Arab efforts to thwart the creation of a Jewish haven read like one more chapter in a lachrymose narrative of Jewish history. Arabs could be perceived as just another recurring nightmare of Cossacks threatening Jewish existence in new form.

In the 1930s and 1940s, films and literature produced by Jews and Westerners portrayed Arabs as belligerent tyrants defending a stagnant society and standing in the way of progress for their own people. Alexander Ford's 1933 film, *Sabra*, for example, portrays Jews as saving Arabs from their own corrupt leaders.[2] The film portrays Russian immigrants in Palestine bringing socialism to Palestine to free Arabs and Jews together from class oppression. Arab women in the film symbolize static, oppressive Arab culture: they carry jugs of water on their heads to and from the well, like their biblical sisters, suggesting that nothing has changed for millennia. The women are exotic ornaments who dance together in a mosaic of beautiful dresses.

The Jewish men trudge out to the rocky fields with tools slung over their shoulders to work with backs bent towards the sun. This scene cuts to Arab women also engaged in heavy labor in the fields. These two images contrast with Arab men who sit idly watching them both. Zionists imagined Arab men as emasculated, outmoded aristocrats or lazy, greedy overlords, both types shunning manual labor. Instead, women and camels performed the heavy work for them.

While the film's Shaykh shoots lascivious glances at Arab women who come to the well, his evilness is ultimately proved by his refusal to give water to Arab peasants during a time of drought. Unless they can afford to pay him, he refuses them the most basic life-sustaining resource. The parasitic Arab landlord is portrayed as a threat to the survival of his own people, compared with the young Jewish socialist Zionist who will save Jews and Arabs. This message comes from the lips of a young Arab man. As the camera pans the mud hovels of peasants who will perish if they do not gain access to the Shaykh's water, the Shaykh refuses the young man's pleas: "No money, no water." So the young Arab man warns him: "Your rule is not for long. The new immigrants will give everybody water without payment."

In the same year this film was made, the literature of the Hagaddah (telling of the ancient story of Jewish slaves' liberation from Egypt) was rewritten at Golda Meir's seder (ritual meal to celebrate freedom). The ritual question and answer chanted by the youngest child, "Why is this night different from all other nights?" was changed to: "Why are there rich and poor in the world? Because of an unjust economic system which [the Palestinian Jewish] cooperatives strive to rectify. Why do the Arabs live on hills and we in valleys? Since we think only of peace and of reclaiming the soil, we are not afraid of settling in a valley." Meir envisioned the children of these seders as those who would eventually defend the land against "warrior" Arabs.[3]

In the novel *Thieves in the Night*, published after World War II, Arthur Koestler implicitly justified Jews' claim to Palestine through particular renderings of male and female characters. The narrative compares and contrasts the manliness of Arabs and Jews on issues of authority, work, and ability to protect one's women. Jews who build the settlement Ezra's Tower are rebels who epitomize the modernist hero by railing against traditional authority of parents, religion, European and Russian masters in host governments, and class-based societies. In fact, they rationalize the justice of their quest for land in Palestine by their rebelling against convention, rejecting hierarchy, and improving the lives of both Arabs and Jews.

Koestler portrayed Arabs as everything despised by modernizers: docile and blindly obedient to parental authority. Even their claims to land are based on tradition, continuity of family life, fathers' legacies to sons. An old Arab says angrily to a young Jewish man, "we do not want your women, whose sight offends the eye." Meanwhile, his own women sit huddled with the children at a little distance from the men, giggling and pointing at Jewish girls with bare legs in short shorts.[4] Koestler contrasted this faceless mass of Arab women to the upright and proud individual Jewish women protagonists of his novel.

But these bronzed Jewish beauties sustain deep scars from treatment by Nazis in Europe, where their men were unable to protect them. The heroine Dina personifies this tragedy. When Joseph attempts to kiss Dina for the first time, the independent, hardworking, sexy, and intelligent woman goes rigid, trembles, then flings him away and vomits. He discovers that she has been the victim of sexual torture by Nazis. Dina flees Joseph's caresses and rides out alone on horseback into the night of a *khamsin*, a stifling heat wave. When she is found dead, stabbed twenty-seven times and her fingernails broken, the conflation of Nazis and Arabs is complete. The kibbutz men complain to the *mukhtar*, who responds, "She was a whore," and "Who can blame them? You are strangers, bringers of whores and corruption."

Created in the 1950s about the 1948 war, Thorold Dickinson's film *Hill Twenty-Four Doesn't Answer* portrays Zionists as profoundly human and manly in contrast to the brutality and cowardice of their enemies.[5] As soldiers, Jews epitomize humanity's highest virtues. There are four fighters and three dramatic flashbacks that trace their journeys to this life-and-death moment in defense of Hill Twenty-Four. In one dramatic flashback we witness the protagonist's heroic attempt to save the life of an Egyptian enemy soldier shot in a battle against the Jews. The Jewish man staggers under the weight of his dying Arab enemy amidst dropping bombs. The dying man reaches for the grenade in the belt of the Jewish man in a final attempt to kill his Jewish savior, demonstrating the irrationality and incorrigibility of his hatred. They wrestle for a long tense moment until the Jewish man gets the grenade away from him and gets him to safety.

The dying Egyptian then reveals that he is actually a German Nazi in disguise, trying to finish the job he began in Europe. The film achieves the elision of difference between Arabs and Nazis as the Egyptian-dressed, German-speaking enemy launches into a long invective of hatred of Jews. When he hallucinates the tall Jewish soldier to be a stooped religious Jew with yellow star and *payot*, or sidelocks, he is compelled to rise and shout "Heil Hitler" the moment before he drops dead.

The fourth fighter, the only woman, does not warrant a flashback. She is Esther, an "Oriental" (Arab) Jew. Instead she listens to each man supportively and does not carry a weapon, as the men do. The silencing of a Jewish woman and one of Middle Eastern descent is ironically part of the same silencing or dehumanization of Arabs in the film. Only in the final silence of her death will Esther make her contribution to the nation, clutching the Israeli flag to her bosom as proof (to the United Nations) that Jews have indeed captured Hill Twenty Four for Israel.

Gender in Arab Attitudes towards Jews

Arabs had ideas about Jews long before the first Zionists stepped onto Palestinian shores. For centuries, Jews lived under the laws of Islamic empires as one of many tolerated but subordinated minorities. As non-Muslims, Jews were benevolently protected but restricted from accruing power, which they occasionally did to a limited degree anyway. Christian Arabs as a minority under Muslim rule alternately treated Jews with camaraderie, regarded them as competitors, or saw them as a smaller and weaker minority to whom they felt superior.[6] With European encroachment in the Middle East, Ottomans passed new laws that in principle gave Christians and Jews legal equality with Muslims but in fact aggravated resentment towards them. Expanding European influence stirred things up further as Europeans introduced their particular brand of anti-Semitism. By 1840 there was actually a blood libel in Damascus mimicking the medieval European attack on Jews, which was based on the accusation that Jews had killed a Christian child for its blood to bake matzah.

As early Zionists entered Palestine, they contributed to an aggravation of intercommunal relations. Zionists ignored traditional *musha'*, communal grazing rights. They arrived on a scene in which peasant dispossession from land was already on the increase because of changes wrought by Ottomans, Arab absentee landlords, and processes of modernization that reduced peasants' usufruct rights.[7] They acted above all to further their own autonomy in Palestine. Increasing Zionist presence fermented a heady brew of vintage antagonism based on traditional beliefs of Jews' inferiority to Muslims and a contemporary anti-Zionist sentiment.

Historian Muhammad Muslih noted the combination of Jewish ignorance of the local habits, peasant dispossession, and a mix of European-brand anti-Semitism responsible for the hostility among Palestinian Arabs in the earliest years of Zionist settlement. Although he oversimplified and romanticized Arab-Jewish "tranquility" before it was "ruptured" by these incidents, he astutely observed that anti-Semitism was especially virulent among Arab writers who had gained a Western-style education or spent time in the West. Nagib Azuri's *Le Réveil de la nation arabe* (The Awakening of the Arab Nation) of 1905 is an example of the infiltration of a European-brand anti-Semitism into Arab nationalism. Azuri was a Maronite Catholic Arab who had also been an Ottoman official. His anti-Semitism reflected the influence of the Dreyfus trial when he was living in France and exposed to reactionary French Catholic propaganda.[8]

By the 1920s, Arab-language publications articulated the Zionist threat to Palestinian aspirations. Plays, stories, novels, and newspaper articles employed metaphors of gender to portray the Jew as enemy. In January 1920, for example, the Arab club of Nablus hosted a performance of a play titled "The Ruins of Palestine."[9] A wily, seductive, and treacherous female represents Jews in Palestine. Two wealthy Arab men sit in a cafe where the hostess is a young "flirtatious Jewess" who flatters them. They leave her a large tip and return the next day. This time the woman finds a way to get them drunk. In this way she tricks them into agreeing to go out with her in the evening and steals their money. Another Jewish character in the play is portrayed as a kind of old pimp referred to as a "Zionist leader"; he caresses the woman saying, "do your best for your country and nation."

The hostess threatens to break her relations with the two men if they don't register their property in her name. They are so drunk by this point that they comply and a British officer certifies the transfer of title, symbolizing the complicity of the British in the betrayal of the Palestinians. When the two rich Arabs return to the coffee shop, the hostess turns them out. They've lost all their property. The only option left for them is to commit suicide. They kill themselves in the middle of the market, crying: "The country is ruined, the Jews have robbed us of our land and honor!" Anti-Jewish and anti-Zionist sentiments conflate in these sexualized images of Jewish women, symbolizing a corrupt, seductive, and morally inferior enemy.

In 1925, when Lord Balfour visited Jerusalem, the poet Iskandar al-Khuri al-Baytjali used a gendered metaphor to critique British deception of the Jews. He compared the Balfour Declaration to mother and lover, characterizing it as

> a unique declaration, meant only to deceive the Jews, as a mother lulls her baby to sleep, deceiving him by her singing, like a lover, satisfied by being put off with promises. In political life trickery is not something new.[10]

What They Did to Our Women

How one group treated the other group's women became part of the expression of outrage and resentment. The desire to defend one's women or the inability to do so was a measure of the degree of power or powerlessness with which one group regarded the other. Ability or lack of ability to defend women or of women to defend themselves implied success or failure of men and their movements.

Jewish women's stories are full of contradictory elements that include fear of rape in the face of overpowering military force, a sense of relative powerlessness against an overarching Turkish authority, British power, or Arab majority. Hannah Trager told the story of an Arab attack on a Jewish settlement in pre–World War I Palestine. The women gathered together with the children and barricaded themselves in a house. They each held guns, proud that "all we girls knew about fire-arms." One of the women told the story of their self-defense:

> Almost a hundred Arabs came. . . . They found the houses with women and children and shot at the windows terrifying the children who were screaming. Arabs shouted to the mothers to open the doors and they'd do no harm—they only wanted cattle. . . . We girls stood armed with whatever weapons we could find bravely deter-

mined to sell our honor dearly, which was more precious than life.[11]

Arab attitudes towards the British were influenced by Arab perceptions of British treatment of Arab women. In 1936, for example, at the start of the Arab revolt, the *ulama*, religious authorities, sent a memorandum to the British high commissioner complaining about an incident: on May 30 at 4:00 A.M. British soldiers forcibly entered the houses where men, women, and children resided at Bab Hutta. The Muslim women were still in their pajamas, but the soldiers did not allow them to get dressed when the British stormed their houses to search for weapons. The soldiers threw the Quran on the floor and then stopped and searched men on their way to the mosque to pray.[12] The blatant disregard for sociosexual norms mingled with disrespect for Islamic practice fueled Palestinian Arab hatred of the British.

Fear of rape had many implications for power and hierarchy in a colonizing society. In Europe, Jewish communities had often been powerless to prevent the rape of their women when their villages were pillaged. In Palestine, fear of the rape of Jewish women by Arab men justified many levels of arming and militant nationalist policies. Arab men were also portrayed, however, in the usual fashion by colonizers who feared the unleashed rage of the colonized people carried out through rape of their women.

For Jews, a raison d'etre of the state was to counter the powerlessness of *galut* life. After World War II, as the Jewish terrorist group Irgun stepped up its attacks on the British, Jewish men complained about British retaliation on Jewish women. In one case, a soldier dragged a pregnant woman by her hair to her room when she did not hurry to carry out a curfew order quickly enough. Soldiers also attempted to break into Jewish girls' rooms at night but were deterred by their screams. Although these acts obviously cannot compare with the brutality of the Nazis, some couldn't resist the conclusion that the British were no better than the Germans.[13]

Power hierarchies dictated which men were threatening to which women. Incidents of rape and murder fed the stereotype, born of fear and anger, of an Arab majority capable of inflicting sexual violence on Jewish women. But such incidents also fed Palestinian Arabs' fear when Jews finally became fully armed during the 1948 war. The most infamous incident of Jewish brutality towards Arab women was at Deir Yasin. Jewish soldiers attacked the Palestinian village and included Arab women in their wrath. News of the massacre triggered some Palestinians' abandonment of their homes during the war in hopes of protecting their women from harm.

Humanizing the Other

Not all the images of the "other" were dehumanizing. From Zionism's earliest days, Jewish men wrote about the courage and integrity of Arab men and the possibilities of Arab women's influence. Later, Arab men and women in Palestine who viewed modernization as a path to a more powerful future sometimes referred to Jews as models to emulate, often with a contradictory mix of admiration and desire to accrue enough power to defeat them. Some Arab writers described Jewish women in a more idealized light, calling on Arab women to assume similar roles. Arab writers and leaders who saw the process of modernization as leading towards Palestinian independence and power expressed respect for certain aspects of Jewish presence.

Moshe Smilansky wrote short stories on the daily life of ordinary people in Palestine in the 1870s and 1880s. In his fiction, Arab men and women were symbols of thoughtful integrity. Smilansky wished to debunk myths both of Arabs and of Jews, so his stories were full of Jews who could work the soil and Arabs who were intelligent with a deep sense of humanity. He wrote his stories in Hebrew under the pseudonym Hawaja Musa and the stories became popular among readers of Hebrew. Both Arabs and Jews of his stories find adventure and romance, triumph and tragedy.[14]

Michael Halpern wrote before World War I about Arab women constructively engaged in building a new society. Arab women would become part of schemes of cooperation and mutual support. In one fantasy, he advocated a "brotherly" alliance between Muslim Arabs and Jews against the common enemy, Christianity. To accelerate what he envisioned as "cultural assimilation" of the two peoples, he proposed that there be intermarriage between Jews and Muslims on a mass scale. Women and their children would thus become conduits for a new Arab-Jewish union realized through sexual and familial ties. Halpern's stories of Arab life and customs influenced a generation of Eastern European *halutzim* (pioneers), who imbibed notions of respect for, as well as romanticized views of, Arab culture.[15]

Arab men and women wrote with admiration about the involvement of women and teens in Jewish activities. Fakhri al-Barudi, for example, observed that the Zionist movement was enhanced by the participation of women and youth. Therefore Arab youth had it in their power to save their country. The Arabs of Palestine, he urged, should stop dreaming about the glory of the past and not underestimate the power of the Jews whom they had known to be so weak in the past. He called on all women, as well as men, between the ages of sixteen and sixty to go into an army that would defend Palestine against the Jews.[16]

One woman argued that Palestinians must learn from Jews that the role of women in nationalism would make all the difference between a weak and a strong movement. She noted that Jewish women played many roles in building their state, working with men in all activities, not only in "feminine" jobs. The Jewish woman, she observed, worked on the land, in road construction, and in the building trades, as well as helping people find suitable jobs. But Arab women faced limitation on social, political, and economic levels. The author complained that while Jewish women worked in these arenas, Arab women sat at home without knowledge of what was happening outside her walls.[17]

Al-Barudi expressed outrage that Arab women's hands were tied and all their energies consumed by attempts to free themselves from old traditions in their own homes. Other women sought blueprints of progress from the ways Jewish men and women treated each other and worked together towards national fulfillment. One Palestinian woman, Mrs. Shukri Deeb, functioning in public under her husband's name, recommended emulating some aspects of Jewish nationalism to strengthen the Palestinian movement. In a speech delivered to other Palestinian women, she urged:

> We have to fight the Jews with their weapons. They raise money from other concerned Jews all over the world and buy the land in Palestine. We, too, must collect money and build schools and hospitals as they do. The Jews raise their children in schools which teach them to love their homeland and to be loyal nationalists. So we must do the same.[18]

Deeb warned that when two nations fight each other, as in the case of the Palestinians and the Jews, the nation that wins is the one that gives its women full rights. The nation that loses is the one in which women have no rights. Jewish women had rights; thus, Deeb urged, so must Arab women of Palestine.

Images of women and men in the fiction and nonfiction of Jewish and Arab writers, filmmakers, playwrights, and poets functioned as markers of difference and inequality between the peoples of Palestine. Zionists and Palestinian Arabs used these images to demonstrate that the other people were a threat to their own desires for independence as well as being inferior, immoral, and treacherous. There were also remarkable exceptions to this dominant discourse of "the other" in which Jews and Arabs noticed and articulated things about each other that were admirable and human.

IV

Founding and Confounding the Boundaries

11

Challenging Patriarchy

For the Sake of the Nation

Who delivered you men and trained you to be so strong and brave
as lions? Who taught you to be honest and who helped you to
reach high?
This is woman, don't forget her goodness.
If you forget, we are lost.
Help her when she begs you for education and is willing to pay
the price with her spirit and money.
Eastern men, listen to her and give her what she asks.
Because she brings you happiness and honor.

> Salwa Sardah, *Sawt al-Mar'a al-Hur*

Now is the time for us colony women to take a stand for our fair
share in communal matters. Here we are, helping to build up a
new commonwealth in a country where we are all really free to do
as we like. Are we going to build on the basis of equality or not?

> Hannah Trager, *Pioneers in Palestine*

Nationalism was a Pandora's box for women. The growth of nationalism everywhere offered women opportunities to break out of old roles whether they wanted to or not and whether nationalists intended it or not. Arab and Jewish women in Palestine were no exceptions. The rise of women into public life accompanied the growth of nationalism despite the fact that many men and women vociferously opposed it. The catch for women, however, was that when they took unprecedented steps away from their traditional roles they did so for the most part not for their own sake but for the sake of their nation. This meant that although nationalist struggles opened doors for women, their own needs for freedom and equality were subordinated to the needs of the emerging nation as defined by men.

Women as well as men created and reproduced discourse. Real women, as opposed to those imagined in the literature, accepted or rejected aspects of nationalism and altered the discourse about women according to who they wished to become. They confirmed or contested the imagination of male leaders. Jewish and Arab women in Palestine were never homogeneous groups. They came from different class backgrounds, religious orientations, ideological preferences, levels of ability to articulate and act on their interests, and different senses of entitlement regarding their own desires.

Discourse on citizenship opened a secular space in which the rhetoric of "rights," "freedom," and "independence" gained currency. Arab and Jewish women, whether religious or not, entered this secular space to challenge colonialist constraints on their nations and patriarchal constraints on their lives. This chapter looks at what happened to Arab and Jewish women in Palestine from the latter part of the nineteenth century to the mid-twentieth century. How did they respond to the imperatives of political, economic, and social change? How did changes in identity and community affect them and how did they affect evolving political collectives? Here are some elements in the history of Arab and Jewish women of Palestine, first under Ottoman and then under British rule, that illuminate the importance of the actions of women in shaping notions of gender and nation.

Women in Ottoman Palestine

Most Arab and Jewish women of Palestine functioned within the bounds of patriarchal, gender-segregated societies. Even in the domestic sphere, in their own arena of action, they were subordinated to patriarchal will. The changes taking place in Ottoman Palestine affected these women in a mixture of different ways depending on whether they were urban or rural, upper or lower class, Christian, Muslim or Jewish, new foreign immigrants or old subjects of the sultan. Wealthier urban Palestinian Arab women, for example, remained cloistered within a strict social order, although higher status could also afford them opportunity to act ouside the home. Poorer urban and rural peasant Arab women had to leave the walls of their homes to contribute economically to the survival of their families but had less latitude in taking public initiative. Some new Jewish immigrant women had come from relatively cloistered situations in Europe but as uprooted women living in a strange place were forced to move beyond old patriarchal boundaries. Other Jewish women who had been part of egalitarian socialist groups found themselves newly constrained in Palestinian Jewish society.

However we come to understand the multiple factors that shaped Palestinian women's lives under Ottoman rule, Donna Robinson Divine has argued that "no inference can be drawn about the position of women from the situation of their male counterparts."[1] Wives of prominent Palestinian notables had to entertain the men who met in their homes. Peasant women had to start grinding grain into flour in the middle of the night to provide bread for their families. Divine stated that

"of all Palestine's economic sectors, those dominated by agrarian capitalism fostered the most troubling and painful social relationships. Marriage between urban notable families from distant centers—Jaffa, Haifa, Beirut, Damascus—became more common. On one hand, the loneliness of women who were brought to live in cities far from their parents' homes could be overwhelming. On the other hand, the new mobility helped women of the upper classes awake to a new awareness of themselves and their world."[2]

Ottoman land laws marked increasing privatization of land ownership, leaving Arab peasants increasingly landless or without sufficient means to support their families. Arab men would leave their villages to find work elsewhere in these early stages of proletarianization, but very few women could leave their villages. The women left behind had to cope with a widening realm of responsibility. Some girls became servants or wet nurses for wealthier families. At harvest time both men and women could work close to home picking olives or fruit or reaping. Peasants, feeling the brunt of hardships induced by privatization of lands, took out their frustration on new Jewish immigrants moving onto the lands they had worked. Village women joined in one of the earliest protests (1884) against a Jewish settlement near Afula.[3]

By the end of the nineteenth century, the education of Palestinian Arab women was under way. At this point there were a disproportionate number of Christian girls in school compared with their Muslim counterparts. In 1889, Quakers established the first girls' school in Ramallah, followed by a boys' school in 1901. A Muslim girls' school was set up in Jerusalem soon afterward. Jerusalem eventually became the place of highest concentration of educated Muslim and Christian women and of opportunities for education later, when the British took over Palestine.[4] Expanding educational opportunities resulted in a growing readership of women. Women were a substantial part of the reasons for the burgeoning of newspapers and magazines that promoted national causes. Women not only read these new journals and dailies but wrote for them as well.

These literary and journalistic forums became a way for Arab women to contribute to emerging national cultures in Palestine. In the last decades of the nineteenth century, middle- and upper-class women began to write and publish their ideas. Whether they railed against age-old limitations or defended traditions, their ability to enter into written public conversation was a radical step. In their books, articles, journals, pamphlets, political treatises, and poetry women participated in the construction of new national collectivities.

The debate about women's rights in Palestine and throughout the Arab world flowered with the rise of the press and literacy at the turn of the century. Credit for the first written feminist expression in the Middle East generally goes to educated men such as Qassim Amin in Egypt or Ziya Gokalp in Turkey. But educated Arab women such as Malak Hifni Nasif in Egypt and Halide Adib Edivar in Turkey shaped the contours of the debates through their own writings. As early as the 1880s educated Arab women wrote from their homes in Egypt, Lebanon, and Palestine, exchanging ideas with each other in new journals, newspapers, books, and poetry. Hind Nawfal, a Beiruti, published the first women's magazine in the Arab world, in which Palestinian women published their ideas.

The "modernizing" newspaper, *Al-Jarida*, 1907–1915, published an Egyptian woman's call for emancipation by Malak Hifni Nasif. Zaynab Fawwaz of South Lebanon (1845–1914) researched a biography of prominent women in the Arab world. May Ziyada was born in Palestine and moved to Egypt in 1908. She received a convent education and proceeded to write articles, essays, short stories, and poetry. She became known as the "Princess of Poetry," and founded a salon for poets and writers in Cairo in 1912.[5]

Jewish women, who came to Palestine from Europe and Russia, also faced limitations on their actions in the public sphere. Like Palestinian women, they began to make their own interventions and interpretations of nationalism according to their own experiences. Most of the Jewish immigrant women of the first aliya, 1882–1903, came from Russia and were affiliated with the Hibbat Tzion movement to settle Palestine. Some of the women had been a part of radical movements in Russia and continued to seek ways to break with tradition. Most women and men of this wave of immigration, however, tended to uphold more traditional patriarchal gender relations. Girls and women came with lower–middle-class families and established *moshavot,* which were supported financially by Baron de Rothschild.[6]

Jewish women immigrants dealt with enormous challenges in a foreign land. Like frontier situations everywhere, one could find both the tendency to entrench in old ways to preserve a sense of the familiar, and the impossibility of upholding old traditions in new places. Most women came willingly, but some followed their husbands. Regardless of how willingly or unwillingly they came, they faced poverty and hard physical labor. Yet their very presence in Palestine was a political act whether they remained at home or broke out into the male-dominated public domain of work or politics. As the women experienced hunger, lack of adequate shelter, disease, overwork, and danger, they developed new perspectives.

Hannah Trager's personal narratives of the first settlement at Petah Tikva, for example, capture the tensions produced by challenging old gender roles. Women's desire for wider participation in the life of the community was aggressively opposed on religious, social, biological, and political grounds.When several women of the settlement, for example, decided to attend a lecture on hygiene by a young Russian doctor, the male elders prohibited the women from going. In another incident, when a young woman decided to act in the role of a female character in a dramatic theater piece to celebrate a Jewish festival, the male religious establishment bucked. At first, the young people obeyed the authority of their religious leader, the *rav:*

> 'We are done for! . . . The Rav has heard that Leah is to be Potiphar's wife and he will allow no such thing. No Jewish maiden can play together with a man, and such a part! . . .' So a young man was chosen in Leah's place. Leah took her seat with the audience. The play was a great success.[7]

Men made unilateral decisions in "democratic" forums on all matters. But as contradictions within the system grew, young women of Petah Tikvah began to organize for the right to vote. The young men joined with their elders to oppose the women's vote on the basis of education:

the boys had attended high school and some had been to university in Russia; the girls had not been permitted to go to university and some had not even finished high school. To counter these arguments the girls turned to their own religious system using biblical metaphors to argue for suffrage:

Look at the old days when the daughters of Zelophe had stood up for themselves and claimed their inheritance. Look at Deborah, without whom the leader of the Israelites refused to go into battle. Look at Judith, look at the many Jewish women of Biblical times who had as much wisdom and courage as the men.[8]

The men at first rejected their argument and accused the petitioners of succumbing to degenerate influences of secular Westernization. "What next will you be introducing from America? Strikes, perhaps. We do not want such things in a Jewish colony in the Holy Land."[9] Through a combination of religious and secular arguments the women fought this classic reaction and eventually won their voting rights:

Now is the time for us colony women to take a stand for our fair share in communal matters. Here we are, helping to build up a new commonwealth in a country where we are all really free to do as we like. Are we going to build on the basis of equality or not? Have not we women taken our part in the founding of this colony as fully as the men have? Did not our mothers suffer and struggle as well as our fathers? Have we girls ever refused to help in any kind of work, indoors or out? Have we not weeded in the vineyards in the burning sun, made the hay, milked the cow? Have we not done our best in times of sickness and trouble? . . . Let us go forward together, not struggling against one another.[10]

Other Zionist women continued to press for the right to vote in piecemeal fashion within their own organizations. When twelve women were among the two hundred delegates of the First Zionist Congress in Basle in 1896, they participated without full voting rights and were excluded from leadership.[11]

Jewish women who emigrated to Palestine in the years between 1904 and 1918 constituted around 18 percent of the second aliya. Most women and men of this wave of immigration were unmarried young people who saw themselves as *halutzim*, pioneers, and defined themselves as Labor

Zionists.[12] Those who identified with idealistic socialist Labor Zionists and A. D. Gordon faced the widest discrepancy between ideals and reality. These women believed that personal and national transformation occurred through hard physical labor on the land, that socialism would eradicate hierarchical class society, and that in classless societies women would have equal rights.

Thus many women were shocked by the opposition of male comrades, who advocated the abolition of class society as long as the women continued to cook for them, do their laundry, and raise their children. But women fought these dictates and organized to work on the soil and do all manner of hard physical labor to "build up" the land. From the battles of this small minority of women, the myth of the liberated Israeli woman grew: working side by side with men in the fields, carrying in one hand a hoe and in the other a rifle.

In 1911, on the Kinneret Farm, there was a meeting to discuss the problems of women workers. The women who organized the meeting prohibited men's attendance so they could address women's issues. They recognized the failure of male comrades to attend to the problems of women workers, acknowledged the limited opportunities for women, protested women's confinement to food preparation, and discussed women's desire to train themselves in all skills. The women were careful to couch their demands in terms that appeased men's fears that women's equal participation would hinder their roles as mothers. They also based their arguments for equality on its contribution to increasing the strength of the nation.

In 1915, women announced a manifesto that demanded their participation in the secular paramilitary group Hashomer. These demands expanded their roles but did not gain them the right to vote. The "Decisions Regarding Female Membership in Hashomer" proclaimed that "the wives of the Shomrim," watchmen, would be allowed passive membership only. They would have the right of discussion, they could be present at meetings, but they would not have the right to make motions or vote.[13] In 1918 the Hashomer women Atara Struman, Devora Dracler, and Yehudit Horowitz drew up "Demands for Female Equality in Hashomer":

We the young women who have worked together with you for several years and who have always been at your side under the most difficult conditions, do not feel it is possible for us to continue our work in the manner which we have done thus far. . . . We have come to the decision that joint work and joint responsibility is possible only when there are equal conditions in all areas. . . . And if we are equal members in our daily work, let us be equal members in all aspects. No meetings which exclude us, no secrets from us.[14]

During World War I, Ada Maimon called for the establishment of a women workers' organization, *Moetzet Hapo'alot,* and demanded that the Histadrut reserve two seats for a delegation from the women's organization to vote in Histadrut Council decisions.[15] In 1914, at the first Women Workers' Convention, Yael Gordon confirmed the importance of motherhood in the nation while broaching the subject of women's rights. Basing her arguments on a traditional foundation, she made a radical plea:

Equality and emancipation for women . . . will enable them to fulfill their roles both as mothers and as effective individuals in society. . . . The young Jewish women who come here want not only to fulfill their national roles as daughters of our nation, but also to find themselves . . . to find the roots of their souls and to give them expression . . . in the workers' sector of our land.[16]

These women wanted to build partnerships with other women and men that were not based on economic or emotional dependency. Rachel Yanait explained that "in the thick of that passionate movement towards the land the women workers suddenly found themselves thrust aside and relegated once more to the ancient tradition of the house and kitchen."[17] To this end, women formed the Women's Equal Rights League. For years they defended this league as an outcome of the opposition they experienced from all quarters—from the Ottoman government, the British administration, the Muslim community, the Orthodox Jewish community, and their own secular Zionist leaders. Women created separate organizations that served men and women, established vocational training for women workers, and initiated collective activity enabling them to earn a living during severe economic crises.

In 1918, Sarah Azaryahu organized to expand suffrage for women in towns. Azaryahu was a Jewish mother of three and a schoolteacher who had won recognition for being the first woman in Palestine to teach science in Hebrew. She organized three thousand Oriental Jewish women to vote in Haifa municipal elections. This first election by such a broad base of women managed to elect a woman, Rachel Lunz, to the city council.[18]

Women in Mandatory Palestine

In the decade following World War I, under British rule, Palestinian women openly shared their discontent about the limitations on their lives in their writings and their meetings. They enumerated complaints that as Muslims they could have no free association with men and no political suffrage, and that no matter how keen their interests were in politics, as Muslim women they could not speak publicly in a mixed gathering.[19] Yet despite these limitations, Palestinian women made an indelible impact on debates about women and nationalism in Palestine and in the Arab world through their words and actions.

Towards the end of the war, middle- and upper-class women participated in demonstrations to protest the Balfour Declaration and Britain's support for the creation of a Jewish national home in Palestine. After the war, with the Ottoman defeat and the installation of British Mandate rule, Palestinian women formed the Arab Women's Society. Established in 1921, it lasted two years and continued to protest Zionist settlements.[20]

For Palestinians under British rule, the family was the most important unit of production and consumption; households were the locus of work. Women's marriages could augment alliances and rifts between leading families and boost new families aspiring to leadership. The practice of linking families of landowners with merchant families or families of administrators with business families was common. During the Mandate period, these marriages increased the material wealth of extended families but created hostilities by bringing into one family unit different cultural values and levels of education.

The spread of technical and secular knowledge could also be divisive in these families.[21] Divine noted that British policies assaulted Palestinians' economy and weakened its family structure. For example, bride price increased along with the practice of bringing brides from outside the *hamula*; complaints increased concerning financial hardships that prevented or postponed marriages; and divorce rates climbed, especially in cities.[22]

Women's magazines published articles by women on social criticism and domestic instruction. The magazines provided a significant way for Palestinian women to make contact with other women in the Arab world and for Arab women throughout the region to participate in the debate on Palestine and women's rights. During these interwar years, when Palestinian women wrote articles or poetry, they most often wrote on behalf of all Arab women, while women outside Palestine often wrote about the problems in Palestine. *Al-Ahram*, the Cairo daily, opened its columns to women and received letters and contributions from all over the Middle East including Palestine.[23]

The ways that women participated in politics of the nation expanded. Throughout the first decade of the British Mandate, Palestinian women acknowledged that an important task for them was to help the poor and others who had suffered the most from political and economic changes. Women also organized on international levels. For example, Atufa al-Husayni, the wife of the Jerusalem leader Amin al-Husayni, traveled to England to speak to prominent English women about Palestine. In meetings with British women, she accused their government of policies that gave up Palestine to strangers.[24] Other women attended demonstrations, boycotted foreign goods, and vowed to buy Arab-made goods.[25]

Palestinian women were active in the 1920s in response to both the imposition of British Mandate rule and the growth of the Yishuv. In 1929, two hundred Palestinian Arab women, both Muslim and Christian from upper- and middle-class families, organized the First Palestinian Arab Women's Congress. They elected a fourteen-member executive committee and then held another congress on economic issues in Haifa. Some Palestinian women participated in protests and demonstrations against British policy and action. Others sent letters to the king of England and the League of Nations. A fourteen-member delegation went to meet with the British high commissioner of Palestine to demand revocation of the Balfour Declaration and to halt Jewish immigration.[26]

These activities were spurred in part by the expansion of the Yishuv with the third aliya from 1919 to 1923 and by the founding of many protonational Zionist institutions. In 1921, the British allowed Jews to organize themselves into a parliamentary body, Assefat Hanivharim.

Orthodox Jewish men opposed women's right to vote, but after intense fighting, the women achieved victory.[27] Of particular importance was the creation of the Histadrut, the General Federation of Labor; in the same year, 1920, the Women's Workers' Movement was officially established.[28]

Inequality was institutionalized in evolving policies of the Histadrut even though one of its goals was to raise the standards of living and culture of Jewish women workers of Palestine. It sought to do this through the establishment of facilities that would relieve women as much as possible from the "cares of the household." To this aim, it created training farms, trade courses, kindergartens, and day nurseries. Women democratically elected a Women's Secretariat, organized conventions of the central council of women workers, and organized thousands of members.[29]

Women of the third aliya were influenced by the victory of the Communist Revolution of 1917. They assumed that they had an absolute right and ability to work. People such as Miriam Schlinowitch could not understand the opposition to the women workers' movement of Palestine. Brought up with the Communist Revolution, she had shared with other women important economic and cultural positions, and took equality for granted. She was surprised to see how small a contribution women were permitted to make in Palestine.

Schlinowitch joined a women's farm where "the work was the main thing and aside from it nothing mattered."[30] On the farms founded by men, she could be "swallowed up again by the powerful traditions of our feminine past," and "no longer know the joy of independent, self-supporting work." Golda Meir writes that kibbutz women of this time had hated kitchen duty and traditional feminine tasks, but not because they were hard work. "Their struggle wasn't for equal 'civic' rights . . . but for equal burdens."[31] The women of this period broke down barriers to work. They entered road building, carpentry, sewer digging, and farmwork. They had self-confidence, initiative, and readiness to express themselves. But this was not enough. Opposition to their efforts by men and difficult economic conditions reinforced recalcitrant gender boundaries.

Men defended their positions in all industries and trades. They argued that from a scientific point of view women shouldn't work in heavy jobs such as construction. They insisted that they wouldn't marry a woman who worked in construction, that women had no right to choose what they wanted to do because men knew better what was good for them, and that women's work was only temporary anyway until they got married. When one of the large contractors fired a number of women, he lectured:

> You really did do an excellent job but do you actually intend to be construction workers? . . . It's difficult enough for Jewish men. As far as they are concerned, we hope to make Jewish builders out of them; but women, there is no need for women builders. Believe me—there is no need for them at all.[32]

From 1924 to 1931 Jewish families, mostly from the Polish petit-bourgeoisie, emigrated to Palestine on the fourth aliya. They came with small amounts of capital and larger numbers of women owing to both increased numbers of families and single women who came with the Labor Movement. These immigrants settled in urban areas. Although most women remained housewives, women workers and those who had to find work outside the home had a hard time finding employment. The majority of urban jobs created during the 1920s were in construction work where women were excluded in all but a few instances.[33]

As the city of Tel Aviv expanded, thousands of Jewish workers entered the building trades for the first time. After a long fight, the workers' council decided to permit two women to enter every building *kvutza* (cadre). One woman recalled showing up for work to the sound of men jeering. They gave her the lightest work in the cement crew, pouring water. When she insisted on taking turns as they'd done before, they gave her a heavier load than anyone else until she demanded equal share. On each different job these ordeals were repeated.

Contracts for women in industry gave women with four years' experience lower pay than men just starting, and women faced obstacles to advancement. The number of women working in the trades was low. Out of 55,429 members, 12,426 "wives" were not employed outside the home. Seventeen women worked in the building trade out of 1,569, three worked in wood out of 615, five worked as painters out of 229, thirteen worked in bakeries out of 256, and one woman worked in a technical or mechanical trade out of 126. No women worked in metals, plumbing, electricity, leather, porterage, or stevedoring; no men worked as domestics.[34] Women who married ceased to be members of the Histadrut in their own right but were officially "wives of workers."

In the 1930s, 46 percent of all employed women were in domestic ser-

vice, including teenage and school-age girls and Oriental women. A Tel
Aviv survey found that 34 percent of all domestic workers were between
the ages of twelve and eighteen. They worked under poor conditions, for
long hours, low pay, and under the control of employers and even "pimp"
managers. Women were considered fit to do labor-intensive, low-
strength, low-skill, and low-paid jobs. Jewish women in Palestine were
hired in labor-intensive industries that had to compete with plants and
workshops that employed Arab women workers for even lower wages.[35]

On the kibbutzim, collectivized production, rejection of marriage, and
establishment of collective child care helped free women for "productive"
work. But women who ventured beyond conventional roles, going to
work in the fields, orchards, nurseries, cowshed, or chicken coop, remained exceptions to those left in child care, kitchen, and laundry.[36]
Women even had difficulty becoming members of the kibbutz. Hierarchical work values defined in male socialist terms placed "productive"
work at the highest end of the scale and mending, cooking, washing, and
child care at the lowest end. This reinforced disregard for traditional female work and relegated women to menial tasks. Instead of "public" versus "domestic" the kibbutz developed a parallel distinction between "productive (male) work," and "maintenance (female) work."[37] "One-way
equality" allowed women to do men's work but prevented men from doing so-called women's work.

Rejecting traditional forms of security for women and initiating
nonfamilistic divisions of labor, the kibbutz reduced women's engagement in social services and drew them into production efforts. Women
attempted to adopt male values and appearance in a continual battle for
inclusion in what was believed to be the central work of nation building.
As socialists, the men were ideologically committed to gender equality,
but as Zionists they "defined the problem of Jewish existence as the fundamental and overriding social issue to which all efforts had to be directed." This cast "women's rights" in a subversive light.[38]

Jewish women who came on the fifth aliyah, between 1932 and 1939,
comprised 50 percent of the last pre-state wave of immigration spurred
by the rise of Hitler. The immigrants were middle-class families and
brought with them the largest influx of capital so far. During the 1930s
employment opportunities for women expanded in the area of professional work. Women demanded the right to vote and broke into many
male-dominated areas as skilled laborers and professionals. Middle-class

women created new welfare services that reached out to poorer Jewish families and offered sustenance and advice about modern child rearing and housekeeping.[39]

The politicization of Arab women increased throughout the 1930s. Arab women of upper- and middle-class urban areas took new opportunities to act outside the domestic sphere on behalf of the national cause. An expanding number of these women continued to respond to the multiple changes occurring throughout Palestine and to foment change themselves. In 1930 Palestinian women held two agricultural conferences in Hebron and Haifa. An Arab Women's Committee protested a proposal to partition Palestine. The Arab Women's Society in Jerusalem had Muslim and Christian women working together even if their husbands were in opposing factions.

Arab women raised money through flower days, bazaars, and lotteries to buy land in Hebron, which they gave in trust to three families whose men were hanged by the British in 1930 for their involvement in the 1929 riots. They protested discrimination of British policies towards Arab educational and economic matters. The Arab Women's Society in Jerusalem opened welfare centers in 1931 to provide better services to poor families and nurses to teach mothers modern hygiene and methods of child care.[40]

In 1933 Palestinian women joined in the riots and demonstrations in Nablus, Jaffa, and Jerusalem. In 1936 the Palestinian revolt against British rule and Jewish settlement erupted and continued for three years, during which women expanded their participation in the national movement by supporting the revolt in several ways. They held rallies opposing British treatment of Arab detainees and protesting military searches in the villages. Women collected funds, contributed their own money, distributed funds to needy families, hid and transported arms, cooked for and delivered food and water to fighters, and safeguarded leaders.[41]

Throughout the 1930s, Palestinian dailies gave voice to at least four different approaches to the "woman question." Some articles lauded women's new roles as women; others praised them for their national service through conventional and unconventional means; still others reminded them of the traditions they must uphold for the nation; and some, finally, cited women's liberation as proof of progress of the nation.

Articles in the Palestinian dailies *Al-Difa'* and *Filastin*, for example, praised the fund-raising efforts of Palestinian women on behalf of poor families and families whose men died in fighting. Palestinian women used the paper to print political appeals for aid or policy changes. One woman published a letter to the British governor in *Filastin*, asking him to give adequate medical treatment to those wounded in fighting and to put them in private hospitals.[42] Another Palestinian woman asked Arab countries for help in changing the death penalty for three Arab men held by the British for instigation of Arab uprisings in the late 1930s.[43]

Filastin published a letter from a Palestinian woman to the Saudi King 'Abd al-'Aziz and to Huda Sharawi to enlist their support in obtaining the release of Sadhij Nassar, the first Palestinian woman to be held in British jails.[44] *Filastin* reported Asma Tubi's speech at the Arab Women's Conference of 1939 in which she celebrated the bravery of Arab women in the revolts of 1936–39. Tubi cited the presence of women on front lines of battle, where they helped the wounded. This proved, she said, that Arab women in Palestine could do everything.[45]

When Huda Sharawi launched publication of *The Egyptian Magazine* in 1930s Cairo, she printed letters and articles from Palestinian women, including a copy of a declaration sent by a delegation of Palestinian women to the British high commissioner condemning British treatment of female and young prisoners. The letter complained of British tactics to search women in the streets for weapons.

Palestinian women who wrote letters to Sharawi solicited help from Egyptians for Palestinian families whose fathers or brothers were jailed by the British. Sharawi sought to raise these issues in the international community outside the Middle East. She published letters that she had drafted and sent to the International Women's Union. In them she declared, "in the name of the widowed, bereaved, and orphaned in Palestine, I ask the British women to demand from the British authorities to stop the massacre of human beings immediately."[46]

In 1936, Christian Arab writer and activist Matiel Mogannam wrote *The Arab Woman and the Palestine Problem*. It was both a plea for and an illumination of Palestinian women's political activism. She dedicated her book both to King Hussayn of Jordan, whom she described as firing the first shot in the revolution of the Arab nation for freedom, and to "innocent Arab women" who died in 1936 as a result of "an unjust policy." Her book exemplifies efforts by some upper-class, educated Arab women to link the issue of women's rights with Palestinian nationalism.

The book begins with a history that highlights precedents of power for

Arab women. Women of the Jahiliyya, the pre-Islamic period of "igno-rance," were not ignorant but brilliant. They attained "high standing in culture and learning."[47] Before and after the advent of Islam, women were outstanding rulers (Queen Zubayda), musicians (Princess Alawieh), patriots and poets (Al-Khansa), politicians (Khaizuran, Shajarat Al-Durr, Sitt al-Mulk), jurists (Zaynab and Taqlabint Abu Faraj), and soldiers.[48]

Mogannam believed that Arab nationalism would provide opportuni-ties for women to take on new roles and allow greater public expression. She blamed British Mandate authorities for their fear of angering the religious establishment and thus reinforcing traditional obstacles for women. In this way the British added difficulties to women's organiza-tions in Palestine, compared with Egypt and Turkey where they could make more progress. Although this collusion between religious and im-perialist forces limited women's organizations to social and charitable matters, the political situation of Palestine infused even these types of organizations with a political dynamism.[49]

With the outbreak of World War II, thousands of Arab and Jewish men enlisted in the Allied forces leaving behind thousands of wives to live more independently. Husbands of Palestinian Arab women who had been active in the Arab revolt and had been consequently exiled by the British now were allowed to return. Almost two thousand Jewish women en-listed in military service in auxiliary organizations. Some entered into active duty. The most famous was the young Hungarian immigrant Han-nah Senesh, who left the relative safety of her home in Palestine to para-chute back into Europe to help save Jews. She was caught by the Nazis, tortured, and executed.

During the war, Palestinian and Arab women continued to organize. By the 1940s, pages of Palestinian dailies were full of examples of wom-en's actions and opinions. One article in *Al-Difa'*, for example, recognized women's national service, describing A'isha Abu Khadrah's donation of a substantial sum of money to build a hospital in Gaza for those too poor to afford health care.[50] A few days later, an article by a Palestinian woman argued that the rights of women could not be separated from the progress of the nation. It was necessary to grant women the right to study and to achieve high positions to improve the country as a whole. Egyptian women, she argued, were already working as doctors, lawyers, and jour-nalists, and Palestinian women could do these things as well. Her article concluded with a plea: "Fathers! Let us serve our country with our education and knowledge."[51]

Palestinian women were subjects of study at a conference held in Egypt in 1944. Mufidah Abd al-Rahman argued that there were connections between the politics of Palestine and the politics of Palestinian women. All nations progressed, she contended, when their women acquired political rights. There was no lack of intelligence among Arab women, yet they still did not have rights. Al-Rahman gave a double declaration: she would fight to achieve equality for women and would send blood, money, and children to fight in Palestine.[52]

After the war, Palestinian women's voices exerted an even greater presence in the public arena. As the middle classes grew during the war because of the economic boom in Palestine, more women began to enter the professions. Many of the women who participated in public debates about women's rights did so because they themselves were entering new territory and believed that the success of their nation depended on the rising status of women.

Pleas for equality by Palestinian women would soon become eclipsed by the intensifying threat to their survival in Palestine after World War II. By 1947, thousands of displaced refugee Jewish women in Europe were risking their lives to reach Palestine on leaking, overcrowded ships. Many lost their lives but many were able to enter Palestine illegally despite the British ban. Some Jewish women became members of terrorist groups that fought a guerrilla war against the British in Palestine. When the United Nations voted to partition Palestine, women on both sides became fighters in the civil war between Palestinian Jews and Arabs. Some Palestinian Arab women picked up arms to fight when their sons or husbands were killed. When Helwa Zaydan saw her husband and son killed, she picked up their guns and fought until she was killed.[53] Jewish women were forced to fight because the Zionist forces were outnumbered by Palestinian fighters.

Israel declared its independence on May 14, 1948. When the fighting ended later that year, Jewish women were elected as representatives to the Knesset. Women's participation in politics were at a peak and would gradually decline in the following decades while Israeli women labored under a myth that they were already liberated. "The woman question" would lie buried until the 1970s, when the constraints on women's lives became visible in the light of a fledgling woman's movement.

In the process of the war to establish the state of Israel, thousands of Palestinian women lost their homes, parts of their families, and their land. Some were exiled to often-hostile Arab countries and many landed in refugee camps. This left them with the task of preserving lifelong traditions that were difficult to maintain in new situations. But the pressure on Palestinian women to hold together a fractured society only served to strengthen the force of patriarchy in their lives. Yet like pioneering women everywhere, they found themselves in situations that forced them to step outside the prescribed boundaries. By the 1970s, the awareness of their predicament and the demand for changes in women's lives became part of the debate over strategies for national liberation.

Despite patriarchal and economic restrictions on their lives, Arab and Jewish women's contributions to emerging political identities were significant. Palestinian women were part of resistance movements against foreign domination and Jewish women participated in "building-up" the land. The politics of nationalism engendered unprecedented outcomes for women. For Arab and Jewish women of Palestine, the rise of Palestinian nationalism and Zionism signaled an expansion of their direct involvement in politics and in the public domain.

But women broke through these conventional limits almost entirely for the sake of their nation rather than on behalf of their own rights. As long as the motor force behind their actions remained nationalistic, the gains for women remained limited. On one hand, their writings and actions for the nation succeeded in widening opportunities for women in the public arena. On the other hand, liberation politics privileged national liberation over women's liberation. Thus the rights of women could be dismissed as irrelevant or opposed as subversive. Never in this struggle were Palestinian and Jewish women able to turn to each other to strengthen their cause. Placing national liberation above women's liberation separated them from each other and undermined each group's ability to win the very rights that would have been a true victory for both nations.

Sacrificing Sisters

Difference versus Power

Difference doesn't mean simply diversity, but hierarchies and inequalities of power.
Alice Kessler-Harris, "Women's History and Public Policy"

Some problems we share as women, some we do not. You fear
your children will grow up to join the patriarchy and testify
against you, we fear our children will be dragged from a car and
shot down in the street, and you will turn your backs upon the
reasons they are dying.
Audre Lorde, *Sister Outsider*

Power relations between Jewish and Arab women of Palestine were at
least as complex as what existed between respective peoples. The relations are only partially similar to those described by Audre Lorde above
regarding white and black women in the United States. Jewish women
who settled in Palestine from Europe could perhaps be seen in a position
similar to "whites," as representatives of an expanding Zionist hegemony. Yet they were a minority in Palestine and their support for their
people's access to arms and land was in part a minority defense against
the violence that had dogged them for so long. Palestinian Arab women
could perhaps be seen as "black," or as increasingly powerless in the face
of a double Zionist and British colonialism. But they were a majority in
Palestine and in part trying to claim the supremacy to which they felt
entitled. The limits of Lorde's analogy for the Middle East are particularly telling.

European Jewish women did not become part of a majority Jewish
population or dominant class in Palestine until after the creation of Israel
in 1948. Only then did they become beneficiaries of official military and

state authority, nevertheless remaining subordinate to their own male establishment. Palestinian women remained part of the majority population until 1948 and also subordinate to male domination. Ultimately women of each culture remained vulnerable to the other as well as to the men in their own cultures. Jews remained in danger from threats by surrounding Arab majorities, including Palestinians. Palestinians remained in danger from expanding Zionist presence. So both Palestinian and Jewish women feared that their "children . . . [would] be dragged from a car and shot down in the street." Not only would the other women "turn . . . [their] backs upon the reasons they . . . [were] dying," but also they would continue to act in ways that perpetuated the killing of their children. Jewish and Palestinian women who embraced nationalism sacrificed each other.[1]

The ongoing vulnerability of Jews in an Arab world, even as they increasingly wielded power as colonizers in Palestine, intensified their subjugation of Palestinian women and men in search of an illusive "security." That threat made it almost impossible for Jews to realize they had to take responsibility for the way they endangered Palestinian lives. The Zionist threat to Palestinians would make it almost impossible for Palestinians to understand they had to take responsibility for the ways they endangered Jewish lives as part of a larger Arab majority in the Middle East.

Yet there were moments when Jewish and Arab women refused to sacrifice each other. Some women defied danger to support other women on the opposing side. Some took responsibility for reaching across boundaries to make contact even when it seemed treasonous to do so. In the first section of this chapter, we look at women's actions that transgressed nationalist boundaries and humanized the intractable "other." In the final sections of the chapter we conclude the study with ways that women and issues of gender became linchpins of international conflict as well as possibilities for connection between two peoples of Palestine.

Confounding the Boundaries

The process of formulating group identity is never neat, linear, absolute, or final. During the time in which fledgling modern collective identities were forming in Palestine, individuals and groups were testing the boundaries. Before 1948 countless daily contacts between Arabs and Jews nuanced the "other" as human and, more treacherously, as part of "self." Women acted in ways that blurred nationalist boundaries by making contact with each other and challenging mainstream assumptions of separation, difference, and hostility.

This section presents a few instances of these kinds of interactions between Jewish and Arab women in Palestine. It is neither accidental nor incidental that the data come almost entirely from Jewish sources, with few exceptions. Jews would have found these interactions with Arabs significant. Jewish settlers wanted acceptance from Arab neighbors to remove them as an obstacle to national goals. Those Zionists who didn't completely resign themselves to the enmity of Arabs found the possibilities for contact and cooperation meaningful, hopeful, and important. Also, for Europeans who had learned inhuman ideas about indigenous peoples in other lands, these contacts meant taking a stance, whether consciously or not, against racism.

The oldest generation of Palestinians today still has memories of Jewish friends, coworkers, and contacts from the pre-1948 period. Their anecdotes are intimate, daring, compassionate, and ordinary, accentuating how much less segregated both peoples were then.[2] But these contacts are not as evident in the published accessible sources of this study, although they may be located in private archives. Palestinian Arabs would have taken these contacts for granted in that they were not dissimilar to centuries of amiable contacts with non-Muslim minorities within Muslim empires. They certainly did not see a need for positive contact with Jews to realize their national aspirations. So although both Jewish and Arab women and men in Palestine acted in ways that challenged emerging nationalist boundaries by cooperating with each other, for the most part the evidence here comes from Jewish sources.

Having said this, there is the story of a Palestinian Arab woman who exercised her own judgment and countered prevailing political dictates. She is the mother of Arab-Israeli writer Atallah Mansour. He portrays his mother during the Mandate years as someone who bucked the nationalist establishment. As a girl, she had formed friendships with Jewish girls from Safed and through them got work with a group of new immigrants from Russia in Moshava Migdal, near the Sea of Galilee. Her experiences there were ones of great discovery and pleasure. They were one factor that molded the attitudes she and her children harbored for the next seventy years towards Jews and Israelis.

Mrs. Mansour told her children stories about how Jews had treated her and each other as equals. No foreman stood over the workers to see that they worked hard. This was not a kibbutz, so they all received pay every week. Her main jobs had alternated between child care and almond picking in the fields. For the rest of her life she defended the Jewish settlers to her friends, even during the Deir Yasin massacre, which, she argued, was expected Jewish revenge for the 1929 Hebron massacre. Her son became a journalist in Israel who critiqued Israeli government policies from inside the system.[3]

Jewish women, too, repeatedly made contacts, took risks, and had insights that went against mainstream view of Arabs as threatening or inferior. Through exchange of information, Arab women as well as Jewish women who came from Arab countries made contributions to the survival of the Yishuv in countless crises and mundane moments. One kind of story common to many colonialist ventures was the one in which the settlers learned survival skills from indigenous people even though the dominant narrative claimed that there was nothing to learn from them and everything to teach.[4] Arabs provided Jews with vital information that enabled them to survive. The conduit for this survival information was often a woman.

Arab women and Jewish women from Arab countries, who were supposed to be recipients of advanced knowledge from the Europeans, imparted crucial information, supplies, and skills that enabled Europeans to survive in a foreign land. In one settlement, a Palestinian Arab woman taught an immigrant woman from Europe to wash the grain that came mixed with red earth. She showed her how to mix grain with water and to watch three layers form: the bottom layer of earth, the next layer of seeds of wild grass, and the top layer of clean wheat. After spending whole days with this Arab woman, the Jewish woman went on to become the expert in grain washing in her settlement.[5] In 1907 in Sedjera, the first settlement to accept Jewish women workers, four of the workers came from Europe but most others came from Kurdistan, the home of the non-Arab, Kurdish-speaking ethnic group. The Kurdish Jewish women taught the European ones how to sift barley "in the old Arab fashion."[6]

One of Hannah Trager's earliest memories of childhood in the settlement of Petah Tikva was of long, hard hours spent in the sun learning from Arab women how to make bricks for mud huts. The settlers needed to move from tents to houses before the onslaught of autumn rains. At first it was the Arab women who made bricks for the huts as Jewish women and children fetched and carried things for them. Eventually the Jewish women learned from the Arab women to make the bricks themselves. The children continued to carry earth, lime, or straw. When the Arab and Jewish women mixed the materials and added water, children stamped on the mixture and kneaded it with their feet. Trager remembered how "at first we were told to look on and watch mother and the Arab women [knead and shape the clay into boxes] and then we did it ourselves."[7]

In another incident, an Arab woman who had been selling eggs to colonist women for a long time came running to the settlement to tell the women that they must take their families away into hiding. She warned that neighboring Arab villagers were angry and intending to surround the colony and kill everyone. The Arab woman feared being killed herself for giving the Jewish women this information, but she felt compelled to do so because of the relationship of mutual kindness that had developed over time.[8]

Arab neighbors repeatedly risked their lives to defend Jewish friends against the anger of other Arabs. During the 1921 attacks on Jews of Jaffa, the Jews defended their houses without ammunition but with iron rods, stones, and bottles, except for one old woman who wielded an axe. In most neighborhoods, Jews and Arabs lived side by side so that any kind of organized defense was impossible. Some Jews fled to Tel Aviv and many died, but those who stayed and survived did so through the aid of Arab friends.

Friendships were often based on the contacts made between the women of the households. In one Sephardic Jewish family the mother had contact with the mother of the Arab family next door (both spoke Arabic) and their children played together. The Jewish family was in danger during the Jaffa riots, and their Arab neighbors hid them. When the attackers arrived, the Arab family refused to give up their Jewish friends. The attackers beat the father of the Arab family so that he would disclose the Jewish family's whereabouts. But he declared to his family that he was ready to give his own life rather than sacrifice his neighbors.[9]

Once when members of a fledgling Jewish settlement had no more food, the men left to find food in a distant town. Rains washed out the roads, preventing their return. As the situation grew worse for the women and children who were starving, they defied the orders of their men not to make contact with surrounding Arab neighbors. One girl went into the tent of an Arab woman nearby. She watched the woman make barley bread with meal and water. The woman gave her some barley cakes and an onion that the girl gulped down ravenously. The Arab woman sent her husband to fetch barley meal from his village because the Jewish men had forbidden their women to buy food there. The Arab woman baked barley cakes for the settlers, softening the hunger of the children and enabling them to all to survive until the men returned with supplies.[10]

Arab and Jewish women exchanged mutual support as mothers. A Jewish woman's memoirs refer to both Jewish and Arab women who helped her care for her children and whom she in turn helped.[11] Another Jewish woman settler formed a friendship with an Arab woman who lived outside Palestine in Beirut. When her friend was about to give birth she was summoned for help and support; this experience deepened their friendship. The Arab woman was a member of the Bak family of the Lebanese Christian elite. After the family lost favor with the French regime, the Jewish woman gave them refuge for months in her home on Kfar Giladi. When the British came to arrest Ahmad Bak, the Jewish villagers refused to turn the family over to the authorities.[12]

Arab women introduced Jewish women to Arab family traditions. One such tradition arranged for a woman who had just given birth to a male child to nurse another male child born in her area around the same time, making him and her son foster brothers. Musa al-'Alami, from a prominent Palestinian Jerusalem family, gave an account of his Jewish foster brother. A few days after Musa's birth, according to custom, the midwife who delivered him informed his mother that she had delivered another woman of a son around the same time.[13] In this case the woman was not only poorer than the 'Alamis but Jewish as well. Nevertheless, each woman breast-fed the other's baby, making the two of them foster brothers; they expected to regard each other as such for the rest of their lives.

The families became friends despite religious, national, and class differences. In Musa's case, his foster brother was the son of a Jewish grocer down the street. For the next thirty years the two families visited each other, exchanged gifts on feast days, and offered congratulations and condolences. Contacts continued until escalating violence between Arabs and Jews rendered such intimacies impossible.

Beyond childhood, motherhood, and neighborhood, women made

contact with each other and helped one another in a myriad of ways. Jewish and Arab girls were able to find work in an Arab-owned enterprise called the Nur Match Factory. The owner preferred hiring nonunionized girls, and these young Arab and Jewish women worked side by side under dangerous conditions, terrible sanitation, and low wages. At one point, the women organized a strike that included Arab and Jewish men and women alike. They kept the strike going for four months and twelve days, despite the arrest of the men, the beating of the women, and their removal to prison.[14]

Prominent Jewish women active in the leadership of the Yishuv also challenged the boundaries of conventional nationalist policy. On Beatrice Magnes's first visit to Palestine from the United States in 1912 she was impressed with the "majority population of Arabs." She came to the conclusion that there would never be peace unless Jews and Arabs could rule the country together. Magnes settled in Palestine in 1922. After the 1929 riots, she became part of a small group of dignitaries from the Jewish community who explored binationalism. She critiqued mainstream Zionism and offered an alternative: a political entity that would have joint rule by Arabs and Jews.[15] Between 1933 and 1939, Beatrice rented a house from a wealthy Arab property owner, the mother of Musa al-Husayni, who at the time was a student in Nazi Germany. The Magneses moved with their three little boys into this Jerusalem neighborhood peopled by Jews, Muslims, Christians, and British. Beatrice lived long enough to see her ideas on binationalism rejected by the Jewish community and the Arabs who accepted it murdered.[16]

Manya Shohat sought friendship with her Arab neighbors despite her stance that the Jews' return to Israel was a right, not a favor. She fought the devaluation of the learning of Arabic in the Yishuv and insisted that Jews must learn Arabic. Shohat and her women friends became fluent in the language. This enabled them to initiate relationships with Palestinians and to build friendships over time. Shohat formed friendships of mutual respect with Arab women as well as men. In one story, Manya was limping along in an Arab marketplace with an injured foot. One of the organizers of a planned attack on Jews in Haifa recognized her and helped her to safety before issuing the order to commence the attack.

Shohat apparently did not see a contradiction between receiving help from these attackers or supporting groups that advocated Arab rights, while making all-out efforts to obtain weapons to fight Arabs. She also argued that Jews must help Arabs form a democratic national party. In a letter to Rachel Yanait in 1930, she elaborated some of her ideas about Arab-Jewish relations. She recommended a "wide range of activity within the Arab community" including communication with the *fallahi* and "joint clubs for Jewish and Arab workers in the cities."

Shohat proposed the establishment of a Jewish-Arab League for the purposes of negotiating compromises with Arab leaders and building direct relationships with the "masses." She advocated education for Arab children through literature steeped in "a humanitarian spirit which will release them from the fascist-chauvinistic poison which has thus far been fed to the Arab youth." Shohat recommended that the Jewish and Arab chambers of commerce unite and that joint labor unions be created.[17]

Henrietta Szold, founder of the international Zionist women's organization Hadassah, explicitly expressed appreciation for Arab knowledge, practice, and individuality. Whereas volumes of treatises on Palestine ignored the existence of the Arab population of Palestine, Szold recognized its existence and its political desires. Most remarkably, where others saw only "stagnation" or "neglect," she acknowledged the evolution of agricultural techniques that were appropriate to the environment of Palestine. Szold observed the specialization of Arab knowledge and methods of working the soil in ways particularly befitting to unique conditions of that land. On a journey to Tiberias she examined the soil and observed its richness. She remarked that "the terraced fields near the river bank [gave] evidence of the most loving cultivation."

Szold learned that Arabs plowed between the prolific stones of their hills and that their yields of grain were extraordinary under these conditions. She discovered that whereas Arabs still used wooden plows, the deeper plowing of modern Western technology ruined certain soils. She concluded, in a way extraordinary for her time and orientation, that the inhabitants used the appropriate technology of superficial scratching of the wooden plowshare, with its small iron attachment, in exactly the most beneficial ways.[18]

Szold argued that the settlers in Palestine had failed to create economic opportunities for Arabs and that they must "reinspect their national aspirations" and remove from them "every possible admixture of injustice."[19] She eventually broke off from the core of the binationalist Brit Shalom along with Beatrice and Judah Magnes, Martin Buber, and Ernst Simon to advocate Arab nationalism as something healthy and desirable. She believed that Arab leaders would be open to cooperation with sympathetic Zionist leaders. Szold called a meeting of one hundred supporters of binationalism and Arab-Jewish rapprochement and joined the "presidential board" of the new group, *Ihud,* or union. During World War II, as rumors of Nazi slaughter began to reach the Yishuv, *Ihud* received terrible press coverage in Jewish periodicals as well as in the *New York Times,* which criticized the group for extending a hand to Arabs who were "sympathetic" towards Germany.[20]

It was not only progressive, left-wing Jews who made contact with Arabs. Geula Cohen, an Arab Jew engaged in right-wing terrorist operations against the British, eventually became a member of the Israeli parliament. She saw herself as an outlaw in both British and Zionist establishments and as such made contact with Arab women regarded as outlaws. She recorded friendships with several Arab women during the time she served in British prisons. Arab and Jewish women helped Cohen escape from prison. She described one of her Arab inmates as full of "dignity and thoughtfulness." Another of her prison allies was Fatima, who gave birth to a baby boy while in prison. One might speculate that it was easier for Cohen to make these contacts with Arab women because she herself was a Yemenite Jew, spoke fluent Arabic, and struggled against an Ashkenazi establishment in ways that perhaps echoed Arab women prisoners' own struggles against upper-class Arab society.

Individual, isolated, occasionally public, and more often private resistances to nationalist imperatives were mostly not recorded. Yet many women, some known in history and others nameless, acted according to their own consciences and personal values in ways that confounded political dictates. At the most public end of the spectrum, this meant that Jewish women attempted to change national policies detrimental to Palestinians; at the most personal end, it meant that Arab women risked their own lives to help save Jews from fatal attack. Whether blatantly public or quietly personal, these moments had immeasurable repercussions on the microcosmic level of individual lives. Yet they could not alter the macrocosmic realm of international conflict.

Conclusions: Possibilities of Interconnection

Palestinian and Arab women both experienced marginalization and invisibility in their respective nationalist texts. Direct references to women in nationalist texts by Arabs and Jews both in and out of Palestine were rare. Both sides' nationalist texts spoke in the gender-neutral language of universal political truths. Yet both were in fact written by and for a particular group of men who, even as they judged their goals to be universal, relegated women's (as well as some men's) issues to the margins.

Jewish and Arab women of Palestine appeared in their nationalist texts to represent very specific issues: motherhood, sexuality, proof of equality, civilizers, and markers of difference and power. Women came to inhabit nationalist narratives in cameo appearances symbolic of survival, identity, and transformation. In the process of imagining women, whether as wives or mothers or as symbols of freedom or tradition, Palestinian nationalists and Zionists used gender in similar ways to defend their own legitimacy and reject the other's claims.

Arab and Jewish men, like men all over the world who organized nationalist movements in the nineteenth and twentieth centuries, sought power, dignity, and freedom. Through these two conflicting and seemingly contradictory national movements in Palestine one gets a vivid sense of the similarities with which nationalists seized upon ideas about women and men to formulate new political identities. In these two opposing movements women and men altered or reinforced their roles and dreams. But no matter how similarly nationalists gendered political identity, and no matter how similar were the needs of Arab and Jewish women and men, each side coopted gender in ways that confirmed the difference, hostility, and illegitimacy of the other in Palestine.

Manipulation of gender became yet one more piece of evidence of the impossibility of forging potential alliances against Ottoman and British rulers, class oppression, and cultural hardships. Instead, Arab and Jewish men perceived each other's struggle for manhood as essentially different. They saw the other's *shahada* or *haganah* as a danger to their own survival. Jews rejected Arab men's martyrdom as a powerless stance. Arabs rejected Jewish men's self-defense as imperialist. In this way each took the gendered trope of the other that uplifted masculinity to a new political height and dashed it to pieces, rejecting at once the nationalism and the masculinity of the other.

Zionists used metaphors of barrenness as an accusation that Arab men had neglected the land. It was a way of saying that Palestinians were not fully men and didn't deserve to rule Palestine. "Neglect" of land was tantamount to a crime, punishable by exile, or at least, subordination. Palestinian men interpreted Jewish rebirth on the land as a veritable death knell to their own potential sovereignty and independent manhood. They lumped it together with their fight against all imperialist claims on Palestine, just as Jews lumped Arabs together with all the host cultures that had sought their destruction. So although Palestinian and Jewish men tapped into the power of '*ird* and *ard,* and into the marriage of *adam* and *adama* for their own inspiration, they used these metaphors to define the other side as ultimately illegitimate.

The nation's men had to possess woman and land completely, guard them, go to war for them, and suffer humiliation from loss or desecration of them. Feminization of the land was part of the project of developing nationalism based on the constructs of manhood and power. Both sides feminized the land to articulate their own sacred devotion and eternal tie to it as the basis of life for their people. Yet both peoples also used these gender tropes to delegitimize the other's claim to the land. In this way, nationalists co-opted gender to reinforce boundaries between "self" and "other," and to construct the relationship between the two as irreconcilable.

Jewish and Arab men argued both for the preservation of women's conventional roles and for the breaking of convention to expand women's roles in the new nation. The irony of these debates over equality is that no matter what stance men took, the pragmatic and idealistic aspects of nationalism in fact opened new possibilities for women. As Arab and Jewish women stepped into these new domains, they encountered opposition from their men no matter how liberal or traditional these men were.

However egalitarian the claims of Palestinian or Jewish nationalists, women were still seen as wives, mothers, nurturers, and general supporters of men's goals. Productivity for women remained synonymous with reproductivity. Women who did not carry out these functions constituted a problem for nationalists. Women's worth was measured on a limited and biased basis of how they helped or hindered, fit or contradicted men's visions of the world. Men envisioned women as part of their own cosmology of self, as a critical though often unconscious vehicle for becoming a man among men, and a nation among nations.

The debate about women was a field upon which men competed for power. Texts wrestled with explicit or implicit comparisons between Arab and European, Jewish and European, or Arab and Jewish women. Status and treatment of women became a measure by which men judged their capacities to civilize Palestine and thus prove their worth as sovereigns. Sternhell refers to equality in early Zionism as a mobilizing myth.[21] This is true for much older democracies too, where nationalism takes precedence over gender and class equality.

Concern for modernization and progress highlighted women's roles in the conflict over Palestine. Because the project of modernization postulated a human race divided into realms of civilized and backward, rational and irrational, secular and religious, modern and traditional, it contributed to perceptions of essential and eternal difference between the two peoples. Thus Christian Arab women who believed that Muslims were backward reinforced class and confessional divisions amongst Arabs. Jewish women who accepted the Zionist idea of Palestine as uncivilized rendered other Palestinian-Arab and Arab-Jewish women invisible or inferior. Seeing Arab or Jewish women as in need of being saved, or as nameless obstacles to progress, meant not seeing them at all.

Concerns with progress drew attention to girls' education. Tibawi's and Nardi's studies of education in mandatory Palestine became weapons in the war between Arabs and Jews in Palestine to prove the legitimacy of their claims to Palestine as modernizers. Tibawi's study assumed that obstacles to girls' education were obstacles to Palestinian national development. Nardi's study was based on the belief that educating girls was proof of the progressiveness and innate goodness of the Jewish national project.

Both writers inhabited a shared terrain at the crossroads of nationalism and modernization that lauded education of their children and especially their girls. Both assumed that their success in this endeavor would affect the success of their national struggles. But when Nardi noted that Arabs educated only their more privileged boys and a small fraction of girls who were most often Christian, he was attacking them for failing to meet a basic civic responsibility; in his mind this weakened the legitimacy of Arab claims to Palestine.[22] A subtext of his work was that Jews were better equipped than Arabs to form a civil society in Palestine because they educated a higher percentage of their children. A subtext of Tibawi's work was that education would fortify Palestinians for their ongoing struggle against Zionism.

Gendered tropes contributed to ideas about civilization, education, and progress, in the process of negotiating boundaries between "us" and "them." Each people passed judgments on the other in part by making assumptions about the other's women. "Their" women were seen as irrevocably different: too backward or too lewd, too oppressed or too liberated, too cloistered or too unfettered.

Even as Palestinian and Jewish women challenged the limits on their lives, even as they strode farther into the public sphere, they widened the gulf between their two peoples. Because the expansion of rights of women on both sides occurred in the context of nationalist movements, it reinforced women's sense of the other as the major obstacle to liberation rather than as an ally in a struggle for rights. Women in each culture saw their own struggle for liberation, whether as women or as members of a new nation, in opposition to rather than in alliance with the freedom of the other. So although some Jewish and Arab women fought against their respective patriarchal strictures, they rarely recognized this as a bridge between them.

As Palestinian and Jewish women took unprecedented actions in their respective national movements, they became boundary markers for their nations. Yet there were always remarkable women who did in fact confound the boundaries and reject demonization of the other. The women who sought solidarity, who challenged notions of essential difference, who recognized the legitimacy and urgency of the other's needs for sovereignty and security in Palestine remained a small but significant minority. For in their alternative vision there were seeds of a more tenable future.

The fact that some Arab and Jewish women took actions that complicated, challenged, and even transgressed nationalist boundaries did not alter their deepest loyalties to their own people. Rather, they pushed gently or boldly on boundaries of loyalty and identity to make possible human exchange and connection. Although individual acts or even organized actions by Jewish and Arab women could not alter the conflict of two peoples over one land, they managed nevertheless to create new possibilities of interconnectedness. They spoke and acted in ways that created options outside the dominant nationalist narratives of hegemony and hierarchy. They pointed to possibilities of life in Palestine that might not necessitate obliterating the other. Their actions offered fragile alternatives for a less violent future.

Potential for connection and relationship grew in Jewish and Palestinian women's struggles against the patriarchal strictures of their lives, in the love Jewish and Palestinian men felt for Palestine as bride and mother, in the yearnings women and men had for home, community, and safety, in the many gendered ways that both peoples bound themselves to Palestine and Israel. But the evolution of gender roles occurred in the context of a power struggle that rendered potential connections between the two peoples virtually impossible. Similarities in the ways that they co-opted gender were all the more remarkable for the differences that existed between them. Differences in social structures, cultural norms, historical experience, and political leadership created very different realities for Arab and Jewish women. So while women and issues of gender continued to embody the difficulties between two peoples in one land, they also created the potential to make those connections happen in the future.

The inaugural years of this new millennium are a critical time for the peoples of Palestine and Israel. The final years of the last century witnessed unprecedented initiatives to resolve the over one-hundred-year-old conflict in the Middle East. Just as women and issues of gender have been part of the production of conflict, they will be part of the solution. In the last decades of the twentieth century, it was not accidental that as Jewish and Arab women in Israel and Palestine took new steps toward freedom, so did nationalists toward a negotiated solution. Neither is it a coincidence that as the official "peace process" excluded women and ignored the gains they had made as leaders, the situation exploded into violence.

In the patriarchal view of nationalism, the other side is always to blame for the humiliating, violent things one must do to them. In this process, women are sacrificed and expected to sacrifice all that they love. "Soldiers and mothers [are] the sacrificial couple, honored by statues in the park, lauded for their willingness to give their lives to others."[23] Two extreme expressions of patriarchal nationalism, fascism and religious nationalism, distort reality by elevating war and death to an act of noble humanity. Feminist nationalism rejects this notion and emphasizes instead that only through relationship and honoring difference as strength, even with a so-called enemy of the nation, can people achieve dignity and security.

Understanding the ways that women and issues of gender operate in patriarchal nationalism helps to untangle the gnarled skein of injustices that fuel the conflict. As Israelis and Palestinians broaden the discourse on what it means to be a man or a woman, an Arab or a Jew, a citizen of Israel or Palestine, they loosen the stranglehold of the conflict's "deadly embrace."[24] When women breach the divide between nations as some Israeli and Palestinian women are doing today in a plethora of cooperative initiatives, they create alternatives to endless war and turn the nation into a crucible of life. As Israeli women become advocates to end the brutalities to Palestinians and as Palestinian women stand up against the threat to Israeli lives, they create alternatives to endless war with productive, dynamic, unpredictable relationships also called peace.

Notes

Preface

   1. Scott, *Gender and the Politics of History,* 24.

   2. McClintock, *Dangerous Liaisons,* 89.

   3. Kimmerling and Migdal, *Palestinians,* 54.

Chapter 1. (En)Gendering Nations

   1. McClintock, *Dangerous Liaisons,* 2.

   2. For ways that feminist theory has challenged the field of international relations, see also Enloe, *Bananas, Beaches and Bases;* Grant and Newland, *Gender and International Relations;* Stearns, *Gender and International Relations;* Amy Swerdlow, "Engendering International Relations Theory," 160–63; Tickner, *Gender in International Relations.*

   3. Cockburn, *The Space Between Us,* 44.

   4. For further discussion see introduction and "Gender: A Useful Category of Analysis," in Scott, *Gender and the Politics of History,* 1–11, 28–50.

   5. Tucker, *In the House of the Law,* 10.

   6. Ibid., 10.

   7. Sharoni, *Gender and the Israeli-Palestinian Conflict,* 6.

   8. Ibid., 152.

   9. Khalidi, *Palestinian Identity,* viii.

   10. There are excellent studies of women's lives in Palestinian and Israeli history including works by Deborah Bernstein, Barbara Swirski, Marilyn Safir, Judith Tucker, and Julie Peteet as well as many others whose work is indispensable to this book.

   11. Joan W. Scott, *Gender and the Politics of History,* 49.

   12. Anderson developed his theory of nationalism linked to the growth of capitalism, printing, and vernacular language in his book *Imagined Communities.*

   13. Patricia Yaeger used this phrase in her keynote address at the Conference on Nationalisms and Sexualities at Harvard University, June 1989. Benedict Anderson presented a paper there that explored issues of masculinity in nationalism including the "imagined brotherhood" of nationalism that created its highest symbols, its armies, by excluding women and mobilizing them only during national crisis.

14. Showalter, *Speaking of Gender*, 1.

15. See discussion of the links between dominance of male over female and West over East in Norton, "Gender, Sexuality and the Iraq of Our Imagination," 26–28.

16. Accad, *Sexuality and War*, vii.

17. Ibid., 2.

18. Swedenburg, *Memories of Revolt*, 7.

19. For examples of revisionist histories, see Flapan, *The Birth of Israel;* Lockman, *Comrades and Enemies;* Shafir, *Land, Labor.*

20. See Hunt, ed., *The New Cultural History*, 17, for her discussion of her work on the French Revolution.

21. Anderson, *Imagined Communities*. For theoretical approaches to discourse and narratives of power and knowledge see Foucault, *Discipline and Punish*, and *The Archeology of Knowledge.*

22. On the construction of nationalism, see Gellner, *Nations and Nationalism;* Hobsbawm, *Nations and Nationalism since 1780;* Nairn, *The Break-Up of Britain.*

23. Greenstein, *Genealogies of Conflict*, 21.

24. Ibid., 23.

25. Schulz, *Between Revolution and Statehood*, 1.

26. Abdo, "Nationalism and Feminism," 148–70.

27. Lockman, in Pappe, *The Israel/Palestine Question*, 101.

28. Lockman, *Comrades and Enemies*, 367.

29. Boyarin, *Palestinian and Jewish History*, 3.

30. Doumani, "Rediscovering Ottoman Palestine," in Pappe, *The Israel/Palestine Question*, 30.

31. Enloe, *Bananas, Beaches, and Bases*, 44.

32. Wood, *The Boundless Courtyard*, 82–83.

33. Ibid., iii.

34. Shohat, *Israeli Cinema*, 6.

35. Scott, *Gender and the Politics of History*, 24.

36. Cooke, *War's Other Voices*, 2.

37. Rejwan, *Israel in Search of Identity*, 2.

38. *Ahl al-dhimma*, people of the book, were non-Muslims with specific legal rights and obligations in Islamic societies.

39. Rogan and Shlaim, *The War for Palestine*, xi.

40. Boyarin, *Palestinian and Jewish History*, 15–16.

41. Bernstein, *Constructing Boundaries*, 9.

42. Lockman, *Comrades and Enemies*, 363.

43. Rouhana, *Palestinian Citizens*, 229–31.

44. Greenstein, *Genealogies of Conflict*, 271.

Chapter 2. Reframing Questions

1. Fanon, *A Dying Colonialism*, 42.

2. Rowbotham, *Women, Resistance and Revolution*, 204–5.

3. Temma Kaplan, *Anarchists of Andalusia*.

4. See, for example, Bridenthal, "Butter and Guns: German Countrywomen as Producers and Nationalists," Tim Mason, "Women in Nazi Germany," and Koonz, *Mothers in the Fatherland*.

5. Theweleit, *Male Fantasies*, vol. 1, Barbara Ehrenreich's foreword xiii–xiv, also 76, 348, 401.

6. Theweleit speaks of susceptibility to fascism as explicable in terms of economic degradation of large sections of the middle class, but argues that this does not explain German fascism, *Male Fantasies*, vol. 2, 398.

7. Theweleit, *Male Fantasies*, vol. 1, 30, 221.

8. Ibid., *Male Fantasies*, vol. 1, 32, 301, 310.

9. Mosse, *Nationalism and Sexuality*, 23, 90.

10. Martin, "Imagined Brotherhood," unpublished paper from Nationalisms and Sexualities Conference, Harvard University, 1989.

11. Hunt, *Politics, Culture, and Class*, 25.

12. Warner, *Monuments and Maidens*, xix–xxiii, 3–17, 27–30.

13. Spivak, *In Other Worlds*, 184, 186, 215.

14. Jayawardena, *Feminism and Nationalism*, 2–9, 18, 23, 254–59.

15. Sangari and Vaid, *Recasting Women*, 1–26.

16. Peter Stallybrass and Ann Jones, unpublished paper, Nationalisms and Sexualities Conference.

17. Ellen Goodell, unpublished paper, Nationalisms and Sexualities Conference.

18. Vera Kreilkam, unpublished paper, Nationalisms and Sexualities Conference.

19. Purnima Bose, unpublished paper, Nationalisms and Sexualities Conference.

20. Ketu Katrak, unpublished paper, Nationalisms and Sexualities Conference.

21. Paul Brophy, unpublished paper, Nationalisms and Sexualities Conference.

22. Nancy Paxton, unpublished paper, Nationalisms and Sexualities Conference.

23. Yuval-Davis and Anthias, *Woman-Nation-State*, 2.

24. Fernea, *Women and the Family*, 162.

25. Schipper, *Unheard Words*, 10.

26. Ibid., 162.

27. See, for example, Augustin, *Palestinian Women*, and Sabbagh, *Palestinian Women of Gaza and the West Bank*.

28. Graham-Brown, *Palestinians and Their Society, 1880–1946*.

29. See Tucker's writings *Arab Women; In the House of the Law* and "Marriage and Family in Nablus."

30. Kazi, "Palestinian Women and the National Liberation Movement," Peteet, *Gender in Crisis*.

31. Moors, *Women, Property and Islam*.

32. Taqqu and March, *Women's Informal Associations in Developing Countries*, 1–18, 34, 48, 121.

33. Muhawi and Kanaana, *Speak, Bird, Speak Again*, 2–4, 17–18, 30–31, 37–38.

34. Hazelton, *Israeli Women*, 18, 21, 23, 35, 65, 121.

35. Tiger and Shepher, *Women in Kibbutz.*

36. Safir, "The Kibbutz: An Experiment in Social and Sexual Equality?" 100–29.

37. Izraeli, "The Zionist Women's Movement in Palestine," 87–114.

38. Bernstein, *The Struggle for Equality*, 2, 155.

39. Bernstein, *Pioneers and Homemakers*, 2, 8, 9.

40. Yuval-Davis, "The Jewish Collectivity;" *Israeli Women and Men;* and *Woman-Nation-State.*

41. Young, *Keepers of the History*, 4–18, 155–57.

42. Sharoni, *Gender and the Israeli-Palestinian Conflict*, 9–10, 150–52.

43. Deniz Kandiyoti, "Contemporary Feminist Scholarship and Middle East Studies," *Gendering the Middle East*, 17.

Chapter 3. Historicizing Narratives I

1. Doumani analyzed this aspect of Palestinian historiography in his article "Rediscovering Ottoman Palestine," in Pappe, *The Israel/Palestine Question*, 30.

2. Doumani, *Rediscovering Palestine*, 5.

3. Shafir, *Land, Labor*, 23–40.

4. Alexander Scholch, "European Penetration and the Economic Development of Palestine, 1856–1882," in Owen, *Studies in the Economic and Social History of Palestine*, 10–87.

5. Kimmerling and Migdal, *Palestinians*, 7.

6. Greenstein, *Genealogies of Conflict*, 76–87.

7. Butrus Abu-Mannah, "The Rise of the Sanjak of Jerusalem in the Late Nineteenth Century," in Pappe, *The Israel/Palestine Question*, 46.

8. Bishara Doumani, "Rediscovering Ottoman Palestine," in Pappe, *The Israel/Palestine Question*, 16.

9. For a detailed discussion of these changes see Greenstein, *Genealogies of Conflict*, 75–80.

10. Muslih, *Origins*, 1, 223.

11. Idinopulos, *Weathered by Miracles*, 123.

12. For detailed discussion of changes in land laws and their repercussions see Stein, *The Land Question.*

13. Doumani, "Rediscovering Ottoman Palestine," in Pappe, *The Israel/Palestine Question*, 18.

14. Tessler, *A History*, 56–57.

15. Greenstein, *Genealogies of Conflict*, 34.

16. Divine, *Politics and Society*, 1–5.

17. Hourani, *Arabic Thought*, 39.

18. Ibid., 40.

19. Ben-Sasson, *A History*, 915.

20. Ibid.

21. Ibid., 916.

22. Sicker, *Reshaping Palestine*, 4.

23. Hourani, *Arabic Thought*, 53.

24. Kimmerling and Migdal, *Palestinians*, 8–9.

25. Tessler, *A History*, 57–58.

26. Kimmerling and Migdal, *Palestinians*, 20.

27. Ben-Sasson, *A History*, 917.

28. Tessler, *A History*, 59.

29. Ben-Sasson, *A History*, 850. The alliance formed in reaction to the 1858 Edgardo Mortara affair, in which the Vatican kidnapped an Italian Jewish six-year-old boy to raise as a Catholic. The alliance aimed to defend Jews against attacks around the world.

30. Tessler, *A History*, 59.

31. Ben-Sasson, *A History*, 893.

32. BILU manifesto in Laqueur and Rubin, *The Israel-Arab Reader*, 3–4.

33. For analysis of six stages of Zionist settlement see Shafir, "Zionism and Colonialism," in Pappe, *The Israel/Palestine Question*, 81–96.

34. Tessler, *A History*, 60.

35. "The Jewish State," in Laqueur and Rubin, *The Israel-Arab Reader*, 6–11.

36. "Zionist Congress, Basle," in Laqueur and Rubin, *The Israel-Arab Reader*, 11–12.

37. Tessler, *A History*, 53–54.

38. Reference to Ahad Ha'am's 1891 article in Greenstein, *Genealogies of Conflict*, 42.

39. Reference to Ahad Ha'am's 1891 article in Lockman, *Comrades and Enemies*, 36.

40. Reference to "The Jewish State and the Jewish Problem," in Tessler, *A History*, 48.

41. Ibid., 55.

42. Ben-Sasson, *A History*, 898–905.

43. Ibid., 906.

44. Shafir, "Zionism and Colonialism," in Pappe, *The Israel/Palestine Question*, 81–96.

45. For information about the split labor market in Palestine see Shafir, *Land, Labor*, and Bernstein, *Constructing Boundaries*.

46. Syrkin, "The Jewish Problem and the Socialist-Jewish State," in Hertzberg, *The Zionist Idea*, 333–50.

47. Ber Borochov (1881–1917), "The National Question and the Class Struggle," in Hertzberg, *The Zionist Idea*, 355–60.

48. Gordon, "Logic for the Future," and "People and Labor," in Hertzberg, *The Zionist Idea*, 371–74.

49. Ben-Sasson, *A History*, 921–24.

50. Tessler, *A History*, 135–37.

51. Greenstein, *Genealogies of Conflict*, 74–75.

52. Kimmerling and Migdal, *Palestinians*, 70–71.

53. Ibid., 72.

54. Ibid., 45.

55. Ibid., 46.

56. Ibid., 25–26.

57. *Le Réveil,* excerpt from Laqueur and Rubin, *The Israel-Arab Reader,* 5; discussion in Hourani, *Arabic Thought,* 277–79.

58. Tessler, *A History,* 131–32.

59. Yaacov Roi, "The Zionist Attitude to the Arabs, 1908–1914," in Kedourie and Haim, *Palestine and Israel,* 44.

60. Kimmerling and Migdal, *Palestinians,* 71.

61. Mandel, *The Arabs and Zionism,* 37.

62. Greenstein, *Genealogies,* 38–39.

63. Tessler, *A History,* 127.

64. Sternhell, *Founding Myths,* 44.

65. Tessler, *A History,* 127.

66. Mandel, *The Arabs and Zionism.*

67. Idinopulos, *Weathered by Miracles,* 137.

68. Tessler, *A History,* 128–29.

69. Ibid., 126.

70. Hourani, *A History,* 309.

71. Divine, *Politics and Society,* 145–49.

72. Ibid., 158.

73. Tessler, *A History,* 126.

74. Hourani, *Arabic Thought,* 283.

75. Ibid., 286.

76. Greenstein, *Genealogies of Conflict,* 76–87.

77. Kimmerling and Migdal, *Palestinians,* 26–27.

78. Tessler, *A History,* 126.

79. Ben-Sasson, *A History,* 926.

80. "The McMahon Letter," in Laqueur and Rubin, *The Israel-Arab Reader,* 15–17.

81. "The Balfour Declaration," in Laqueur and Rubin, *The Israel-Arab Reader,* 17–18.

82. "Sykes-Picot Agreement," in Laqueur and Rubin, *The Israel-Arab Reader,* 12–15.

83. Greenstein, *Genealogies of Conflict,* 89.

84. Tessler, *A History,* 155.

85. Greenstein, *Genealogies of Conflict,* 202.

86. Tessler, *A History,* 218–19.

87. Mogannam, *The Arab Woman,* 116.

88. Tessler, *A History,* 155.

89. Muslih, *Origins,* 91, 174, 177.

90. Mogannam, *The Arab Woman,* 127.

91. Tessler, *A History,* 222.

Chapter 4. Historicizing Narratives II

1. "The British Mandate," in Laqueur and Rubin, *The Israel-Arab Reader,* 34–42.

2. Greenstein, *Genealogies of Conflict,* 230.

3. Divine, *Politics and Society,* 193.

4. Wasserstein, *The British in Palestine,* 10–17.

5. "The Churchill White Paper—1922," in Laqueur and Rubin, *The Israel-Arab Reader,* 45–50.

6. Tessler, *A History,* 185–89.

7. Myers, *Re-inventing the Jewish Past,* 6.

8. Tessler, *A History,* 195–204.

9. Ibid., 210–12.

10. Ibid., 214–18.

11. Porath, *Palestinian-Arab National Movement,* 1:74.

12. Tessler, *A History,* 223–25.

13. For detailed studies of land issues see Stein, *The Land Question,* and Granott, *The Land System.*

14. Granott, *The Land System,* 41, 80–82, 221–27; Stein, *The Land Question,* 14–15, 34.

15. Porath, *Palestinian-Arab National Movement,* vol.2, 80–108.

16. Ruedy, "Dynamics of Land Alienation," in Abu-Lughod, *Transformation of Palestine,* 119–38.

17. Greenstein, *Genealogies of Conflict,* 142, 223.

18. Ibid., 136.

19. Tessler, *A History,* 228.

20. On the revolt see Kimmerling and Migdal, *Palestinians,* 96–123; Porath, *Palestinian-Arab National Movement,* chs.6–9; 'Abd al-Wahab Kayyali, *Palestine,* 155–227.

21. "From the Report of the Palestine Royal Commission (Peel Commission, 1937)," in Laqueur and Rubin, *The Israel-Arab Reader,* 56–58.

22. Kimmerling and Migdal, *Palestinians,* 114–22.

23. Ibid., 96.

24. Ibid., 97.

25. Ibid., 123.

26. "The White Paper of 1939," in Laqueur and Rubin, *The Israel-Arab Reader,* 64–75.

27. "The Zionist Reaction to the White Paper," in Laqueur and Rubin, *The Israel-Arab Reader,* 76–77.

28. Sachar, *Modern Jewish History,* 460.

29. "Declaration Adopted by the Extraordinary Zionist Conference," in Laqueur and Rubin, *The Israel-Arab Reader,* 77–79.

30. Kimmerling and Migdal, *Palestinians,* 133–34.

31. Khalaf examines the persistence of factionalism, the "vertical cleavages" in Palestinian agrarian society, the impact of the development of the working class, and the roles of the urban notables in nationalist development of this decade. Khalaf, *Politics in Palestine,* 1–5.

32. Smith, *Palestine,* 122–23.

33. Kimmerling and Migdal, *Palestinians,* 137.

34. Morris, *Palestinian Refugee Problem,* 45–46.

35. Glazier, "The Palestinian Exodus in 1948," *Journal of Palestine Studies* 9 (Summer 1980): 104, claims the lower figure and Morris, *Palestinian Refugee Problem,* 30, claims the higher figure.

36. Kimmerling and Migdal, *Palestinians,* 143–44.

37. Morris, *Palestinian Refugee Problem,* 62–64, 73–95.

38. Rashid Khalidi, *Palestinian Identity,* 193.

Chapter 5. Politicizing Masculinities

1. See, for example, Jayawardena, *Feminism and Nationalism,* and Ahmed, *Women and Gender,* part 3: "New Discourses," 125–234.

2. See Ahmed, "Early Feminist Movements in the Middle East," in Frida Hussain, *Muslim Women,* 118.

3. Amin, *Tahrir al-Mar'a* (The Liberation of Woman); and *al-Mar'a al-Jadida* (The New Woman).

4. 'Abd al-Rahim Mahmud (1913–1948) came from a small village near Nablus named 'Anabta. This line is from a poem in Rashid, *al-Kalimah al-Muqatilah,* 15.

5. *Tomorrow Is a Wonderful Day* (1952), film directed by Helmar Lerski and produced by Hadassah, about young Jewish refugees coming to Palestine after the Holocaust.

6. Hazelton, *Israeli Women,* 94.

7. Gonen, *A Psycho-History,* 14.

8. Max Nordau, "Jewry of Muscle," in Reinharz and Mendes-Flohr, *Jew in the Modern World,* 434–35.

9. Golda Meir, *My Life,* 88, 113–46.

10. Ahad Ha'am, "Moses," 1904, *Selected Essays,* 306–29.

11. Peretz Smolenskin (1842–1885) was a Russian-born writer. The quotation is from "A Time to Plant," in *Ha-Toeh Be-Derech Ha-Hayim,* an essay written in response to the 1881 pogroms, in Hertzberg, *The Zionist Idea,* 145.

12. For a discussion of some of the problems of gender in Herzl's writings, see Michael Berkowitz, "Transcending 'Tzimmes and Sweetness,'" 8–9.

13. Louis Dembitz Brandeis (1856–1941, appointed to the U.S. Supreme Court by President Woodrow Wilson in 1916) had "converted" to Zionism in 1912. Excerpts are from "The Jewish Problem and How to Solve It," *Brandeis on Zionism,* 25.

14. 'Abd al-Rahman 'Azzam became the secretary of the League of Arab States, where he continued to work on behalf of Arab unity. Excerpt is from "Arab League and World Unity," in Haim, *Arab Nationalism,* 159.

15. Abdullah al-Alayili, *"Dustur al-'Arab al-Qawmi,"* in Haim, *Arab National-ism,* 127.

16. Moses Hess, *Rom und Jerusalem* (1862), in Hertzberg, *The Zionist Idea,* 131.

17. Bentwich, *Palestine,* 60.

18. Emma Lazarus, "Banner of the Jews" (1882), in Friedman, *The Rise of Israel,* vol.1, 34.

19. Translated in Sulaiman, *Modern Arab Poetry,* 20.

20. 'Ajaj Nuwiyhid, *"Kul shabab,"* in *Filastin al-Damiyyah,* 107.

21. Theodor Herzl (1860–1904) was born in Budapest and was a writer in Vienna. Excerpt is from *The Jewish State,* preface and 72.

22. Herzl excerpt from *The Jewish State,* in Hertzberg, *The Zionist Idea,* 225.

23. 'Alush, *al-Muqawamah al-'Arabiyya,* 109.

24. Leon Pinsker (1821–1891). Excerpt is from "Auto-Emancipation," in Fried-man, *Rise of Israel,* vol. 1, 169.

25. Ibid., 167.

26. Bernard Lazare (1865–1903) was a French Zionist. Excerpt is from "Jewish Nationalism and Emancipation, 1897–1899," in Hertzberg, *The Zionist Idea,* 475.

27. Ishaq Musa al-Husayni, *Mudhakkirat Dajajah* (Recollections of a Hen). Al-Husayni was an educator in Jerusalem. Jayyusi remarked that this work gained im-mediate fame in the Arab world and was the "first work of contemporary fiction to benefit from the Arab traditional literary heritage." See *Anthology,* 13, and discus-sion in Abu-Ghazaleh, *Arab Cultural Nationalism,* 65.

28. Benedict Anderson, in *Imagined Communities,* postulated nationalism as a set of created cultural artifacts and asked, "[W]hy are people ready to die for these inventions," observing that "colossal numbers [of people have been] persuaded to lay down their lives" for "the idea of the ultimate sacrifice." Anderson found an-swers in language, the capitalist press, race, and class but overlooked gender.

29. Khalah, *Filastin wa'l-Intidab al-Britani,* 14.

30. Ibrahim Tuqan, "Al-Shahid," in al-Sawafiri, *al-Shir al-'Arabi,* 225.

31. See discussion of his work in Jayyusi, *Anthology of Modern Palestinian Lit-erature,* 9.

32. "Al-Shahid," in Sulaiman, *Palestine,* 32.

33. Myers, *Re-inventing the Jewish Past,* 179.

34. Rabbi Zvi Hirsch Kalischer (1795–1874) was born in Poland. Excerpt is from "Derishat Tzion" (1862), in Hertzberg, *The Zionist Idea,* 114.

35. Norman Bentwich, *Palestine,* 5.

36. Abu Salma, translated in Jayyusi, *Modern Arabic Poetry,* 298–99.

37. Diqs, *A Bedouin Boyhood,* 78.

38. Michel Aflaq, "Nationalism and Revolution" (1940), in Haim, *Arab Nation-alism,* 248.

Chapter 6. Feminizing Lands

1. "Al-Nafa'is al-'Asriyya," in Sulaiman, *Palestine,* 8–9.

2. Sulaiman, *Palestine*, 21.

3. Davida Wood described how funerals for martyrs become enacted as weddings: "The wedding becomes at once a celebration of national identity and the ritual bestowal of personhood on the young [male] martyr. In this way the construction of (im)mortality in Palestinian social life is recast as national vitality" ("The Boundless Courtyard," 151).

4. Iskandar al-Khuri al-Baytjali (1920s), in Sulaiman, *Palestine*, 19.

5. 'Ajaj Nuwiyhid, "Kul Shabab," in *Filastin al-Damiyyah*, 107.

6. Abu Salma (1911–1981). Excerpt is from Jayyusi, *Trends and Movements*, vol. 1, 300. For further discussion see Sulaiman, *Palestine*, 157.

7. Ibrahim Tuqan (1905–1941). Excerpt is from Jayyusi, *Trends and Movements*, 294.

8. Jayyusi, *Trends and Movements*, 290.

9. al-'Arif, *Bedouin Love*.

10. Fawaz Turki, "Meaning in Palestinian History," 374.

11. Ginat, *Women in Muslim Rural Society*, 177.

12. Pinsker, "Auto-Emancipation," in Hertzberg, *The Zionist Idea*, 187.

13. Elon, *The Israelis*, 142–43.

14. A. D. Gordon (1856–1922) was born in Russia and emigrated to Palestine in 1904, where he articulated the ideology of redemption through physical labor on the land. Excerpt is from "Some Observations" (1911), in Hertzberg, *The Zionist Idea*, 375.

15. Gordon, "Our Tasks Ahead" (1920), in Hertzberg, *The Zionist Idea*, 382.

16. In anticipation of receiving the commandments from God at Mount Sinai, Moses spoke to the "people" but actually addressed himself to the men to warn them: "And he said to the people, 'Be ready for the third day; do not go near a woman.'" (Exodus 19:15). See also Plaskow's interpretation of the significance for women of this Biblical event in *Standing Again at Sinai*, 25–28.

17. Edmond Fleg, born in 1874 in Switzerland and raised in France, became a Zionist after the Dreyfus affair. Excerpt is from "Pourquoi je suis Juif," Paris, 1927, in Hertzberg, *The Zionist Idea*, 483.

18. Buber, "An Open Letter to Mahatma Gandhi," *Israel and the World*, 253.

19. Ibid., 233.

20. Koestler, *Thieves in the Night*, 356.

21. Sulaiman discusses blood and pagan images in nationalist poetry, *Palestine*, 75.

22. Sulayman al-Taji al-Faruqi (1912), in Sulaiman, *Palestine*, 11.

23. Abu Salma, "Filastin," in al-Sawafiri, *al-Shir al-'Arabi*, 222.

24. Ilyas Farhat (1891–1976, Lebanon), in Sulaiman, *Palestine*, 72.

25. 'Umar Abu Risha (born 1908, Egypt), in Sulaiman, *Palestine*, 75.

26. Ahmad Muharram, in Sulaiman, *Palestine*, 75.

27. 'Ali Mahmud Taha, "Nida' al-Fida'," in Sulaiman, *Palestine*, 63.

28. Muhammad Mahdi Al-Jawahiri, in Sulaiman, *Palestine*, 65.

29. Rashid, "To the Martyr," in al-Sawafiri, *Al-Shir al- 'Arabi*, 455.

30. Tuqan, in Jayyusi, *Trends and Movements*, vol. 1, 286.

31. Ahmad Makhrum, in Rashid, *Al-Kalimah al-Muqatilah*, 127.

32. Max Nordau, "Zionism" (1902), in Hertzberg, *The Zionist Idea*, 244.

33. Ber Borochov, "The National Question and the Class Struggle" (1905), in Hertzberg, *The Zionist Idea*, 352–59.

34. A. D. Gordon, "Logic for the Future" (1910), in Hertzberg, *The Zionist Idea*, 371.

35. Ibid., "People and Labor" (1911), in Hertzberg, *The Zionist Idea*, 374.

36. *Sabra* (1933), film directed by Alexander Ford, a Tzabar production.

37. Revusky, *Jews in Palestine*, 269.

Chapter 7. Imagining Women

1. Khalah, *Filastin wa'l-Intidab al-Britani*, 12.

2. al-Ghuri, *Filastin 'abra sittina 'aman*.

3. al-'Arif, *al-Nakbah*.

4. Alkalai in Hertzberg, *The Zionist Idea*, 103–4.

5. Lilienblum in Hertzberg, *The Zionist Idea*, 167.

6. Ahad Ha'am in Hertzberg, *The Zionist Idea*, 250.

7. Hertzberg, *The Zionist Idea*, 201.

8. Alex Bein's biographical preface to Theodor Herzl, *The Jewish State*, 23.

9. Marvin Lowenthal's biographical preface to *The Diaries of Theodor Herzl*, xiv.

10. Herzl, *Altneuland*, 24.

11. Ibid., 74.

12. Ibid., 75.

13. Ibid., 76.

14. Ibid., 77.

15. Trager, *Pioneers in Palestine*, 207.

16. Katz, *The Lady Was a Terrorist*, 140.

17. For elaboration of the significance of this shift from subject to citizen, see Schama, *Citizens*, 858–59.

18. Amin, *Tahrir al-Mar'a;* and *al-Mar'a al-Jadida*.

19. Sabri, *Qawli fi al-Mar'a*, 9.

20. Himadeh Sa'id, *al-Nidham al-Iqtisadi fi Filastin*, 110.

21. Ahmad Husayn, *al-Zawaj wal-Mar'a*, 25–27, 84, 92.

22. al-Khuli, *al-Mar'a bayna al-Bayt wal-Mujtama'*, 43, 51, 151.

23. Sarna referred to the Pittsburgh Platform of 1918 as a kind of "sacred agenda." See Sarna, "Louis D. Brandeis," 26–27.

24. Revusky, *Jews in Palestine*, 131.

25. For a refutation of the myth of equality in the early settlements see Fogiel-Bijaoui, "From Revolution to Motherhood," and "On the Way to Equality?" in Bernstein, *Pioneers and Homemakers*, 211–34, 261–82.

Chapter 8. Civilizing Women

1. Jacob Klatzkin (1882–1948), born in Russia, was trained as a rabbinic scholar but embraced secular culture, philosophy, and Zionism when studying in Western Europe. "Boundaries" (1914–1921), in Hertzberg, *The Zionist Idea*, 327.

2. Charles Beard, introduction to Bury, *The Idea of Progress*, xxxi.

3. Jamal al-Din al-Afghani, translated in Patai, *The Arab Mind*, 270–75.

4. Qustantin Zurayq and Musa al-'Alami, translated in Abu-Ghazaleh, *Arab Cultural Nationalism*, 159.

5. Furlonge, *Palestine Is My Country*, 3–4.

6. Herzl, *Altneuland*, 45–46.

7. Ibid., 112.

8. Revusky, *Jews in Palestine*, 179.

9. Ibid.

10. Michel Aflaq, "*Fi Sabil al-Ba'th*" (Toward the Ba'th), in Haim, *Arab Nationalism*, 240.

11. Tibawi, *Arab Education*, 16.

12. Miller, *Rural Palestine*, 106.

13. An interview with Antoinette Khoury, in Stern, *Daughters from Afar*, 35.

14. Mansour, *Waiting for the Dawn*, 15.

15. Ibid., 10.

16. Ibid., 19–20.

17. Trager, *Pioneers in Palestine*, 195.

18. Ibid., 31.

19. Ibid., 195.

20. Ibid., 196.

21. Berkowitz, "*Tzimmes*," 21.

22. Loeb, *Palestine Awake*, 115.

23. Ibid., 180.

24. Ibid., 188–89.

25. Bentwich, *Palestine*, 199.

26. Berkowitz, "*Tzimmes*," 21.

27. Bar-David, *Women in Israel*, 33.

28. Ibid., 95.

29. Katz, *The Lady Was a Terrorist*, 99–100.

30. Mordecai Kaplan (born in 1881 in Lithuania and raised in United States), *The Future of the American Jew*, 129.

Chapter 9. Educating Girls

1. This chapter was originally presented as a paper for the World Union of Jewish Studies Conference, Jerusalem, 1997.

2. Jayawardena, *Feminism and Nationalism*, 12.

3. Anderson, *Imagined Communities*, 74–79.

4. Ahmed, "Early Feminist Movements in the Middle East," 114, 116–18.

5. Woodsmall, *Moslem Women*, 187.

6. Tibawi, *Arab Education*, 20.

7. Woodsmall, *Moslem Women*, 187.

8. Tibawi, *Arab Education*, 24.

9. Ibid., 34–35.

10. Ibid., 43–47.

11. Miller, "From Village to Nation," 186, 103, 104; and Tibawi, *Arab Education*, 52.

12. Miller, *Rural Palestine*, 106.

13. Woodsmall, *Moslem Women*, 188.

14. Miller, *Rural Palestine*, 64.

15. Tibawi, *Arab Education*, 229.

16. Woodsmall, *Moslem Women*, 188.

17. Miller, *Rural Palestine*, 62.

18. Ibid., 103.

19. Tibawi, *Arab Education*, 108.

20. Miller, *Rural Palestine*, 104.

21. Woodsmall, *Moslem Women*, 189.

22. Miller, *Rural Palestine*, 103.

23. Tibawi, *Arab Education*, 228–29.

24. Beth Baron, "The Making and Breaking of Marital Bonds in Modern Egypt," in Keddie and Baron, *Women in Middle Eastern History*, 275–91.

25. Cole, "Feminism, Class, and Islam," 387–407.

26. al-Bindari, *al-Mar'a wa-Markazuha al-Ijtima'i fi al-dawlah*.

27. Sabri, *Qawli fi al-Mar'a*, 23.

28. Miller, *Rural Palestine*, 317.

29. Ibid., 65.

30. Nardi, *Education in Palestine*, 83.

31. Ibid., 22.

32. Ibid., 153.

33. Ibid., 199.

34. Lesch, *Arab Politics in Palestine*, 57.

35. Nardi, *Education in Palestine*, 58.

36. Bentwich, *Mandate Memoirs*, 254.

37. For the difficulties women had in finding training outside of traditional roles, see writings of immigrant women in Katzenelson-Rubashow, *The Plough Woman;* and Dafna Izraeli, "The Women Workers' Movement: First Wave Feminism in Pre-State Israel," in Bernstein, *Pioneers and Homemakers*, 183–210.

38. Nardi, *Education in Palestine*, 89–90.

39. On differences between European and Yemenite women, for example, see Nitza Druyan, "Yemenite Jewish Women—Between Tradition and Change," in Bernstein, *Pioneers and Homemakers*, 75–93.

40. Nardi, *Education in Palestine,* 173.

41. A. Fierst, *"Dvar Hapoelet,"* 152.

42. Nardi, *Education in Palestine,* 175.

43. Ibid., 88.

44. Ibid., 80.

45. Ibid., 174.

46. Ibid., 175.

47. Ibid., 176.

48. Miller, *Rural Palestine,* 102.

Chapter 10. Essentializing Difference

1. For a discussion of the justification of racism and sexism with Victorian science, see Russett, *Sexual Science,* 181–206.

2. *Sabra* (1933), film directed by Alexander Ford and produced by Tzabar. The movie was banned by the British as propagandist, leftist, anti-Arab, and dangerous.

3. Syrkin, *Golda Meir,* 125.

4. Koestler, *Thieves in the Night,* 37.

5. *Hill 24 Doesn't Answer* (1955), film by Thorold Dickinson.

6. For histories of Jews in the Middle East, see Stillman, *Jews of Arab Lands,* and Lewis, *The Jews of Islam.*

7. Usufruct rights meant that even though peasants didn't own their land, they had a right to work the land, as did their children and children's children.

8. Muslih, *The Origins of Palestinian Nationalism,* 70, 78, 80.

9. Mattar, *The Mufti of Jerusalem,* 24.

10. Sulaiman, *Palestine,* 25.

11. Trager, *Pioneers in Palestine,* 106–7.

12. Jbara, *Hajj Amin al-Husayni,* 144.

13. Katz, *The Lady Was a Terrorist,* 12–13.

14. See, for example, Smilansky, *Palestine Caravan.*

15. Walter Laqueur, *A History,* 241.

16. al-Barudi, *Karitha Filastin,* 11, 54.

17. Ajlal, *al-Mar'a wa-Qadiyyat Filastin,* 9–11.

18. Mrs. Shukri Deeb, a Palestinian woman, spoke at the Arab Women's Conference in Egypt in December 1944, as noted in *al-Mu'tamar al-Nisa'i al-'Arabi,* 16.

Chapter 11. Challenging Patriarchy

1. Divine, *Politics and Society,* 6.

2. Ibid., 7.

3. Graham-Brown, *Palestinians,* 80; Kazi, "Palestinian Women," 26.

4. Graham-Brown, *Palestinians,* 152.

5. Schipper, *Unheard Words,* 75.

6. Bernstein, *Pioneers and Homemakers,* 4.

7. Trager, *Pioneers in Palestine,* 65.

8. Ibid., 68.

9. Ibid., 70.

10. Ibid., 69.

11. Berkowitz, "*Tzimmes,*" 10.

12. Deborah Bernstein, *Pioneers and Homemakers,* 5.

13. Yanait Ben-Tzvi, *Before Golda, Manya Shohat,* 168.

14. Ibid., 172.

15. Bar-David, *Women in Israel,* 75.

16. Bernstein, *The Struggle for Equality,* 21.

17. Rachel Yanait, in Katzenelson-Rubashow, *The Plough Woman,* 137.

18. Bar-David, *Women in Israel,* 71.

19. Mogannam, *The Arab Woman and the Palestine Problem,* 67.

20. Kazi, "Palestinian Women," 27.

21. Divine, *Politics and Society,* 6–8.

22. Ibid., 210.

23. Schipper, *Unheard Words,* 76.

24. Ajlal, *Al-Mar'a wa-Qadiyyat Filastin,* 24–26.

25. Ibid., 38.

26. Kazi, "Palestinian Women," 26–28.

27. Bar-David, *Women in Israel,* 71.

28. Bernstein, *Pioneers and Homemakers,* 6.

29. Revusky, *Jews in Palestine,* 248–49.

30. On women's farms, see Margalit Shilo, "The Women's Farm at Kinneret," in Bernstein, *Pioneers and Homemakers,* 119–44.

31. Miriam Schlinowitch, in Katzenelson-Rubashow, *The Plough Woman,* 159–62; Golda Meir's words are taken from her autobiography, *My Life,* 88.

32. Bernstein, *The Struggle for Equality,* 48.

33. Ibid., *Pioneers and Homemakers,* 6.

34. Revusky, *Jews in Palestine,* 245.

35. Bernstein, *The Struggle for Equality,* 77–82.

36. For a critique of gender roles on kibbutzim see Safir, "Kibbutz: An Experiment," 100–29.

37. For a discussion of these distinctions, see Ridd and Callaway, *Caught up in Conflict,* 17.

38. Dafna Izraeli, "The Zionist Women's Movement," 4.

39. Bernstein, *Pioneers and Homemakers,* 6–7.

40. Lesch, *Arab Politics in Palestine,* 63.

41. Kazi, "Palestinian Women," 26–28.

42. *Filastin,* August 13, 1938.

43. Ibid., February 16, 1939.

44. Ibid., March 26, 1939.

45. Ibid., February 1, 1939.

46. Ajlal, *Al-Mar'a wa-Qadiyyat Filastin,* 79.

47. Mogannam, *The Arab Woman and the Palestine Problem*, 19.

48. Ibid., 20–24.

49. Ibid., 50–55.

50. *Al-Difa'*, November 12, 1943.

51. Ibid., November 16, 1943.

52. *Al-mu'tamar al-Nisa'i al-'Arabi* (Arab Women's Conference), 17–27.

53. Kazi, "Palestinian Women," 27–28.

Chapter 12. Sacrificing Sisters

1. Lorde, *Sister Outsider*, 119.

2. From my own conversations (1975–80) with older Palestinians who came of age before 1948 in Jerusalem, Haifa, Shefar'am, and Nazareth.

3. Mansour, *Waiting for the Dawn*, 9.

4. For analysis of this kind of unacknowledged information exchange in which colonizers depend on the colonized for knowledge and help, see Francis Jennings, *The Invasion of America*.

5. Zipporah Seid, in Katzenelson-Rubashow, *The Plough Woman*, 43.

6. Shifra Betzer, in Katzenelson-Rubashow, *The Plough Woman*, 31–32, mistakenly conflates Kurdish with Arab culture.

7. Trager, *Pioneers in Palestine*, 9.

8. Ibid., 105.

9. Yanait Ben-Tzvi, *Before Golda, Manya Shohat*, 90.

10. Trager, *Pioneers in Palestine*, 15–17.

11. Bernstein, *Struggle for Equality*, 118.

12. Yanait Ben-Tzvi, *Before Golda, Manya Shohat*, 126.

13. Furlonge, *Musa 'Alami*, 6.

14. Malchah, in Katzenelson-Rubashow, *The Plough Woman*, 121–23.

15. Magnes, *Episodes*, 27–39.

16. Ibid., 78, 95, 100.

17. Yanait Ben-Tzvi, *Before Golda, Manya Shohat*, 128–31.

18. Dash, *Summoned to Jerusalem*, 81.

19. Ibid., 171.

20. Ibid., 297.

21. Sternhell, *The Founding Myths of Israel*, 3–4.

22. Nardi, *Education in Palestine*, 58.

23. Gilligan, *The Birth of Pleasure*, 4. For a discussion about the tension between democracy and patriarchy, see 3–5, 207–8.

24. Kass and O'Neill, *The Deadly Embrace*, 313.

Bibliography

Abdo, Nahla. "Nationalism and Feminism: Palestinian Women and the Intifada—No Going Back?" in Valentine M. Moghadam, ed. *Gender and National Identity*. London: Zed, 1994.

Abu-Ghazaleh, Adnan M. *Arab Cultural Nationalism in Palestine during the British Mandate*. Beirut: Institute for Palestine Studies, 1973.

Abu-Lughod, Ibrahim, ed. *The Transformation of Palestine: Essays on the Origin and Development of the Arab-Israeli Conflict*. Evanston, Ill.: Northwestern University Press, 1971.

Accad, Evelyn. *Sexuality and War: Literary Masks of the Middle East*. New York: New York University Press, 1990.

Ahad Ha'am. *Essays, Letters, Memoirs*. Oxford: East and West Library, 1946.

———. *Selected Essays*. Philadelphia: The Jewish Publication Study of America, 1912.

Ahmed, Leila. "Early Feminist Movements in the Middle East: Turkey and Egypt," in Frida Hussain, ed. *Muslim Women*. London: Croom Helm, 1984.

———. "Western Ethnocentrism and Perceptions of the Harem," *Feminist Studies* 8, no. 3 (Fall 1982): 521–34.

———. *Women and Gender in Middle East History*. New Haven: Yale University Press, 1992.

Alcoff, Linda. "Cultural Feminism versus Post-Structuralism: The Identity Crisis in Feminist Theory," in *Constructing the Academy: Women's Education and Women's Studies*. Chicago: University of Chicago Press, 1988.

'Alush, Naji. *Al-Muqawamah al-'Arabiyya fi Filastin 1914–1948* (The Arab Resistance in Palestine 1914–1948). Beirut: PLO Research Center, 1967.

Amin, Qassim. *Al-Mar'a al-Jadida* (The New Woman). Cairo: J.M.A. Sina, 1987.

———. *Tahrir al-Mar'a* (The Liberation of Woman). Cairo: Maktabat al-Taraqi, 1899.

Anderson, Benedict. *Imagined Communities*. London: Verso Editions, 1983.

al-'Arif, 'Arif. *Bedouin Love, Law and Legend: Dealing Exclusively with the Badu of Beersheba*, trans. by H. Tilley. Jerusalem: Cosmos Publishing, 1944.

———. *Al-Nakbah* (The Disaster). Beirut: The Modern Library, 1952.

Augustin, Ebba, ed. *Palestinian Women: Identity and Experience*. London: Zed, 1993.

Bar-David, Molly Lyons. *Women in Israel*. New York: Hadassah Education Department, 1952.

al-Barudi, Fakhri. *Karitha Filastin* (Palestine Disaster). Damascus: Ibn Zaydun Press, 1950.

Ben-Sasson, H. H. *A History of the Jewish People*. Cambridge: Harvard University Press, 1976.

Bentwich, Norman. *Palestine*. London: Ernst Benn, 1934.

Bentwich, Norman, and Helen Bentwich. *Mandate Memoirs, 1918–1948*. New York: Schocken Books, 1965.

Berkowitz, Michael. *Zionist Culture and West European Jewry before World War One*. Cambridge: Cambridge University Press, 1993.

———. "Transcending 'Tzimmes and Sweetness': Recovering the History of Zionist Women in Central and Western Europe, 1897–1933." Unpublished paper presented to the Jewish Feminist Research Group, University of Southern California, 1991.

Bernstein, Deborah. *Constructing Boundaries: Jewish and Arab Workers in Mandatory Palestine*. Albany: State University of New York Press, 2000.

———. *The Struggle for Equality: Urban Women Workers in Pre-State Israeli Society*. New York: Praeger, 1987.

———, ed. *Pioneers and Homemakers: Jewish Women in Pre-State Israel*. New York: State University of New York Press, 1992.

al-Bindari, Muhammad. *Al-Mar'a wa-Markazuha al-Ijtima'i fi al-Dawlah* (Woman and Her Social Status in the State). Cairo: n.p., 194-.

Borochov, Ber. *Nationalism and Class Struggle*. Westport, Conn.: Greenwood Press, 1972.

Boyarin, Jonathan. *Palestinian and Jewish History: Criticism at the Borders of Ethnography*. Minneapolis: University of Minnesota Press, 1996.

Brandeis, Louis Dembitz. "The Jewish Problem and How to Solve It," in *Brandeis on Zionism*. Washington, D.C.: Zionist Organization of America, 1942.

Bridenthal, Renate. "The Dialectics of Production and Reproduction in History," *Radical America* 10 (1976): 3–11.

Buber, Martin. *A Land of Two Peoples*, ed. by Paul M. Flohr. New York: Oxford University Press, 1983.

———. *Israel and the World: Essays in a Time of Crisis*. New York: Schocken Books, 1948.

Bury, J. B. *The Idea of Progress: An Inquiry into Its Origin and Growth*. New York: Macmillan, 1932.

Canaan, Taufik. "Unwritten Laws Affecting the Arab Women of Palestine," *Journal of the Palestine Oriental Society* 11 (1931): 172–203.

Cockburn, Cynthia. *The Space between Us: Negotiating Gender and National Identities in Conflict*. London: Zed, 1998.

Cohen, Geula. *Woman of Violence: 1943–1948*, trans. by Hillel Halkin. New York: Holt Rinehart Winston, 1966.

Cole, Juan R. "Feminism, Class, and Islam in Turn-of-the-Century Egypt," *IJMES* 13 (1981): 387–407.

"Collection of Official Documents Relating to the Palestine Question, 1917–1947," submitted to the General Assembly of the United Nations. New York: Arab Higher Committee, 1947.

Cooke, Miriam. *War's Other Voices: Women Writers in the Lebanese Civil War.* Cambridge: Cambridge University Press, 1988.

Dash, Joan. *Summoned to Jerusalem: The Life of Henrietta Szold.* New York: Harper and Row, 1979.

Davin, Anna. "Imperialism and Motherhood," *History Workshop* 5 (1978): 9–66.

Davis, Natalie Zemont. "Women's History in Transition: The European Case," *Feminist Studies* 3 (1975–1976): 90.

Al-Difa' (The Defense), Jerusalem daily (November 12, 1943; November 16, 1943; January 3, 1944).

al-Din, Lamya' Baha'. "For the Girl of Today," *Al-Difa'a* (January 3, 1944).

Diqs, Isaak. *A Bedouin Boyhood.* New York: Praeger, 1969.

Divine, Donna Robinson. *Politics and Society in Ottoman Palestine: The Arab Struggle for Survival and Power.* Boulder, Colo.: Lynne Reinner Publisher, 1994.

Doumani, Beshara. *Rediscovering Palestine: Merchants and Peasants in Jabal Nablus, 1700–1900.* Berkeley: University of California Press, 1995.

Elon, Amos. *The Israelis: Founders and Sons.* New York: Penguin Books, 1971.

Enloe, Cynthia. *Bananas, Beaches and Bases: Making Feminist Sense of International Politics.* Berkeley: University of California Press, 1990.

Fanon, Frantz. *A Dying Colonialism,* trans. by Haakon Chevalier. London: Writers and Readers, 1980.

Fernea, Elizabeth, ed. *Women and the Family in the Middle East: New Voices of Change.* Austin: University of Texas Press, 1985.

Fierst, A. "Dvar Hapoelet," *Women's Labor Magazine* (November 1942): 152.

Filastin (Palestine). Jaffa daily (August 13, 1938; February 1, 1939; February 16, 1939; March 26, 1939).

Filastin al-Damiyyah (Bloody Palestine). Damascus: Al-Itidal Press, 1937.

Flapan, Simha. *The Birth of Israel: Myths and Realities.* New York: Pantheon Books, 1987.

Foucault, Michel. *Discipline and Punish: The Birth of the Prison,* trans. by Alan Sheridan. New York: Random House, 1977.

———. *The Archeology of Knowledge and the Discourse on Language,* trans. by A. M. Sheridan Smith. London: Tavistock, 1972.

Frankel, Jonathan. *Prophecy and Politics: Socialism, Nationalism, and the Russian Jews, 1862–1917.* New York: Cambridge University Press, 1981.

Friedman, Isaiah, ed. *The Rise of Israel: A Documentary Record from 19th Century to 1948,* vol. 1. New York: Garland Publishing, 1987.

Furlonge, Geoffrey. *Palestine Is My Country: The Story of Musa 'Alami.* London: John Murray, 1969.

Gellner, Ernest. *Nations and Nationalism.* Ithaca: Cornell University Press, 1983.

Ghorayeb, Rose. "May Ziadeh (1886–1941)," *Signs* 5, no. 2 (1979): 376.

al-Ghuri, Imil. *Filastin 'abra sittina 'aman, 1922–1937* (Palestine through Sixteen Years). Beirut: Dar al-Nahar Publishing, 1973.

Gilligan, Carol. *The Birth of Pleasure.* New York: Alfred A. Knopf, 2002.

Ginat, Joseph. *Women in Muslim Rural Society: Status and Role in Family and Community.* New Brunswick: Transaction Books, 1982.

Glazier, Steven. "The Palestinian Exodus in 1948," *Journal of Palestine Studies* 9, no. 4 (Summer 1980): 96–118.

Gonen, Jay. *A Psycho-History of Zionism.* New York: Meridian, 1976.

Graham-Brown, Sarah. *Images of Women: The Portrayal of Women in the Photographs of the Middle East 1860–1950.* London: Quartet, 1988.

———. *Palestinians and Their Society, 1880–1946: A Photographic Essay.* London: Quartet Books, 1980.

Granott, Abraham. *The Land System in Palestine: History and Structure,* trans. from Hebrew by M. Simon. London: Eyre & Spottiswoode, 1952.

Granqvist, Hilma N. *Birth and Childhood Among the Arabs: Studies in a Muhammadan Village in Palestine.* Helsinki: Soderstrom, 1947.

Grant, Rebecca, and Kathleen Newland. *Gender and International Relations.* Bloomington: Indiana University Press, 1991.

Greenstein, Ran. *Genealogies of Conflict: Class, Identity and State in Palestine/Israel and South Africa.* Hanover: Wesleyan University Press, 1995.

Haim, Sylvia, ed. *Arab Nationalism: An Anthology.* Berkeley: University of California Press, 1962.

Harper, M. "Recovering the Other: Women and the Orient in Writings of Early Nineteenth-Century France," *Critical Matrix* 1, no. 3 (1985): 1–31.

Hazelton, Lesley. *Israeli Women: The Reality behind the Myths.* New York: Simon and Schuster, 1977.

Hertzberg, Arthur, ed. *The Zionist Idea: A Historical Analysis and Reader.* New York: Atheneum. Reprinted by arrangement with the Jewish Publication Society of America, 1959.

Herzl, Theodor. *Altneuland* (Old New Land), trans. by Lotte Levensohn. New York: Herzl Press, 1960.

———. *The Diaries of Theodor Herzl.* New York: Grossel and Dunlap, 1962.

———. *The Jewish State: An Attempt at a Modern Solution of the Jewish Question,* trans. by Harry Zohn. New York: Herzl Press, 1970.

———. *The Jewish State.* New York: American Zionist Emergency Council, 1946.

Hill 24 Doesn't Answer, film by Thorold Dickinson, 1955.

Himadeh, Sa'id. *Al-Nidham al-Iqtisadi fi Filastin* (The Economic Organization of Palestine). Beirut: The American Press, 1939.

Hobsbawm, Eric, and Terence Ranger, eds. *The Invention of Tradition.* Cambridge: Cambridge University Press, 1983.

———. *Nations and Nationalism since 1780: Programme, Myth, Reality.* Cambridge: Cambridge University Press, 1990.

Hourani, Albert. *Arabic Thought in the Liberal Age 1798–1939.* Cambridge: Cambridge University Press, 1983.

———. *A History of the Arab Peoples.* Cambridge: Harvard University Press, 1991.

Hunt, Lynn. *Politics, Culture, and Class in the French Revolution.* Berkeley: University of California Press, 1984.

———, ed. *The New Cultural History.* Berkeley: University of California Press, 1989.

Husayn, Ahmad. *Al-zawaj wal-mar'a* (Marriage and the Woman). Cairo: Egypt House Books, 1946.

al-Husayni, Ishaq Musa. *Mudhakkirat Dajajah* (Recollections of a Hen). Cairo: Education Publishing House, 1940.

Idinopulos, Thomas. *Weathered by Miracles: A History of Palestine from Bonaparte and Muhammad Ali to Ben Gurion and the Mufti.* Chicago: Ivan R. Dee, 1998.

Ijlal, Kalifah. *Al-Mar'a wa-qadiyyat Filastin* (Woman and the Palestinian Case). Cairo: Al-matba'ah al-'arabiyyah al-hadithah, n.d.

Ingrams, Doreen. *Palestine Papers, 1917–1922: Seeds of Conflict.* London: J. Murray, 1972.

Izraeli, Dafna. "The Zionist Women's Movement in Palestine, 1911–1927: A Sociological Analysis," *Signs: A Journal of Women in Culture and Society* 7, no. 1 (1981): 87–114.

Jayawardena, Kumari. *Feminism and Nationalism in the Third World.* London: Zed, 1986.

Jayyusi, Salma. *Anthology of Modern Palestinian Literature.* New York: Columbia University Press, 1992.

———. *Modern Arabic Poetry.* New York: Columbia University Press, 1987.

———. *Trends and Movements in Modern Arabic Poetry.* Leiden: E. J. Brill, 1977.

Jbara, Taysir. *Palestinian Leader Hajj Amin al-Husayni: Mufti of Jerusalem.* Princeton: The Kingston Press, 1985.

Jennings, Francis. *The Invasion of America: Indians, Colonialism, and the Cant of Conquest.* Chapel Hill: University of North Carolina Press, 1975.

Jewish Frontier Anthology 1934–44. New York: Jewish Frontier Association, 1945.

Kandiyoti, Deniz, ed. *Gendering the Middle East.* London: I. B. Tauris, 1996.

Kaplan, Mordecai. *The Future of the American Jew.* New York: Macmillan, 1948.

Kaplan, Temma. *Anarchists of Andalusia, 1868–1903.* Princeton: Princeton University Press, 1977.

Kass, Ilana, and Bard O'Neill. *The Deadly Embrace: The Impact of Israeli and Palestinian Rejectionism on the Peace Process.* Lanham, Md.: University Press of America, 1997.

Katz, Doris. *The Lady Was a Terrorist: During Israel's War of Liberation.* New York: Shiloni, 1953.

Katz, Sheila H. "*Adam* and *Adama,* '*Ird* and *Ard*: En-gendering Political Conflict and Identity in Early Jewish and Palestinian Nationalisms," in *Gendering the Middle East.* Deniz Kandiyoti, ed., 85–106. London: I. B. Tauris, 1996.

———. "*Shahada* and *Haganah*: Politicizing Masculinities in Early Palestinian and Jewish Nationalism," *Arab Studies Journal*, vol. 4, no. 2 (Fall 1996): 79–97.

Katzenelson-Rubashow, Rachel, ed. *The Plough Woman: Records of the Pioneer Women of Palestine*, trans. by Maurice Samuel. New York: Nicholas L. Brown, 1932. Reprint, Westport, Conn.: Hyperion Press, 1976.

Kayyali, 'Abd al-Wahab. *Palestine: A Modern History*. London: Croom Helm, 1978.

Kazi, Hamida. "Palestinian Women and the National Liberation Movement: A Social Perspective," in Khamsin Collective, eds. *Women in the Middle East*. London: Zed, 1987.

Keddie, Nikki, and Beth Baron, eds. *Women in Middle Eastern History*. New Haven: Yale University Press, 1992.

Kedourie, Elie, and Sylvia Haim, eds. *Palestine and Israel in the 19th and 20th Centuries*. London: Cass, 1982.

Kessler-Harris, Alice. "Report on the First Conference on Women's History and Public Policy," *Perspectives* 28, no. 5 (May–June 1990): 11.

Khalaf, Issa. *Politics in Palestine: Arab Factionalism and Social Disintegration 1939–1948*. Albany: State University of New York Press, 1991.

Khalah, Kamal Mahmud. *Filastin wal-Intidab al-Britani, 1922–1939* (Palestine and the British Mandate). Beirut: The P.L.O. Research Center, 1974.

Khalidi, Rashid. *Palestinian Identity: The Construction of Modern National Consciousness*. New York: Columbia University Press, 1997.

Khalidi, Tarif. "Palestinian Historiography, 1900–1948," *Journal of Palestine Studies* 10, no. 3 (Spring 1981): 59–76.

Khalidi, Walid. *Before Their Diaspora: A Photographic History of the Palestinians 1876–1948*. Washington, D.C.: Institute for Palestine Studies, 1984.

al-Khuli, al-Bahi. *Al-mar'a bayn al-bayt wa'l-mujtama'* (Woman between House and Society). Cairo: Maktabat Dar al-'Urubah, 1957.

Kimmerling, Baruch, and Joel Migdal. *The Palestinians: The Making of a People*. New York: The Free Press, 1993.

Koestler, Arthur. *Thieves in the Night: A Chronicle of an Experiment*. New York: MacMillan, 1946.

Koonz, Claudia. *Mothers in the Fatherland: Women, the Family, and Nazi Politics*. New York: St. Martin's Press, 1987.

Laqueur, Walter. *A History of Zionism*. New York: Holt, Reinhart, and Winston, 1972.

Laqueur, Walter, and Barry Rubin, eds. *The Israel-Arab Reader: A Documentary History of the Middle East Conflict*. New York: Citadel Press, 1968.

Lazreg, Marnia. "Feminism and Difference: The Perils of Writing as a Woman on Women in Algeria," *Feminist Studies* 14, no. 1 (Spring 1988): 81–107.

Lesch, Ann M. *Arab Politics in Palestine 1917–1939: The Frustration of a Nationalist Movement*. Ithaca: Cornell University Press, 1979.

Lewis, Bernard. *The Jews of Islam*. Princeton: Princeton University Press, 1984.

Lockman, Zachary. *Comrades and Enemies: Arab and Jewish Workers in Palestine, 1906–1948.* Berkeley: University of California Press, 1996.

Loeb, Sophie. *Palestine Awake: The Rebirth of a Nation.* New York: The Century, 1926.

Lorde, Audre. *Sister Outsider: Essays and Speeches.* Trumansburg, N.Y.: Crossing Press, 1984.

Magnes, Beatrice. *Episodes: A Memoir.* Berkeley: Judah L Magnes Memorial Museum, 1977.

Maimon, Ada. *Women Build a Land.* New York: Herzl Press, 1962.

Mandel, Neville. *The Arabs and Zionism before World War One.* Berkeley: University of California Press, 1976.

Mansour, Atallah. *Waiting for the Dawn: An Autobiography.* London: Secker and Warburg, 1975.

Mar'i, Miryam. "Women's Movements in Palestine in the Period before the Disaster," paper presented to the first Conference of Palestinian Thought, Nazareth, May 10–12, 1985.

Martin, R. K. "Imagined Brotherhood." Unpublished paper presented at the Nationalisms and Sexualities Conference, Harvard University, 1989.

Mason, Tim. "Women in Nazi Germany," *History Workshop* 1 (1976): 74–113; 2 (1976): 5–32.

Mattar, Philip. *The Mufti of Jerusalem: Al-Hajj Amin al-Husayni and the Palestinian National Movement.* New York: Columbia University Press, 1988.

McClintock, Anne, Aamir Mufti, and Ella Shohat, eds. *Dangerous Liaisons.* Minneapolis: University of Minnesota Press, 1997.

Meir, Golda. *My Life.* New York: Putnam and Sons, 1975.

Memmi, Albert. *The Colonizer and the Colonized.* Boston: Beacon Press, 1965.

Miller, Ylana. "From Village to Nation: Government and Society in Rural Palestine 1920–1948." Unpublished dissertation, University of California at Berkeley, 1975.

———. *Government and Society in Rural Palestine 1920–1948.* Austin: University of Texas Press, 1985.

Mitchell, Tim. *Colonising Egypt.* Cambridge: Cambridge University Press, 1988.

Mogannam, Matiel. *The Arab Woman and the Palestine Problem.* London: Herbert Joseph, 1937. Reprint, Westport, Conn.: Hyperion Press, 1976.

Moors, Annalies. *Women, Property and Islam: Palestinian Experiences, 1920–1990.* Cambridge: Cambridge University Press, 1995.

Morris, Benny. *The Birth of the Palestinian Refugee Problem, 1947–1949.* New York: Cambridge University Press, 1987.

Mosse, George. *Nationalism and Sexuality: Respectability and Abnormal Sexuality in Modern Europe.* New York: H. Fertig, 1985.

Muhawi, Ibrahim, and Sharif Kanaana. *Speak, Bird, Speak Again: Palestinian Arab Folktales.* Berkeley: University of California Press, 1989.

Muslih, Muhammad. *The Origins of Palestinian Nationalism.* New York: Columbia University Press, 1988.

al-Mutamar al-Nisa'i al-Arabi 1944 (The Arab Women's Conference). Cairo: Dar al-ma'arif al-taba'a wa'l-nashir, December 1944.

Myers, David. *Re-inventing the Jewish Past: European Intellectuals and the Zionist Return to History.* New York: Oxford University Press, 1995.

Nairn, Tom. *The Break-up of Britain: Crisis and Neonationalism.* 2nd edition. London: Verso Editions, 1981.

Nardi, Noah. *Education in Palestine 1920–1945.* Washington, D.C.: Zionist Organization of America, 1945.

Nationalisms and Sexualities Conference. Cambridge, Mass.: Harvard University, 1989.

Nicholson, Linda J. *Gender and History: The Limits of Social Theory in the Age of the Family.* New York: Columbia University Press, 1986.

Norton, Anne. "Gender, Sexuality and the Iraq of Our Imagination," *Middle East Report* (November–December 1991): 26–28.

Owen, Roger, ed. *Studies in the Economic and Social History of Palestine in the 19th and 20th Centuries.* Carbondale: Southern Illinois University Press, 1982.

Pappe, Ilan, ed. *The Israel/Palestine Question.* New York: Routledge, 1999.

Parker, Andrew, et al., eds. *Nationalisms and Sexualities.* New York: Routledge, 1992.

Patai, Raphael. *The Arab Mind.* New York: Scribner, 1983.

Peteet, Julie. *Gender in Crisis: Women and the Palestinian Resistance Movement.* New York: Columbia University Press, 1991.

Plaskow, Judith. *Standing Again at Sinai: Judaism from a Feminist Perspective.* San Francisco: HarperCollins, 1990.

Porath, Yehoshua. *Emergence of the Palestinian-Arab National Movement.* Vol. 1, 1918–1929. London: Cass, 1974. Vol. 2, 1929–1939. London: Cass, 1977.

———. *The Palestinian Arab National Movement: From Riots to Rebellion, 1929–1939.* London: Frank Cass, 1977.

Rashid, Harun Hashim. *Al-Kalimah al-Muqatilah* (The Fighting Word). Cairo: Al-maktabah al-arabiyyah, 1973.

Reinharz, Jehuda, and Paul Mendes-Flohr. *The Jew in the Modern World: A Documentary History.* New York: Oxford University Press, 1980.

Rejwan, Nissim. *Israel in Search of Identity.* Gainesville: University Press of Florida, 1999.

Revusky, Abraham. *Jews in Palestine.* London: P. S. King and Son, 1935.

Ridd, Rosemary, and Helen Callaway, eds. *Caught up in Conflict: Women's Responses to Political Strife.* Hampshire: Oxford University Women's Studies Committee, 1986.

Rogan, Eugene, and Avi Shlaim, eds. *The War for Palestine: Re- Writing the History of 1948.* Cambridge: Cambridge University Press, 2001.

Rouhana, Nadim. *Palestinian Citizens in an Ethnic Jewish State: Identities in Conflict.* New Haven: Yale University Press, 1997.

Rowbotham, Sheila. *Women, Resistance and Revolution.* New York: Pantheon Books, 1972.

Russett, Cynthia Eagle. *Sexual Science: The Victorian Construction of Womanhood.* Cambridge: Harvard University Press, 1989.

Sabbagh, Suha, ed. *Palestinian Women of Gaza and the West Bank.* Bloomington: Indiana University Press, 1998.

Sabra. Film directed by Alexander Ford and produced by Tzabar, 1933.

Sabri, Mustafa. *Qawli fi al-Mar'a* (My Opinion about Women). Cairo: Al-Maktabah al-Salfiyah, 1935.

Sachar, Howard. *The Course of Modern Jewish History.* New York: Dell Publishing, 1977.

Safir, Marilyn. "The Kibbutz: An Experiment in Social and Sexual Equality? A Historical Perspective," in M. Palgi et al., eds. *Sexual Equality: The Israeli Kibbutz Tests the Theories.* Norwood, Pa.: Norwood Editions, 1983.

Sangari, Kumkum, and Sudesh Vaid. *Recasting Women: Essays in Colonial History.* New Brunswick, N.J.: Rutgers University Press, 1990.

Sarna, Jonathan. "Louis D. Brandeis: Zionist Leader," *Brandeis Review* 11, no. 3 (Winter 1992): 26–27.

al-Sawafiri, Kamil. *Al-Shir al-'Arabi al-Hadith fi Masat Filastin* 1917–1955. Cairo: Matba'at Nahdah Misr, 1963.

Sawt al-Mar'a al-Hur (The Free Voice of Woman). Allepo: Maktabah al-Kashaf, 1947.

Schama, Simon. *Citizens: A Chronicle of the French Revolution.* New York: Random House, 1989.

Schipper, Minecke, ed. *Unheard Words: Women and Literature in Africa, the Arab World, Asia, the Caribbean, and Latin America.* London: Allison and Busby, 1985.

Schulz, Helena Lindholm. *Between Revolution and Statehood: Reconstruction of Palestinian Nationalisms.* Gothenberg: Padrigu Papers, 1996.

Scott, Joan Wallach. *Gender and the Politics of History.* New York: Columbia University Press, 1988.

Shafir, Gershon. *Land, Labor, and the Origins of the Israeli/Palestinian Conflict 1882–1914.* Cambridge: Cambridge University Press, 1989.

Sharoni, Simona. *Gender and the Israeli-Palestinian Conflict: The Politics of Women's Resistance.* Syracuse: Syracuse University Press, 1995.

Shohat, Ella. *Israeli Cinema: East/West and the Politics of Representation.* Austin: University of Texas Press, 1989.

Showalter, Elaine. *Speaking of Gender.* New York: Routledge Chapman Hall, 1989.

Sicker, Martin. *Reshaping Palestine: From Muhammad Ali to the British Mandate.* Westport, Conn.: Praeger, 1999.

Smilansky, Moshe. *Palestine Caravan,* trans. by I. M. Lask. London: Methuen, 1935.

Smith, Charles D. *Palestine and the Arab-Israeli Conflict.* New York: St. Martin's Press, 1988.

Spivak, Gayatri Chakravorty. *In Other Worlds: Essays in Cultural Politics.* New York: Methuen, 1987.

Stearns, Jill. *Gender and International Relations.* New Brunswick, N.J.: Rutgers University Press, 1998.

Stein, Kenneth. *The Land Question in Palestine, 1917–1939.* Chapel Hill: University of North Carolina Press, 1984.

Stern, Geraldine. *Daughters from Afar: Profiles of Israeli Women.* New York: Abelard-Schuman, 1958.

Sternhell, Zeev. *The Founding Myths of Israel: Nationalism, Socialism, and the Making of the Jewish State.* Princeton: Princeton University Press, 1998.

Stillman, Norman. *Jews of Arab Lands: A History and Sourcebook.* Philadelphia: Jewish Publication Society of America, 1979.

Sulaiman, Khalid. *Palestine and Modern Arab Poetry.* London: Zed, 1984.

Swedenburg, T. R. *Memories of Revolt: The 1936–1939 Rebellion and the Palestinian National Past.* Minneapolis: University of Minnesota Press, 1995.

Swerdlow, Amy. "Engendering International Relations Theory: The Feminist Standpoint," *Journal of Women's History* 7, no. 2 (Summer 1995): 160–63.

Swirski, Barbara. *Calling the Equality Bluff: Women in Israel.* New York: Pergamon Press, 1991.

Syrkin, Marie. *Golda Meir: Woman with a Cause.* New York: Putnam, 1963.

Taqqu, Rachel, and Kathryn March. *Women's Informal Associations in Developing Countries.* Boulder, Colo.: Westview Press, 1986.

Tessler, Mark. *A History of the Israeli-Palestinian Conflict.* Bloomington: Indiana University Press, 1994.

Theweleit, Klaus. *Male Fantasies,* trans. by Stephen Conway. Minneapolis: University of Minnesota Press, 1989.

Tibawi, A. L. *Arab Education in Mandatory Palestine: A Study of Three Decades of British Administration.* London: Luzac and Co., 1956.

Tickner, J. Ann. *Gender in International Relations: Feminist Perspectives on Achieving Global Security.* New York: Columbia University Press, 1992.

Tiger, L., and J. Shepher. *Women in Kibbutz.* New York: Harcourt Brace and Jovanovich, 1976.

Tomorrow Is a Wonderful Day, film directed by Helmar Lerski and produced by Hadassah, 1952.

Trager, Hannah. *Pioneers in Palestine: Stories of the First Settlers in Petach Tikva.* New York: E. P. Dutton, 1924.

———. *Festival Stories of Child-Life: In a Jewish Colony in Palestine.* New York: E. P. Dutton, 1919.

Tucker, Judith. *In the House of the Law: Gender and Islamic Law in Ottoman Syria and Palestine.* Berkeley: University of California Press, 1998.

———, and Margaret W. Meriwether. *Social History of Women and Gender in the Modern Middle East.* Boulder, Colo.: Westview Press, 1999.

Turki, Fawaz. "Meaning in Palestinian History: Text and Context," *Arab Studies Quarterly* 3, no. 4 (1981): 381.

Warner, Marina. *Monuments and Maidens: The Allegory of the Female Form*. London: Weidenfeld and Nicolson, 1985.

Wasserstein, Bernard. *The British in Palestine: The Mandatory Government and the Arab-Jewish Conflict, 1917–1929*. 2nd edition. Oxford: Basil Blackwell, 1991.

Wood, Davida. "The Boundless Courtyard: Palestinians, Israelis, and the Politics of Uncertainty." Unpublished dissertation, Princeton University, 1994.

Woodsmall, Ruth Frances. *Moslem Women Enter a New World*. New York: Round Table Press, 1936.

Yanait Ben-Tzvi, Rachel. *Before Golda, Manya Shohat: A Biography*, trans. by Sandra Shurin. New York: Biblio Press, 1989.

Young, Elise. *Keepers of the History: Women and the Israeli-Palestinian Conflict*. New York: Teachers College Press, 1992.

Yuval-Davis, Nira. *Israeli Women and Men: Division behind the Unity*. London: Change, 1982.

Yuval-Davis, Nira, and Floya Anthias, eds. *Woman-Nation-State*. New York: St. Martin's Press, 1989.

Index

'Abd al-'Aziz, 161
'Abd al-Hadi: 'Awni, 47, 61; family
    (Nablus), 42; Salim, 46, 47
'Abd al-Rahman, Mufidah, 163
Abdo, Nahla, 8
Abdullah, King, 63
Abu Khadrah, 'Aisha, 163
Abu-Mannah, Butrus, 32
Abu Risha, 'Umar, 90
Abu Salma ('Abd al-Karim al-Karmi),
    79, 84, 89
Accad, Evelyn, 7
Acre: Jewish communities in nine-
    teenth century, 35, 36; *sanjak*, 32
al-Afghani, Jamal al-Din, 111
'Aflaq, Michel, 80
Afula, 149
agriculture: Arab, 172; cooperatives,
    26–27, 38, 40–41, 53, 136, 157, 159;
    Jewish settlements (Degania, 40;
    *Hadera, Rishon Letzion, Rosh Pina,
    Zichron Yaacov,* 38; Kinneret Farm,
    153; Petah Tikva, 36, 115–16, 151–
    52, 168–69; Sedjera, 168); *moshavot,*
    140, 151, 167; Palestinian women's
    conferences on, 160; Palestinian
    women's work in, 24; schools for
    Jews, 26, 36, 130, 131; women's farm,
    157
Ahad Ha'am (Asher Ginsberg), 39, 72,
    97
al-Ahram, 156
al-'Alami, Musa, 61, 111, 170
al-'Alami family (Jerusalem), 43

Algeria, 18, 23
aliya: first, 38, 150; second, 40, 92, 152;
    third, 52, 156; fourth, 158; fifth, 57,
    159. *See also* Jewish immigration
Alkalai, Yehuda, 37, 74, 97
Alliance Israelite Universelle. See Zi-
    onist groups
Altneuland. See Herzl, Theodor
'Alush, Naji, 75
Amin, Qassim, 69, 101, 121, 150
Anderson, Benedict, 6, 8–9, 20, 120,
    189n.28
anti-Semitism: and anti-Zionism, 54,
    139, 139–40; Arab, 56, 117; in
    Dreyfus trial, 39, 139; effects of, on
    Jews' attitudes towards Arabs, 135;
    European, 16, 36–39, 74, 135, 138;
    Hitler's, 56. *See also* racism
anti-Zionism, 16, 44–47, 49, 139; in
    Arabic publications, 139–40;
    conflation of, with anti-Semitism,
    54, 138–39; Hajj Amin al-Husayni,
    54; Palestinian women's, 149, 155
Arab Congress of 1913, 47
Arabia: 'Abd al-'Aziz, 161; Ibn 'Ali
    Husayn, 48; Jamal Pasha, 48
Arabic language: *Al-Difa,* 120, 160,
    162; *Filastin,* 47, 160–61; first book
    on Zionism in, 46; Jews speaking, 41,
    171, 173; journals, *al-Asma'i, al-
    Karmil, al-Najjah, al-Quds,* 46;
    schools, 122–24, 129; versus Turkish,
    46, 122, 128–29
Arab-Jewish relations, 165–79; admira-

Jerusalem, 85, 140; Arab-Jewish relations in, 117, 170; Arab Women's Society in, 160; *Haram al-Sharif,* 56; Jews in, 34–36; journals in, 46; Ottoman, 32, 47; municipal council in, 43; Muslims in, 74, 149; Muslim-Christian relations in, 42–43, 49, 160; Palestinian notables of, 42–43, 45–47, 54, 57, 61, 156, 170; violence in, 56, 160; war of 1948, 62–64; women in, 127, 149, 156, 160

Jewish-Arab relations. *See* Arab and Jewish women's relations, Arab-Jewish relations; violent confrontation

Jewish immigration. *See* aliya

Jewish nationalism: and Arabs, 30, 135–38, 140, 142, 144; and Balfour Declaration, 48; birth of, 34–42; under British Mandate, 51–53, 56, 59–60, 61–65; Declaration of Independence, 64; definition of, 15; factions within, 36–42; historical approaches to, xi–xii, 29–30; growth of institutions of, 53; and Hebrew language, 36, 38–39, 42, 44, 128–29, 142, 155; and identity, 15–16; Jews in Palestine before, 34–36; and Jews outside Palestine, 11, 36–40; legitimacy of, 15–16, 174, 175, 176–79; and manhood, 70–76, 78–81, 91–93; under Ottomans, 29–30, 34–42, 48–49; as rebirth, 86–87; and war of 1948, 24, 63–65; and youth, 131–32; as Zionism, 15. *See also* Zionists

Jewish women, xi, xiii; activism of, 150–55, 157–59, 163–64; in *Altneuland,* 97–99, 112; and Arab women, 27, 165–79; brutality towards, 140–41; and civilizing mission, 109–10, 112, 115–19, 176; elected to Knesset, 163; Hadassah, 112; *halutzot,* 152; immigrants, 150–51; on kibbutz, 26, 157, 159; and La-

bor Zionism, 153–54; and marriage, 142, 152, 157, 158; and motherhood, 153–54, 174; myth of liberation, xii, 25, 129, 153, 163, 191n.25; and nationalism, 25–27, 80–81, 112, 137–38, 141, 147–48, 164, 165–79; and reproduction, 24; struggle of, against patriarchy, 17, 148–49, 164, 165–66, 177–79; struggle of, for equality, 25–27, 147–48, 150–55, 157–60, 174–76; and terrorists, 163, 173; and violence, 56, 137, 140–41, 162; and voting, 151–52, 154–55, 157, 159, 163; Women's International Zionist Organization, 117; workers, 152–54, 157–59, 168–71; writings of and about, 151–54. *See also names of individuals;* women (relations between Arab and Jewish)

Jewish workers: "conquest of labor," 40–41, 56; female, 152–54, 157–59, 168–71; *Kupat Holim,* 41; and Palestinian workers, 75; riots, 52

Jewish youth. *See* youth (Jewish)

Jish, 114

Jordan: King Abdullah of, 63; and Palestinian refugee camps, 64; Transjordanian Arab Legion, 61; in war of 1948, 63–65

Kalisher, Rabbi Zevi, 37, 78
Kallen, Horace, 103
Kanaana, Sharif, 25
Kandiyoti, Deniz, 28
Kaplan, Mordecai, 118
Kaplan, Temma, 19
Katrak, Ketu, 22
Katz, Doris, 118
Kazi, Hamida, 25
Kessler-Harris, Alice, 165
Khalidi, Rashid, 6, 17, 65
Khalidi family (Jerusalem), 42–43, 57
Khalil family (Haifa), 42

modernization: and Arab women, 18,
23, 69, 101–3, 109–10, 162; and
cleanliness, hygiene, 116–19, 124–25,
151, 160; and education, 120–33,
125–27, 132–33; and gender, 109–19;
and health/medicine, 111–12, 117;
and Islam, 125; and Jewish women,
95, 104, 109–10, 112–13, 115–19,
176; and power hierarchies, 110,
113–19, 176; and science, 110–13,
116, 121, 124; versus tradition/reli-
gion, 23, 57, 111, 120–21, 124–28,
132–33, 120–22, 125–27, 132–33,
136–37, 151, 176; and Zionism, 79,
110, 113
Mogannam, Matiel, 161–62
Montefiore, Sir Moses, 35
Moors, Annelies, 25
Morocco, 118
Moshav, 140, 151; Migdal, 167
Mosse, George, 20
Mufti, Aamir, 4
Muhammad 'Ali, 31, 35
Muharram, Ahmad, 90
Muhawi, Ibrahim, 25
Muslih, Muhammad, 32, 139
Muslim Palestinian(s): Bedouin, 24, 32,
54; and Christians, 35, 42, 52, 57, 58,
113–14, 156, 160; Druze, 54; education, 61, 122–26, 150; *Haram al-
Sharif*, 56; and Jews, 13, 35, 36, 56,
170–71; loss of legal privilege under
British, 52; and modernity versus
tradition, 57, 111, 126; municipal
council in Jerusalem, 43, 45; no-
tables' anti-Zionism, 44–45; Quran,
78, 126, 141; resistance to the British, 57–59; and riots of 1929, 55–56;
Shiite and Sunni, 54; Supreme Muslim Council, 54; theater, 74; women,
102, 113, 122–28, 149, 156; Young
Men's Muslim Associations, 57;
youth congress (1932), 57

Myers, David, 78

Nablus, 32, 36, 63, 77; Arab club, 139;
Arab Nationalist Association, 54;
demonstrations in, 160; prominent
Palestinian families of, 42, 47; Youth
Society, 47
Nardi, Noah, 122, 128–29, 131, 176
Nashashibi, 42–43, 50, 55; 'Ali, 46–47;
Fakhri, 61; Muhammad Is'af, 82–83;
and the Palestinian Arab National
Party, 55; Raghib, 45, 57
Nasif, Malak Hifni, 150
Nassar, Najib, 46
Nassar, Sadhij, 161
national histories: discourse of, xi, 7;
exclusion of women in, xi–xii, 9, 69–
81; gender in, xi, xii, xiv, 3–4, 8–9,
12, 73–74; problems with writing,
xi–xii, 29–30; revisionist critiques of,
8–9, 13, 30
nationalism, 51; versus bi-nationalism,
171, 172–73; and bourgeois society,
20; and citizenship, 95, 100–101, 105,
132; and civilizing mission, 109–19;
and claims to land, 9; as contingent,
3, 166–67; as discourse, 6–9, 10–12,
173–74, 178–79, 189n.28; and education in Palestine, 120–33, 176; as ex-
clusive/oppressive, 8–9, 72, 81; and
feminism, 18, 21–22, 178–79; and
gender, xi–xii, 3–7, 17–28, 69–70,
190n.3; and girls' education, 121,
132–33; historical development of,
under British, 51–65; historical development of, under Ottomans, 29–
50; and imagined communities, 3, 6,
8; as inclusive/anti-colonial, 8–9; as
justification for war, xi, 4; and land,
33, 44, 55, 57, 59–60, 69–81, 82–94,
114, 174–75; and language, 128–29;
and manhood, 9, 11, 19–21, 69–81,
174–75, 181n.13; and modernization,

Sheila H. Katz is an associate professor at the Berklee College of Music in Boston, where she teaches history of the Middle East, gender and power, and world civilizations. Her writings have appeared in *Gendering the Middle East, Middle East Journal, Arab Studies Journal,* and the *Harvard International Review,* among others. She is working on a study of grass-roots cooperation between Palestinians and Israelis.